NO-BRAINER

Mike Amos

NO-BRAINER

A Footballer's Story of Life, Love and Brain Injury

Mike Amos

Haythorp Books

First published by Haythorp Books, a division of Canbury Press 2024

This edition published 2024

Haythorp Books

Kingston upon Thames, Surrey, United Kingdom

haythorp.co.uk

Printed and bound in Great Britain

Typeset in Athelas (body), Futura PT (heading)

This is a work of non-fiction

FSC® helps take care of forests for future generations.

ISBN:

Paperback 9781914487231

Ebook 9781914487248

CONTENTS

Contents

Contents

No-brainer is written chronologically between the Spring of 2022 and the Autumn of 2023, focusing on issues around safer sport and neurodegenerative disease. Though several chapters relate to rugby, Dr. Judith Gates now chairs Head Safe Football.

FOREWORD

'That which doesn't kill you makes you strong.'
I am Dr. Judith Gates, wife of Bill Gates. I am a great grandmother: mother of two sons, grandmother of two girls, great grandmother to two precious little boys. Liam was two and a half when Luca was born and, eager to show his skills as a big brother, he reached out to hold Luca. His mum gently intervened: 'You can't pick him up 'cos he's delicate.' Savouring and practising this newly discovered word, delicate, Liam carefully placed his finger on Luca's forehead. 'Delicate forehead' he pronounced with conviction. How true. His words resonate and mobilise my actions.

The brain is fragile. That has been proven scientifically. Repetitive head impacts are identified as the cause of Chronic Traumatic Encephalopathy, CTE, a progressive, incurable brain disease which claims victims to dementia 20 to 30 years after their initial exposure to brain trauma. CTE is a disease which appears in middle to old age but which begins in the brains of the young.

Ex-professional footballers are five times more likely to develop dementia than those in the general population. But the disease is not just limited to the professional game, not just limited to the old. On autopsy, CTE has been found in the brains of young people who have never played for a professional team, it has been found in the brains of both men and women. CTE does not discriminate. It is a disease which can affect anyone who ever heads a football.

Conversations with today's players highlight a fundamental misunderstanding. They assert that 'Dementia was caused by the old heavy leather balls.' The balls of today weigh the same but travel faster. Increased velocity and similar weight mean that today's players experience similar head impacts and are in as great a danger as players in the past. CTE is here to stay unless we take action. The cumulative intensity of head impacts is the cause. Precaution, prevention and protection are the only cure

I co-founded Head for Change, a charity involved with both football and rugby, and was instrumental in organising the first football match in the world which experimented with the rules of heading. International media coverage enabled 50 million people to read about a game in which heading was banned. Now, in order to better meet football's specific needs, I have founded a charity focusing exclusively on football. Head Safe Football is for every player who has ever headed a ball, irrespective of age or gender, grassroots or professional. Our logo, an elephant standing on a ball, symbolises the elephant in the room, namely chronic traumatic encephalopathy, CTE, a progressive and incurable brain disease wholly caused by repetitive head impacts and insufficiently addressed by the footballing community. Head Safe Football is pioneering Football United v CTE in which HeadSAFE Trailblazers pilot HeadSAFE practices within their own football community. We work to protect the players of today from becoming the victims of tomorrow.

No-brainer outlines my fight to make sport safer. Whilst striving to offer support to affected past players and their families, I fight to raise awareness and provide education to prevent this brutal disease from affecting players of the future.

A story has no beginning and no end. Arbitrarily one chooses a moment of experience at which to begin and a moment of history at which to stop. Any story is just a chosen piece of the whole.

No-brainer is a book of separate, yet interwoven, stories, in which each active participant group plays a part in the current epidemic of brain disease in football. The protagonists line up.

There is CTE, the disease itself, with a long and chequered history of recognition, denial and obfuscation. Research has a key role. It has been dominated by the Concussion in Sport Group (CISG), a group aligned with the sporting governing bodies. And then we have the sporting governing bodies themselves, each with a powerful corporate commitment to the business of football. These groups with positional power have the influence to disrupt rational analysis and action. Collectively, their power is virtually unstoppable. Yet surely, the interests of the players themselves should be key, but theirs are the voices which are having to fight to be heard. Footballers beware.

At the core of *No-brainer* is the ongoing story of CTE, Chronic Traumatic Encephalopathy, the incurable brain disease caused by blows to the head, the brain disease which reduces its victims to the description harshly, but honestly, captured by the title of the book. *No-brainer.*

CTE presents a range of symptoms, involving mood, cognition and ultimately physical decline. Often spanning decades after initial damage, it is a protracted death sentence that slowly, but inexorably, takes away every facet that made a person who they were, reducing them to a shell of their former self. First identified in boxers in the 1920s, known then as punch drunk, it has been found in brains of players of contact sports, players both young and old. Although often evidencing itself in later years, it is a disease which starts in youth. CTE is harsh, it is cruel, it is brutally unremitting. But it is preventable by following one simple edict. Be head safe, protect your brain, prevent CTE.

Woven around the CTE story is the story of research into this brutal disease. The Concussion in Sport Group (CISG) has been at the forefront, producing consensus statements on the issue, usually every four years since 2002.

Comprised of members with established links to the sporting governing bodies, their consensus statements were recently described by a DCMS parliamentary inquiry as conservative rather than precautionary. Namely, they are protective of the sports as distinct from being protective of the players. These CISG statements have dominated the international narrative on concussion in sport, from both a legal and a practical perspective, and have influenced the attitudes and actions of decision makers. The CISG group has recently been mired in scandal concerning plagiarism and misrepresentation. Not only did they selectively control research, but theymisquoted it.

The sporting governing bodies in football have their own influential stories. Overseeing and seeking to maintain a billion pound industry, conflict of interest is inevitably endemic. And there are further stories within these stories.

The Premier League, by dint of its financial clout, has the power to direct the actions of other groups and apparently uses it. The Football Association is subject to ongoing legal proceedings for negligence for failing to protect players from permanent brain injury. How do they exercise a 'duty of care' whilst at the same time minimising change?

The PFA Charity, now renamed the Players Foundation, sits with over £50 million in assets. It is the focus of a regulatory alert and an ongoing Charity Commission Inquiry. Involved observers wait with deep interest for this drawn-out investigation to finally publish its findings. After a decade of close involvement between the PFA Union and the former PFA Charity, they now describe themselves as separate entities. However, it must be noted that the PFA Union still continues to be predominantly funded by monies from the Premier League, rather than from member subscriptions. This raises the unavoidable and uncomfortable question. How can a union be independently focused on member needs when funded by the employers of its members?

Against this perfect storm, this backcloth of money and power, are the everyday stories of footballing families, wives, sons, daughters of former professional footballers, each painfully struggling with individual personal tragedies, each trying to make sense of the global and corporate forces which dominate. As they witness the ongoing disintegration of a loved family member they try, often desperately, often bewildered, to access financial support for those suffering for what has been described by coroners as an industrial disease.

In a world of acronyms, the KISS principle has gained traction. 'Keep it Simple, Stupid.' Yet, in the footballing world of profound complexity and competing interests, where does one find simplicity? Simplicity, rationality, for victims of football-related dementia would be financial support for care from a game awash in cash on the basis that their disease was caused by their profession. Simplicity, rationality, for present and future players would be education as to the now irrefutable recognition of repetitive head impacts as a causal factor of CTE. Simplicity, rationality, to meet a duty of care to players would be modification of rules and practices to reduce heading, particularly in training. We now know heading is dangerous. We do not know what level of heading is safe. Let's not be stupid about this. Let's simplify the complex to arrive at actions which protect the players. This is what I am fighting for.

This book, by highlighting the stories of the various protagonists, teases out competing and complex interests, revealing them for what they are. A desire to maintain the status quo at any price, with a canny eye on profitability and corporate interests. Prioritising protecting a sport created by human beings over the needs of the human beings who play it. Players as dispensable commodities in the drive to maintain power and enhance financial gain. All wrapped up in satisficing edicts, giving the overt appearance of constructive action while covertly designed to fundamentally avoid real change where real change is so evidently necessary.

No-brainer grounds these intertwined stories of varying powerful protagonists through the life history, the lens, of a regular footballer, Bill Gates, my husband. Typical of the majority of ex-professionals of his time, Bill was well known in his community, loyal to his club, both loved and criticised by the supporters. A very human man, he is representative of the majority of those players from the sixties and seventies now destroyed by dementia caused by the game they loved.

My story is also part of this book. For over 60 years, Bill and I have stood shoulder to shoulder. Standing next to me when he received the devastating news that advanced medical tests indicated he probably had CTE, he asked me for the promise that now dominates my life. Acknowledging that it was too late for him, he said: 'Promise me that you will do all in your power to protect players of today and tomorrow from this dreadful disease. No other player, no other family, should suffer as we are suffering.' I made a promise. Now, I am trying hard to fulfil it.

I choose to begin my story with my first ever visit to Bill's home in Neale Street, Ferryhill, County Durham in 1960.

Fifteen years old, self-conscious, fashion-conscious, the only child of doting elderly parents, I made my way past redbrick Dean Bank Primary School on the left, past the chapel on the right, down the hill and into the terrace of two up, two down miners' homes, culminating in allotments at the bottom of the street. Number 16 was a narrow house, one window and a front door wide, with a dormer attic that provided bedroom accommodation for two of the five sons. Mam and Dad, Nancy and Jimmy, presided over their family of footballers. It was a male-dominated environment. No nonsense here.

I was immediately a misfit. My lavender mohair belted coat was the epitome of fashion. My winkle-picker stiletto shoes, my long matching umbrella, all indicative of what became the swinging sixties, a decade of rebellion marked by the rise of teenage power.

Nervously confident, I walked through the glass front door, not knowing that I was entering the rest of my life.

Nancy was welcoming. Jimmy was incredulous. Billy was reassuring. Tinned red salmon and chips were for tea, eaten with only a fork. Not a knife in sight. Thickly buttered slices of bread had pride of place in the centre of the table, with the butter kept in a cupboard next to the fire so that it was easy to spread. Red salmon had status and flavour. Pink salmon was for the seriously hard up. The Gates family ate red salmon.

I heard the verdict on me later. 'Why, she is just a little doll.'

How did I get here from there? Where is 'here'? Where was 'there'? What of the journey in between?

'There' was the Durham mining community in the northeast of England. Dean and Chapter pit heap dominated the horizon as I travelled on the bus down the A1 to visit Bill. Slag-heaps surrounded my home town of Spennymoor. The landscape was usually dark, dismal, seemingly permanently November. Local people combined the grey dourness required to survive difficult environments with the colourful, sardonic humour necessary to bring laughter to what was a harsh reality. If you spend two thirds of your life deep in a narrow coal seam down the pit, then you treasure the fresh air moments tending tomatoes on your allotment or berating the referee whilst watching a local football match.

Folks were set in their ways. Men were head of the house. Women looked after the bairns and stirred the sugar into their husband's tea. Everyone knew their unquestioned roles. But difference was gathering momentum and Bill and I became participators in the zeitgeist of the times.

However, our first real act of rebellion, and experimentation, rebounded spectacularly. Even now, over 60 years later, when I think back to the autumn months of 1961 I relive the fear, the panic, the denial of the emerging realisation that I was pregnant. Wakeful nights: 4 am was always the bleakest time. Moments of forgetting followed closely by the horror of remembering. What would my mam say? How would my dad feel? What could we do? Abortion was not an option in the illiberal early sixties. Blame and shame were pervasive across the culture. Jokey references to 'falling wrong' did not mask the disdain for the girl stupid enough to get pregnant without a ring on her finger, while the boy gained status as a 'jack the lad,' doing what boys will do if they get a chance.

As an academic nerd, expected by teachers and family alike to go on to university education, I felt as if my anticipated life had come to an end. My mam fought for me, my dad cried, my heart learned how to break, but Bill and I stood together. Yes, at Mam's insistence, for the first time ever in my life I drank gin. I hated the taste and the smell. It was even more unpalatable drinking gin whilst sitting in a very hot bath, but my pregnancy continued.

On 26th November 1961 Bill and I were married. We had battled for parental permission, had seriously considered eloping to Gretna Green, but finally the consent forms were completed. Bill signed professional for Middlesbrough as the first £50-a-week footballer, the £20 maximum wage having only recently been abolished. He became the target of the press, who waited to photograph him meeting me outside of the school gates. To escape press attention I went to stay with my much loved Uncle Jim and Aunt Nan and Bill and I married in a little parish church close to their home. And so I became a footballer's wife, with our own home in Middlesbrough, 30 miles from our roots in County Durham, and Bill became an articled clerk to a firm of chartered accountants.

I remember the doctor who looked after me during my pregnancy expressing total shock when he realised that Bill and I were living independently from our parents, despite our young age. He rushed out of his surgery and returned with books on childbirth, fearing I may have no understanding of what lay ahead. I remember the sister in the maternity ward treating me with contempt because of my youth. But what I remember most powerfully was my vow to myself. This personal vow became my mantra for life and influences me to this very day, and I have never needed it more.

'That which does not kill you makes you strong.'

The years that followed strengthened us, both separately and together. Much will be said in this book about Bill's footballing career. His was a public life of extreme highs and what felt like desperate lows. The intense praise which followed Saturday's successes, the intense criticism which followed Saturday's mistakes, dominated the mood of the following week. You moved from being a victorious hero to a public failure in less than the time it took to head a football. No other profession has such minute and public surveillance. I think we both learned resilience from an early age.

I launched myself into unplanned motherhood with a fierce determination. My first thought when my blond-haired, blue-eyed baby boy was placed in my arms was 'I will die protecting you.' I applied the same tenacity to baby care as I had to calculus only a few months previously. However my baking skills were less effective. I smile today when I remember the first time I made a cake. How did one know what it meant to 'cream' the margarine and sugar. The outcome was more wafer than cake. The traditional Bero recipe book became my bible and David's christening tea had a table laden with home-made goodies.

However, my heart, and my head, remained in academia. Based on my O-level results I was accepted as a day student into Neville's Cross Teacher Training College at the age of 18. I loved it. Rarely seen without a book in one hand, a toddler under the other arm, sporting a long straight Sandy Shaw hairstyle, somewhat pretentiously I identified as an existentialist and began my lifelong search for the meaning of life. Not unexpectedly, Bill did not share my quest and neither did his dad, Jimmy. Their pragmatic certainties kept me grounded in Northern reality. Never mind Sartre, what's for dinner? My passion for education didn't go unnoticed among Boro footballers. Eric McMordie, who maybe learned how to charm women from his mate George Best, reportedly said the way to chat me up would be to claim to be a salesman for *Encyclopaedia Britanica*.

Son Nick was born just after my 21st birthday, so teaching, two sons and a career ladder were hallmarks of my twenties. At the age of 29, Mam to a twelve- and a eight-year-old, I became a head teacher, said to be the youngest in the country, then, five years later, a school inspector and five years after that, a university lecturer. Bill and I together took on the world. He as a footballer, an accountant and then a phenomenally successful entrepreneur. I as an educator, an academic and a management consultant. Both as loving parents, grandparents and now great-grandparents.

We travelled the world, visiting 115 countries and exploring places as diverse as Papua New Guinea and the Democratic Republic of the Congo. We gazed at the teeth of a great white shark from the relative security of an underwater cage off the coast of South Africa. We trekked mountain gorillas in the remote Bwindi Impenetrable Forest National Park of Uganda. We hiked the Inca Trail. We worked with our son's charity in remote countries, seeking to educate communities to deliver the UN millennium development goals. In between journeys, I was part of a group which advocated against gender violence. Together, we helped change the laws of a small Caribbean island to protect against domestic abuse. Always concerned about social justice, always activists. Always shoulder to shoulder. Until now.

'That which doesn't kill you makes you strong.'

CTE is killing Bill. His brain is decimated by tau protein, dominated by neuro-fibrillar tangles. Confined to a wheelchair, unable to walk, to speak, to do anything for himself, my life partner and I are no longer shoulder to shoulder. Instead, I stand by him, hold his hand and speak for him. His final journey is killing him, but it must strengthen me.

So that is why I have become a great-grandmother with a fierce determination to protect and prevent. That is why I can't turn away from the seemingly simple and essentially rational actions necessary to protect the next kid from Ferryhill who practises heading in a cobbled back lane while dreaming of becoming a footballer.

That is why I advocate, lobby, educate, disturb, disrupt. That is why I ask uncomfortable questions and refuse to accept satisficing replies.

I was always a misfit. Now I am a misfit with a mission. I have a promise to keep.

'That which doesn't kill you makes you strong'

1.

'IT WAS MANY YEARS BEFORE I COULD PROPERLY ENJOY A GIN AND TONIC'

It may not be said that Bill Gates and Judith Curry *had* to get married, that Grade C euphemism of the sinning sixties, not least because Jimmy Gates — Bill's pitman father — was adamant that footballers and girls didn't mix.

Bit late for that one, wasn't it, Jimmy? The lad was 17, she 16 and the lass — to cite another Co Durham euphemism — had fallen wrong.

Nor may it be said that Judith *had* to have the baby, not when parentally obliged to sit in a hot bath with an equally hot gin and hope that Mother Nature (or Mother's Ruin) might at least have second thoughts about it all. 'It was many years before I could properly enjoy a gin and tonic,' she says.

They got together on a school trip to the 1960 Olympics in Rome, he a greatly promising footballer a year and a month and a day her senior, threw their coins in the Trevi fountain but probably never once wished for what happened subsequently. They married in November 1961, the bride still just 16. David was born the following April and his brother Nick five years later. 'People told me that my life and my aspirations were over,' says Judith, then newly possessed of eight good O-levels. 'They said I'd have five kids by the time I was 21.'

Bill had been just 15 when making his senior team debut for Spennymoor United, became Britain's first £50 a week footballer after joining Middlesbrough, captained England's youth team, trained in the morning and studied accountancy in the afternoon.

Love at first sight? 'Attraction at first sight,' says Judith. 'I don't really know how it happened, it was just sexual groping,' (a phrase which might in the circumstances be supposed a mite disingenuous) .Whatever formative forays the footballer may have enjoyed, his new girlfriend truly was an innocent abroad.

Boro gave them a club house, if not a telephone. 'There we were, 16 and 17 and all on our own,' Judith recalls. 'I'd be ringing my mother from the call box at the end of the road to ask her how to make mince.'

It might almost in passing be added that, a dozen years earlier, Middlesbrough had signed Johnny Spuhler from Sunderland and ensured that his club house had a telephone. Johnny told them to take it out again. No one else he knew had one; he said, there was still no one to talk to.

When ever-worsening migraines compelled Bill to retire from football shortly before his 30th birthday, and after 333 first team appearances of the sort euphemistically categorised as uncompromising, he opened a sports shop in Middlesbrough. Thirteen years later the chain had lengthened to ten Monument Sports outlets, the biggest and most successful of them in the bright new Metro Centre at Gateshead. Together they sold for £4.4 million.

Though Bunsen-bright, a maths whizz and aspiring economist, Judith had left Spennymoor Grammar School when the pregnancy was confirmed — 'it was just expected, there wasn't any option' — returned for a fifth and sixth form dance, wore the secondhand engagement ring that Bill had bought from a shop in Newcastle and was asked to leave after comparing it favourably — subversively?

— to the glitter ball thing suspended meretriciously from the ceiling.

'It was a bit as if teenage pregnancy could be transmitted, like Covid,' she says. 'Bill's parents especially were unhappy that I wanted to go to college, but he supported me absolutely. It was a bedrock commitment for him, he never questioned it. My mother was supportive, too.'

At 18 she started teacher training at Nevilles Cross College in Durham, at 29 became the country's youngest head teacher, at 36 a schools inspector and in later years a PhD, visiting professor and, formidably and forensically intelligent, an international management consultant.

Shop sales complete, in 1989 they emigrated for tax and adventure reasons to the Cayman Islands. Their family kept their magnificent home in Castle Eden near the Durham coast but Bill and Judith bought a spacious Cayman apartment overlooking the sun-blessed beach, allowed to return to Blighty for just 91 days each year. Summer days, and summer nights, of course. The Cayman house is alone said to be worth upwards of £4 million, though Bill will never see it again.

Subsequently they bought a third home, overlooking one of Florida's finest golf courses, but still sought worldwide adventure. Judith, in particular, continued to enjoy academic exploration, too.

Though by no means short (as they'd say back in Co Durham when assessing the affluent) Bill would also be confused with the Microsoft founder of the same name and yet greater resources. 'People get quite disappointed when they realise I'm not the other one,' he once said, recalling the time that it took several minutes to persuade an air hostess of her mistake. 'When finally I did it,' said Bill, 'she asked rather plaintively if I might be his dad.'

Though perhaps inevitably they've had their moments — 'blood on the path' Judith likes to say — the couple marked their diamond wedding anniversary in November 2021. 'Celebrated' may not quite be the word.

Concerns about Bill's worsening memory had begun ten years earlier, leading to tests either side of the Atlantic and a diagnosis of probable chronic traumatic encephalopathy, a neurodegenerative disorder that can only conclusively be confirmed after death but which is caused by repeated head impacts — the sort which might be expected of a successful central defender. Slowly, inexorably and ineluctably, it has engulfed him.

For reasons of economy, if not of understanding, it will hereinafter be known as CTE. Perhaps also for future reference it should be made clear at this point that 'football' will generally refer to what the Americans call soccer and that rugby football — or 'rubbery football' as my three-year-old grandson rather appealingly calls it — is simply, here on in, rugby.

In 2014, after returning from London, Bill had forgotten where he'd left the car at Durham station. It took them an hour to find it, Judith remembers. In May 2022, pretty much the starting point for this mostly chronological account, he appears to remember almost nothing, needs a full-time carer, has little speech — even less that seems cogent — might sleep up to 18 hours a day and for his own safety may soon need residential care.

For Bill Gates — footballer, father, entrepreneur, adventurer, innovator — these are harrowing times, though medics assure his wife that he is not unhappy. The man whose 75th birthday cake was topped with a globe, who had visited 115 different countries of the world, who trekked the Inca trail in Peru and tracked mountain gorillas in Uganda, now seldom gets beyond his chair. Judith talks of the Long Goodbye. 'Our Titan diminishes by the day,' she says. 'Every day a little part of him slips away.'

Convinced that her husband's desperate illness was caused by excessively, day after day, heading a football — famous names like Nobby Stiles, Bobby and Jack Charlton, Jeff Astle, Denis Law, Jimmy Robson and Bob Paisley come to mind in similar circumstances — in January 2021 the great grandmother formally co-founded and fuelled Head for Change (H4C), a charity which aims to address concerns, provide care and seek solutions for football and rugby players and other sport participants and to have CTE and other neurodegenerative conditions prevalent among players of professional sport declared an industrial disease.

Denis Law, diagnosed at much the same time that H4C took up arms, was an Aberdeen fisherman's son revered on both sides of the border and the only Scot to win world football's Ballon d'Or. In his early days at Huddersfield Town, he recalled, team mates would take the mickey because after developing headaches he'd started to avoid heading in training because he felt it was doing him no good.

'More research needs to be done,' he told the media before his own diagnosis, 'there's so many old players in the same boat and all the evidence points towards the game being responsible. The football authorities should have acted a lot sooner with money for research. It's been really upsetting seeing those I played with and against suffering from dementia.'

Research at the University of Glasgow, about which we shall hear much more, shows that professional footballers are 3.5 times more likely to suffer a neurodegenerative disorder than non-players, five times more likely to develop Alzheimer's disease.

Anchored to the fundamental medical dictum 'First do no harm,' H4C (as its friends like to call it) has as the book begins already had huge impact at the highest level. Already it has sought answers to many searching and oft-disturbing questions, often with unsatisfactory and evasive outcomes. 'Personally, I would like to see the corrupt lose,' says Judith.

Bob Paisley, a miner's son from Hetton-le-Hole in Co Durham, became Liverpool FC's manager in 1974 after nearly 300 games for the club and a lengthy spell in the bright-burnished boot room at the Anfield ground. In nine seasons as manager he won three European Cups, six English league titles and was six times voted manager of the year.

I'd gone down to interview him in 1989, still in a fairly modest house in the city, a gentle and a generous man dressed in carpet slippers and old cardigan and with a long-familiar habit of saying 'and that' when seemingly lost for words. His only problem was that after all those years in the same house he couldn't for the life of him remember where the coffee was kept. 'Jessie will know when she gets back from fetching the grandchildren, he said and, of course, Mrs Paisley did.

The following year he became yet another former footballer to be diagnosed with dementia, word on the Merseyside street being that family had become worried when he'd got lost driving home from the stadium. Maybe he had, but the really early warning sign may have been when he forgot where Jessie kept the coffee. He did drive me back to Lime Street station, though.

Gordon McQueen is a former central defender with Leeds, Manchester United and Middlesbrough, capped 30 times by Scotland — 'a blonde Clydesdale' the *Glasgow Herald* called him, approvingly. I'd first met him when, as a Middlesbrough youth coach, he'd taken a team to a pre-season tournament in Wensleydale and a little lad ran round excitedly with an autograph book. 'I've got Steve McQueen,' he yelled. Gordon smiled; he'd probably heard it before.

In 2012, days after a boisterously celebrated 60th birthday — 'six in the evening till six the next morning, piper, the lot' — and nine months after he was diagnosed with cancer of the larynx, we met again at his home in North Yorkshire. Though his voice still rasped a bit, radiotherapy's side-effect, he was full of life and laughter, no plans to change. 'The medics blame everything on booze and fags, don't they?' said Gordon. 'If you went in with an ingrowing toe nail, they'd blame it on the beer.'

In 2021 he was diagnosed with vascular dementia, the likelihood being that by the following year that he'd have to go into care. They didn't blame that on beer and fags; they blamed it on football.

In the 1990s I'd gone to see someone at Blackburn Rovers' ground, wandering like a lost soul — a not uncommon experience — when asked by a track-suited chap if he could help. It was Tony Parkes, as much part of the Ewood Park furniture as the board room table — player, scout, six times acting manager and, as with so many former professional footballers, a thoroughly nice guy.

In 2020 Tony was also diagnosed with dementia, one of that cohort — of whom we shall hear more — whose family think he deserved a better deal from the Professional Footballers' Association to which all his career he'd subscribed.

There've been others of my acquaintance, not least Jack Charlton, a very successful manager and player with a wonderfully mischievous light in his eyes and a hypnotic effect on after-dinner audiences, not least because of his unalloyed Ashington accent and his incorrigible ability to cadge cigarettes. Though his family is reluctant to bolster the link between football and dementia, many shared the sadness of seeing the light fade.

I've known Bill Gates for over 20 years, his career greatly successful on and off the football field, a man who flew high but whose feet never left the ground or his heart the Co Durham coalfield. His darkness is now terrible, and no light at the end of the tunnel.

Mostly told sequentially over 2022–23, this is the story of Head for Change and of the subsequent charity Head Safe Football, of the manifest need for change and of the passion which drives Judith Gates and others to campaign for safer sport. It's the story of three coins in the fountain, of that teenage marriage back in 1961 and of the mutual success which followed but it has one perhaps glaring omission. Not for the want of supplication, of patience and indeed of entreaty, there is no direct input from the Football Association, English football's governing body and imagined guardian of the game. The FA has declined to engage, as rather quaintly they phrase it, with the writing of the book. That's unsatisfactory, to put it very mildly, and it's something to which, perhaps less diplomatically, we'll return.

How often during the story's difficult telling will Dr Judith Gates say that she'd give up everything, absolutely everything, just to have the old Bill — 'my Bill' — back in the chair alongside her?

2.

'I WANT TO TELL THEM THERE'S A TICKING TIME BOMB. AS YOU ARE, ONCE WAS BILL'

Bill was one of five sons of Jimmy Gates, a miner at Dean and Chapter colliery in Ferryhill, Co Durham, and of his wife Nancy. Eric, another son, played football at a high level for Ipswich Town and Sunderland and was twice capped by England.

Judith lived in Spennymoor, a couple of miles west, the only daughter of Harry Curry, an insurance man who was 45 when his baby girl was born, and of his wife Margaret, 10 years younger, who worked in a family shop. Though their home was terraced, it had a little balcony above the front window. 'People thought we were posh,' she says.

Bill was forever football daft, organised while still a boy a petition to persuade the council to erect goalposts on waste land near their home in Neale Street. Jimmy always kept a spare pane of glass, in the sure and certain knowledge that it would be needed to address the more wayward efforts of his sons and their friends amid the neighbours' windows.

Keith Telford and Les Walker, friends from those formative years, meet again — the first time in more than 60 years — to recall happy days. They talk of poss tubs and of the store horse, of prize leeks and six-day weeks, of the times when coalface camaraderie surfaced seamlessly to cement the long, lean terraces above.

If Billy No-mates is the symbolic 21st Century pariah — and why pick on poor old Billy, anyway? — then Billy Gates (they all called him Billy in Dean Bank, still do) was his 20th Century antithesis. Everyone liked Billy, everyone wanted to be on the same team, whatever the game and whatever the gang. If it wasn't a team game — maybe marbles, raw-kneed in the coal-black back alley — he'd beat them all at that.

Dean Bank was built around Dean and Chapter colliery, separated from Ferryhill by the Great North Road (as then it was) and by sporadic outbursts of territorial warfare. The lad, they reckon, was a pretty good scrapper, too.

The pit had been sunk in 1902, familiar Durham seams like the Busty and the Brockwell, the Harry and the Five Quarter and with an all-too-familiar death toll. The Durham Mining Museum website lists 177 casualties, concedes there were probably many more, causes of death ranging from falls of stone — probably the most frequent — to the poor lad who died from complications after his pony stood on his foot. He was just 15.

Some causes were rather more arcane. 'The coal fell from a sooty back at the loose end of the jud. A sprag had been set....' Whatever precisely had befallen, that victim was just 14.

There is a tangential curiosity, a little mystery, however. A large fascia board outside the Dean and Chapter pub in Ferryhill, not half a mile from the former pit head, proclaims that the pub is dedicated to the memory of the 73 miners who lost their lives between production starting in 1906 and 1929. Production ended in 1966, it adds.

So what of the other 37 years, of the other 104 men — on the Mining Museum's lugubriously conservative estimate — who were killed thereafter? They were aged from 14 ('killed instantly when he was caught between two trucks on the surface') to 66, putters and pullers-up, screenhands and shaftmen, onsetters, run riders, banksmen, deputies.

A 16-year-old pony lad had 'fallen unconscious into a few inches of slurry,' a washery attendant had (it says) been 'caught up in the machinery and mangled.' Had the mortal coil a break point? Might not Dean Bank and Ferryhill wish to raise a glass in their memory, too?

The colliery terraces had almost all been named after Victorian industrial pioneers, men like Stephenson, Siemens, Bessemer, Faraday and Davy. Neale Street, where seven members of the Gates family lived pretty much harmoniously, might less easily have fallen from an O-level history paper. Who was Neale? Might he, too, have been a father of invention, perhaps even a Dean of Durham? It's a puzzle to which we shall return.

Keith Telford lived next door to the Gates family and was a year younger than Bill. Les Walker, born just a few days after Bill and a classmate at the village primary school, lived in Stephenson Street. Bill's grandfather lived over the road from the family. 'If there was a big football match we'd all be over Bill's grandfather's,' says Keith. 'He was the only one with a telly.'

Unanimously they recall that young Bill was a genuinely nice lad, unanimously that though they didn't have much, they never went short, either. 'We weren't raggy arsed or any of those other things you hear about,' says Les. 'The kids could always properly be turned out.'

The three of us take lunch in a pub a couple of miles away — none, surprisingly, can remember Dean Bank ever having a pub, no matter how great the communal thirst — and there recall the formative fifties.

Keith joined the Midland Bank — '£34 a month, Billy was getting £50 a week,' — retired at 52, devoted himself to charitable works. Les worked in a factory at Spennymoor. Though they live just 25 miles apart, they'd not met since school days.

At Dean Bank primary, they remember, there could be 50 in a class. From his back pocket Les produces the end-of-year report in which — 'excellent progress' — he'd finished 7th. 'If I was 7th then Billy would have been top,' he says. 'Bright lad, Billy.'

They remember Spennymoor Grammar Technical School, as formally it was, and recall Billy Sumner — their first headmaster — patrolling the corridors on his bicycle while wearing an academic gown and carrying a cane as a churchwarden might carry a wand of office, though for a more punitive purpose. Keith almost shudders. 'You didn't want to see Billy Sumner too often,' he says.

They also recall Joe Coulthard, the sports master. 'Funny feller, he'd throw cold water at you as you came out of the shower. Mind, we'd get him back on the football field and he was all right about that. Decent chap, really.'

Though by every account England's youth team captain remained unassuming, just one of the lads, a piece he'd been asked to write for the school magazine — a publication called *Silver Buckle,* a nod to Bonny Bobby Shafto, who'd lived a mile down the road — told tantalisingly of his adventures.

'Apart from visiting Scotland and Wales, I have also been abroad twice this year,' it began, and at a time when the average Dean Bank pitman's son might have been little further than Redcar on the workmen's club trip, and only then if his dad had kept up with the subs.

One fortnight-long trip had been to a 14-nation tournament in Portugal. 'The weather was perfect, just right for sunbathing, but in my haste to pack I had left behind my bathing trunks,' he wrote, also somewhat incredulously referring to the price of 'English things'.

In Portugal a sixpenny bar of chocolate equated to 1/10d, a jar of strawberry jam five shillings and a telegram home nine bob for three words. Chiefly they relied upon letters from Blighty, distributed before dinner at 7pm, though seldom to team manager Billy Wright, capped more than 100 times for his country and married at the age of 34 to Joy Beverley, one of the singing sisters. The skipper was gallant, if unguarded. 'I let him read one or two of mine,' he said.

Back in Dean Bank they'd play endless cricket and football with little regard for neighbours' windows or for overlapping seasons, unless it snowed — it did in those days — when cricket became a bit tricky. Usually it was in the front street, sometimes in the tiled back alley. 'The cobbles were useful for learning how to play spin,' says Les, improbably.

Bill was a good cricketer, too, in the Durham County second team when just 15 and a regular with the Dean and Chapter side. Les remembers batting with him. 'He did particularly well because he didn't have very good eyesight. They hadn't perfected contact lenses in those days and often enough he couldn't see the score-board. People might have thought we were discussing tactics in the middle when really he was asking me what the score was.'

By his Football League days contact lenses were a bit more sophisticated, though still the size of plastic pennies, his myopia cited by club doctor Neil Phillips after Bill had been sent off for what the referee had considered a particularly brutal tackle.

The FA panel listened intently, perhaps incredulously. 'You mean' said the chairman, 'that he can't see the difference between the ball and a leg?' The appeal was lost.

Keith Telford also remembers Middlesbrough manager Bob Dennison's visits to Neale Street, attempts to get the lad ticed, as probably they'd have said down the pit. 'I guess,' he says, 'that the money probably talked loudest in the end.'

Keith himself made several appearances for Ferryhill Athletic, then Northern League 'amateurs', initially surprised to find ten shillings in his boot at the end of the match. 'Do you think the tax man will be round?' he wonders, all those years thereafter.

Whatever the sport, windows were at risk. As Judith Gates had herself recalled, that's where her future father-in-law came in. 'One time when we broke one it was the last people in the street you'd want to upset but fortunately they were out,' says Keith. 'Jimmy produced a pane of glass, removed the broken one, put the new one in, puttied it, painted it and was back in the house before they got home. I doubt if to this day they'd have known what happened, unless they smelled the putty.'

If schoolyard teams were picked in the accustomed manner — what might be supposed devil-take-the-hindmost — then William Lazenby Gates was always on the side of the angels. 'Whatever he turned his hand to, he was the best but he was never big headed, always just one of the lads,' says Keith.

'Just quiet,' says Les. 'I can never once remember him picking on anyone, never bullying anyone. Billy was just a genuinely nice lad, but you could hardly ever walk down Neale Street and not see him playing football.'

Didn't he ever get into schoolboy scrapes, then? 'Oh come on,' says Keith Telford, 'Billy was the biggest catch at Spennymoor Grammar School; don't you think that getting Judith pregnant was a big enough scrape on its own?'

That early move to Teesside, those unexpected changes in circumstances, meant that the old friends had hardly seen one another until a school reunion held in 2014 at the Gates family home in Castle Eden. 'Bill seemed all right,' Keith recalls. 'With hindsight you could see that Judith was looking out for him but he was making sure we had enough to drink, showing us round the lovely house and gardens, seemed OK. To see the way he is now — it's just awful, isn't it?'

Lunch consumed and memories shared, Les Walker kindly offers a lift to Dean Bank and to Neale Street, different in their youth because many of its houses there were owner occupied — 'the posh end' he says.

Nor was it so posh that concessionary coal wouldn't be dumped out the back, stopping play until someone shifted it. Jimmy and Nancy Gates, Keith Telford had supposed, bought their house for £400.

The village school seems outwardly little changed, though doubtless a technological crucible within. A sign proclaims its mantra: 'Believe, achieve, soar with pride.' The allotments still grow at the bottom of the street, though another sign proclaims them to be 'Smart allotments' — that's technological, too. In Jimmy Gates's deep-digging days, a smart allotment was one where they'd creosoted the fence.

'He'd just divide his time between the pit and the allotment and he was the most generous man alive,' says Les. 'Half his produce he'd give to the neighbours just to help them out.' When the pit closed, Jimmy took a newsagent's in Staindrop, about 15 miles south. 'Mind, I never had him down as a shopkeeper,' says Les. 'He'd probably have given half the stuff away.'

John McManners, a retired Church of England priest and scion of another well-remembered Ferryhill family, had also recalled happy days on the allotments. 'Me and my brothers and the Gates boys knocked around everywhere together. Happy days, though it was usually the lads who did the digging while Jimmy Gates and my dad leaned over the gate, gossiping.'

John's sibling Bob, a retired Bishop Auckland GP appointed OBE for services to the community, recalls the annual pig muck derby between the two sets of brothers. It would be around Christmas time, the pig muck — essential for the allotments — collected in old baths from Blackett's Farm near Ferryhill football ground and raced across the Great North Road to Dean Bank. 'They just had an old tin bath and we had a white enamel one with blue facings. They used to call us posh,' says Bob.

Conflict ensued, however, when a McManners family saboteur hid behind a fence to throw wizened old beetroots at the rival bath. 'There was a bit of a fracas, I think our John got thumped,' recalls Bob getting on 70 years later. 'You couldn't blame them, all those beetroots left less room in the bath for pig muck. It was the sort of thing that might only happen in Dean Bank.' And the assailant? 'I fear that it was Bill.'

So what else has changed? Well, obviously the pit has gone and with it that coalface cohesion but the main things, says Les, are the number of working women — 'hardly any of them worked back then' — and the volume of traffic. 'When we lived in Stephenson Street there were 90 houses and one car. Now you can hardly cross the road for them.'

No stone unturned in Neale Street, I seek out acclaimed North-East author and playwright Michael Chaplin, whose father Sid wrote *Close the Coalhouse Door* and whose grandparents lived in Bessemer Street, nearby. Could the street name, Michael very reasonably wonders, be a tribute to Edward Vansittart Neale (1810–92) a pioneer of the Co-operative movement and co-founder of the Northern Wholesale Co-operative Society — 'posh geezer but politically sound.'

There's another memorial to Edward Neale in St Paul's Cathedral, though St Paul's Cathedral never got concessionary coal and nor might it perceive the slightly spectral figure of Billy Gates, forever kicking a football, forever seeking perfection, out the back.

Bill's trip to the Olympics, his wife supposes, was funded by the 'backhanders' siphoned by Spennymoor United to their young star and safeguarded by his mum in a teapot.

'I can't really remember much about him before that,' says Judith. 'He was just one of those people who'd have to stand up at school assembly because he'd captained England or whatever. He also bought me a single rose in Rome, which was quite romantic for a Ferryhill lad.'

Jimmy had once gone to Scotland to watch his son in a youth international, returning to find half the street anxious to know how the lad had got on. 'All Jimmy wanted to talk about was the electric blanket on the hotel bed,' says Judith. 'He'd never had one of those before, probably no one round there had.'

Jimmy, by then 90 and living in Staindrop, had also declined to attend Bill and Judith's lavish golden wedding celebration, held in

Australia, on the grounds familiar to Durham miners that it was ower much clart. 'Besides, he'd added, 'who's ganna look after me allotment?'

Judith had had no interest in sport, supposes that her best game was Scrabble. 'I was always the last to be picked for the hockey or netball teams. You talk about opposites attracting. Bill appeared so confident, so certain of himself, and I was a bookish kind of kid with all of my focus academic. My dad thought I'd be the first woman prime minister, really proud because I could multiply anything by 13.'

Mind, the story goes that Bill's first romantic interest amid the fountains of Rome had been Pauline Blanch, a blonde lass from Shildon. 'There might have been one or two more,' says his wife, cheerfully. 'There were some good looking girls in Shildon.'

So what were his great qualities? 'Tenacity, stubbornness, innate goodness, determination, hard work. He wasn't feckless, he wouldn't run away from anything. He'd stand up.'

He'd thus been characteristically determined that they should marry, sought advice from Middlesbrough FC director Eric Thomas, a solicitor, contemplated a Gretna Green elopement before parental consent, however reluctantly, was wrung out. 'There was still a real stigma about being pregnant at 16,' says Judith. 'We tried to keep it secret, even when I had morning sickness on another school trip.

'One of the worst moments after it became known was my father sitting at the end of the kitchen table with his head in his hands, crying. I just felt absolute guilt. Bill's dad said they'd look after the bairn, my mum and dad did as well, but we were determined to show we could do it — even if I did have to ring my mum to ask her how to make mince. 'It was still a source of great joy when David was born. He remains my precious elder son.'

What of Pauline Blanch, the Shildon blonde? What of Billy Sumner, the stick-wielding, gown-wearing headmaster who'd police grammar school corridors on a push bike? How different might things have been if, when in Rome, they'd chosen not to do as the Romans do?

Pauline was herself a county standard athlete — 'I loved all games except hockey, didn't want to lose my front teeth' — herself became a teacher, twice married and twice divorced 'I haven't had much luck with men,' she says. She's made a plate of tuna sandwiches, as good Co Durham folk do, though it's still just 11am. (Had it been Sunday teatime, there'd have been tinned pears, pears in syrup, to follow.)

Vividly, she still recalls that moment when the handsome young Gates asked her out. 'We were waiting for the bus to the station, after that a steam train all the way to Rome. I was with Pat Cheeseborough, my friend, and we'd promised to support one another. I was 15, Bill was in the year above about to go into the sixth form. Honestly, I'd hardly heard of him, I didn't want it to be a distraction.'

She pulls from a drawer a box of Brownie-box snaps, a couple of the well-groomed young footballer, a third of herself — blonde, bouffant, bonny — relaxing in a deckchair. None of the photographs has them together. They never were.

Spennymoor Grammar Technical School had been established just a few years earlier, formally co-educational but strictly socially distanced. Whatever passed behind the bike shed was nothing more than cigarette smoke, a seductive whiff of Woodbine.

'The school was supposed to be really innovative but the teachers were fogeyish and old-fashioned,' says Pauline. While prefects stood vigilant on every corner, the head would set off on mobile patrol. 'The head was all right with me, because I blew up his tyres.' You did what? 'I just got the job one day and then he'd ask me again. We could have a little joke about it.'

The deputy head, meanwhile, kept a list by the chemi lab blackboard of all those educational incorrigibles seen fraternising with members of the opposite sex — 'If you got on the list two or three times he'd have you in' — while the senior mistress was in the extraordinary habit of lifting girls' skirts as they left assembly to check that regulation navy blue knickers, perhaps any knickers, were in place.

'We'd be filing out in one column, the boys in another. She'd lift the skirts really high. It was supposed to be a modern school but that's how it was, and that was into the 1960s. We were taught together but had to do almost everything else separately. It might seem funny now, but when we went to Rome I was more interested in the Olympic Games than in boys.'

The girls stayed at a convent, where invigilation was every bit as strict. 'One morning at breakfast a nun tapped me on the arm because I was wearing a sleeveless dress. The neck was high but you couldn't even bare your arms. Even when we were allowed to the beach on the last day, every move was supervised.'

It was several months (of course) before the young Judith Curry's pregnancy became public knowledge. 'It was a scandal, the atmosphere in the school was horrible, it was like such a thing had never happened before. People were crying,' says Pauline. 'Judith obviously was believed to have a very bright future. I suppose they thought she'd lose it.'

Coins thrown into the fountain, they returned whence they came, Judith a little closer to her future husband than she'd been on the way out. 'It was fair game, he'd asked me and I turned him down,' says Pauline. 'If he'd asked me out on the way back I might well have said yes. You really do wonder how different things might all have been then.'

It's a lovely March morning in 2022 when first Judith and I begin these conservatory conversations in Castle Eden. Bill no longer able to travel, wings forever clipped, it was their first English spring for several decades. They'd returned the previous May.

She's just missed a call from former England footballer Gavin McCann, like many more an ardent Head for Change champion. 'You think you're invincible,' he'd once said, 'and then you see the consequences.'

Coffee is served alongside a great scree of Tunnock's caramel wafers, to become a familiar accompaniment as the story unfolds. Coffee table books include a collection by the late Norman Cornish, Spennymoor's globally celebrated pitman painter, a photograph album recording the work of Coaches Across Continents — their younger son Nick's award-winning football-centred charity — and a volume about women who've changed the world, from Joan Baez to Golda Meir and from Billie Jean King to Ella Fitzgerald.

Judith delights at the vernal daffodils — 'I didn't know we had any' — equally loves the snowdrops. 'Bill planted those, I think he dug them up from somewhere else,' she says, wistfully.

He comes in silently to say hello, spends much of the rest of the time watching — looking at — football on a large screen television in another room or, head down, walking with his carer around a house the size of a football field, in search of things that he will never again find.

No matter how bright the birdsong, how dancing the daffodils, for Bill Gates it's forever a bleak midwinter. His wife has no doubt that it's repeatedly heading a football, perhaps 100 times a day in training, which is responsible. If it's a game, he's lost.

Judith would take her boys to Middlesbrough matches, one on each arm, enjoyed the social life with other players' families — the first WAGS, she supposes. Those happy days are recalled on the H4C website: 'Sitting in the stand alongside my two proud young sons, we delighted to see him emerge from the dressing room onto the pitch. He ran out with confidence — fit, muscular, alert. Nothing could diminish this man.'

Now she is haunted by the image, his confidence replaced by confusion and alertness by an uncomprehending and all-encompassing anxiety. 'Our Titan is no more,' Judith adds on the website. 'The game that strengthened him is destroying him brain cell by brain cell.

'I want to shout out a warning to the young players of today. I want to tell them that they are not indestructible, that there's a ticking time bomb. As you are, so once was Bill.'

The migraines had started fairly early in his professional career, dismissed by the Middlesbrough club doctor — 'ahead of his time in so many ways' — as something that just went with the territory, perhaps like a kick on the shin pads. 'His aim was just to get players back as quickly as possible,' says Judith. 'I would question his medical objectivity.'

Unmemorable until accumulated, issues with concentration worsened, especially when studying. 'We maybe thought that was just the way it was, but now it seems to have been the start of something.'

In 1966–67 he'd helped Boro gain promotion from the old third division — 12 points behind Queens Park Rangers — and in 1973–74 was part of manager Jack Charlton's squad which won the second division by 15 points from Luton Town. By then, shortly before his 30th birthday and evermore tormented by those crippling headaches, he'd decided upon retirement.

The first shop, simply Bill Gates Sports, opened in the Dundas Arcade in the Boro. It was about the time that trainers were no longer blokes with a mucky towel and a magic sponge but a football fashion statement, that tracksuits were becoming trendy and that a replica shirt spoke not just of loyalty but of young love.

Bill was among the first to discern the trend. Besides, the guys with the magic sponge were becoming physios by then. 'He approached it scientifically, he studied the demographics,' says Judith. 'He didn't just stand there hoping to sell sports gear, everything he did had an entrepreneurial approach. The staff would do anything for him and he for them, including cleaning the toilet.'

Herself a director of the company, she talks of Monument Sports as 'we'. Bill, she says, worked hard and thought things through. 'I had a very satisfactory pay cheque as a head teacher but I was also a shared problem solver with Bill. He was brave, he wasn't afraid to take risks. We'd talk things through in the evening, but it was his baby.'

The migraines temporarily eased. Dormant? 'I'd say quiescent,' says Judith.

The £4.4 million sale complete, the decision on what to do next was complicated because her career had moved on to Durham University. 'I was embedded in it, I loved it,' she says.

Bill favoured emigration, not least because of the expected capital gains tax demand, talked of new opportunities and of chances they might never again have. Their lives, she says, had become separately together. 'It was a very persuasive argument.'

They looked at the Bahamas, thought about other Caribbean escapes, settled on the beach-front apartment in Cayman. 'If we were going to the Caribbean,' says Judith, 'I wanted a place where chickens came in plastic bags, not where you had to wring their necks in the marketplace.'

They also owned a 28ft boat called *Harry C*, named after Judith's dad, a veritable dinghy compared to some of the yachts moored nearby. 'We were comfortable but some of the neighbours were seriously wealthy. It didn't matter and there were no great trappings of wealth, you spent most of the time in shorts or a swimsuit.'

She held visiting professorships at major US universities; became involved in the Cayman community on several levels. 'We didn't want to be typical expats. I don't play bridge and I don't drink much gin and tonic,' she says, perhaps recalling occasions when its intent was most kindly supposed medicinal.

Bill still played football, for Cayman Over-40s and for Coutts' Bank — who no doubt wanted to keep him onside. 'He was already grey haired,' says Judith. 'I think they were surprised that he was still quite good.'

He also remained an adventurer, keen to tackle the Inca Trail, explore the Amazon rain forest or, more inexplicably, to have a heart-to-heart with a big silverback gorilla. 'He once almost did it,' says his wife. 'The silverback put its chin in one hand, Bill did the same and they just looked at one another.'

He was the one, says Judith, who'd just let the day roll out. 'There was still an impulsivity. He'd go off and do things because he could.'

In the early years of the 21st Century they were also asked by Jimmy Gates, one of Bill's brothers, to take a controlling interest in the Whitworth Hall Hotel, near Spennymoor, former home of Bonny Bobby Shafto (who'd also gone to sea and inspired the school magazine.) Still only allowed 91 days' annual home leave, they might be seen waiting at table when in UK residence.

Into his early sixties, however, signs and symptoms of Bill's illness were becoming ever more evident. Extensive tests in 2014 revealed 'mild cognitive impairment'; three years later everything pointed to CTE, though the condition could only be confirmed at post mortem.

The conversation turns — inevitably, almost unwillingly — to his death, after which his brain will be donated for medical research. Judith supposes that, in that event, she will resume a lifestyle either side of the Atlantic. 'It sounds corny but I believe that's what he would want me to do. Bill always said that if you fall on your face, you get back up and start again. He always thought that there was a big interesting world out there, and that we should go and see it. We still had plans.'

Now he sits unresponsively in another room, going nowhere, gazing at that large screen on which 22 well-paid men run athletically around with perhaps never a thought for the neurological consequences, or for what might happen next. It's football, unforgiving football, and it has brought Bill Gates to this.

'The journey isn't going to have a good ending,' says Judith, 'but it's another journey, nonetheless.'

3.

'A RUGGED CENTRE HALF WHO WOULDN'T FLINCH AT A HEAD-ON MEETING WITH CASSIUS CLAY, IF HE WAS WEARING A NO 9 SHIRT'

In more modest homes they might be kept in a cupboard under the stairs. At the Castle Eden mansion the huge scrapbooks pile up in a room that might otherwise double as a single bedroom, chronicling an eventful and sometimes surprising football career.

Who so meticulously maintained them I ask Judith — Bill, her or the butler? 'Bill did,' she replies. 'The butler was too busy serving the sherry.'

The books are hard backed, the size of bakers' bread trays, relevant years gold tooled on the spine. At first — 'Spennymoor boys knock out Kelloe in Shield' — the press cuttings appear to have been pasted with the panache of a five-foot man whitewashing an eight-foot ceiling. Later volumes are pristine, an accountant assiduously at work.

They range comprehensively from early days almost up to his final Middlesbrough match, May 1974, a testimonial against first division champions Leeds United which drew 31,643 spectators to the old Ayresome Park ground. The match alone, said the *Evening Gazette,* would have made the beneficiary around £16,000.

Inflation was running — galloping — at 16 per cent. At 2022 values, it's reckoned, that £16,000 would be worth a dozen times as much. It wasn't a bad start.

The cuttings from the early 1960s offer little suggestion of what might be termed extramural activity, still less of tittle-tattle, not even in the *News of the World.* Margaret Curry, Judith's mum, does however have a pointed paragraph about the forthcoming nuptials. 'We think they're rather young, of course, but they're very fond of one another and we don't want to stand in their way.'

Scant evidence, either, of the tabloids' latter-day passion for punning, though Golden Gates occasionally proves irresistible.

A national magazine cutting, late 1961, details the names to watch in the following year, ranging from Yves St Laurent to Helen Shapiro, from Jackie Kennedy to J D Salinger and from Sean Connery infallibly to Pope John (well you would, wouldn't you?) There's only one footballer — 17-year-old Bill Gates.

If subsequently there's a thread, if not quite a theme, it's that the miner's son from Neale Street, Dean Bank, was rugged, unflinching, hard tackling (as folk sometimes euphemistically have it) and uncompromising. Prisoners were for Durham Jail, a few miles up the old A1; Bill Gates took none.

On one occasion, an FA Cup replay at Manchester United, he'd suffered a double jaw fracture after allegedly being thumped while play, attention and referee were at the other end of the field and with England forward Brian Kidd the principal suspect. Jaw wired after an operation at a Manchester hospital, he'd been interviewed by the *Sunday Express,* philosophically if rather improbably citing the scripture that those who live by the sword must expect to die by it.

'I never squeal,' he said, meaning with anatomical accuracy that he took it on the chin, though he spoke, the paper added, through clenched teeth. 'You have to when your jaw's broken in two places.'

The home side won 2–1 thanks to a contentious late penalty. 'United will never be as lucky again,' said the *Daily Mirror* and in that respect, at least, was manifestly mistaken.

At Spennymoor Grammar School there'd been a dilemma. Though clearly a gifted footballer, though Middlesbrough and other clubs proved sedulous suitors, the youngster had his heart set on becoming a PE teacher. 'My studies will always come first,' he told reporters thronged outside the school gate after being chosen — still an 'amateur' with Spennymoor United — to make his Middlesbrough debut in the match at Luton Town just a few months after his 17th birthday.

First, though, he'd had to seek permission from Donald Cockburn, who by then had replaced Bicycle Billy as headmaster. 'He gave me the Friday off but said it mustn't happen too often,' said Bill, already captain of the England youth team. 'I'll take some school books on the journey, so I can keep up.'

Ever synoptic, the press pack supposed him tousle-haired, a description unlikely to have suited either Bill or his barber. Such is the volume and variety of the scrapbook cuttings, however, the local paper shop owner could probably have retired by the time he reached 35.

The media also appeared as one about the youngster's confident demeanour, the sixth former — like Batman's sidekick — oft-dubbed the Boy Wonder. 'He showed the brainy maturity of a man ten years older,' wrote the near-legendary Charlie Summerbell in the *Daily Mirror* of the lad with the leather satchel over his shoulder and the lapel badges in his blazer. 'Gates smilingly weighed questions and deliberated every answer. He handled reporters as expertly as a Hollywood film star would,' Summerbell added.

Reports after the 3–2 defeat at Luton were rather less unanimous, however. 'Tough time for boy centre half,' said one. 'Gates had a tough debut,' read another. The *Daily Mail* — 'Boro saved from a drubbing by young Gates' — appeared to offer a minority view but one clearly shared by manager Dennison and his board.

Dr Neil Phillips, himself a club director in the 1960s, was also impressed. 'Gates was an unusual professional footballer — articulate, academically very bright, forthright in his views and determined to succeed in both his professions,' wrote Dr Phillips in his self-published autobiography in 2007. Self-published? 'It is a measure of my celebrity status,' he said, self-effacingly, at the time.

Boro's proffered terms, insisted Dennison, were 'attractive', though some might have supposed them drop-dead gorgeous. A few days after vowing that his studies would always be paramount, the Boy Wonder had signed as a full-time professional, the £50-a-week wage widely trumpeted and no matter that part of it was instalments on a signing on fee. 'The richest soccer kid in Britain,' said the *Mirror,* unequivocally. The headmaster's reaction is, perhaps happily, not recorded.

The scrapbooks overflow, embracing contracts that always begin with the perhaps ambiguous stipulation that 'the player shall play in an efficient manner.' Few doubted or defined it. Bonus payments might be £1 a man for every 1,000 in the home crowd over 21,000, maybe an additional fiver apiece were the team to find themselves sitting in the top three.

Neil Phillips, also medical officer to England's 1966 World Cup winning squad, recorded in *Doctor to the World Champions* that such was the contractual contrivance that when Boro were relegated to the old third division at the end of 1965–66 each man received a £330 bonus. 'A bonus for being abject failures,' he added, slightly superfluously.

The scrapbooks include hundreds of programmes from matches in which Bill played — maybe 4d when he began, perhaps 5p by the time it all ended. In the unlikely event of the Gates family finding themselves contemplating supplementary benefit, flogging that lot might keep the wolf from the door for several months.

There are great sheaves of Post Office telegrams, too, one purportedly from young Nick when aged about four and another addressed to Bill Gateshead but safely delivered, nonetheless.

Club rule books, the size of a 1960s workmen's club card, forbid everything from smoking on the premises to bringing friends into the dressing room. Invitations to international trial matches ordain that the player bring his own boots and shin pads and, in capitals, A LARGE CLEAN TOWEL.

Other cuttings reveal him to have been a capable cricketer with Dean and Chapter, a Ferryhill side named after the pit where his father had long toiled, and a decent schoolboy athlete — including in the shot. Judith's name occasionally appears, too, like the time she'd vividly dreamed that Boro would beat first division Everton 2–1 in another FA Cup tie. They lost 3–0.

A business page takes a different slant, supposes that Middlesbrough players' salaries are a closely guarded secret but that some may be on as much as £3,000-£4,000 a year. The club which he joined was also in the hunt for what football called talent money — £220, between the talented lot of them, for finishing fifth in the old second division. (Before the Premiership, Championship, League One and League Two, the old system was simply called Divisions 1 to 4).

Bill and his family had by then moved to Marske, near Redcar. 'He has a detached house that he wouldn't sell for less than £11,000, owns a Singer Gazelle that he bought for £800 in 1968 and doesn't go out much,' it's observed.

In another late 1960s report he admits that he and the family try to live on £12 a week, asking the club directly to bank the rest. 'You tend to spend a lot of money on things like buying a five-a-side goal for your children,' he adds, improbably.

In the mornings he trained, in the afternoons worked in an accountant's office and in the evenings studied — around 26 hours a week, he thought. 'I'm fascinated by figures. Accountancy is almost as intriguing as my football. I've two careers ahead of me and I'm confident I can make a good living at both. I get a lot of ribbing from the lads but I wish that all footballers thought about what happens when they stop playing. Judith never complains, but neither of us has very much spare time.'

The wretched irony, of course, is that the man who so scrupulously sustained memories has now been almost completely robbed of recollection.

Those were the hot metal days when national newspapers sold in molten millions, when Pinks (to resurrect a very old joke) really were black and white and read all over and when the bylines were a story in themselves. Familiar former footballers like Jackie Milburn, Ivor Broadis and Len Shackleton — Shack once naming Bill his North-East player of the year, though he'd spent much of the preceding season at right back and not in his preferred central defensive position — sat in the press box alongside ink-stained old hands like Summerbell, Vince Wilson, Doug Weatherall, Cliff Mitchell of the *Evening Gazette* and dear old Ray Robertson of the *Echo*.

Vince Wilson seemed particularly to admire the Boy Wonder, and to enjoy his company. 'At first glance he might strike you as being a student of medicine, or archaeology or something highbrow like that,' he wrote in the *Sunday Mirror*. 'He certainly doesn't strike you as a footballer.'

The piece said nothing about his hair, tousled or otherwise.

Two weeks after his debut, Middlesbrough played Sunderland, the youngster charged with marking the prodigiously free scoring Brian Clough. Boro won 2–0, Clough so eclipsed that manager Dennison suggested that his new centre half could be in England's team within two or three years and in the £30,000 bracket — by which he meant his transfer value, not his annual income.

By the age of 19, however, he'd unsuccessfully submitted a written transfer request in an attempt to get more first team opportunities elsewhere. Though naturally a central defender, he was also greatly versatile, playing in most positions — including centre forward — but not always happy. On one occasion he was said to have been 'infuriated' after Middlesbrough manager

Stan Anderson — the only man to have captained each of the North-East's oft-diminutive big three — praised his performance in midfield.

'If Boro can't look in the third or fourth division and find a better midfielder than me then something's very wrong,' he told Cliff Mitchell in the *Gazette*. There were to be other issues with Anderson.

That Bill never reached full international heights may partly have been because of a catalogue of illness and injuries, detailed in Neil Phillips's 580-page autobiography. 'He fractured a bone in his spine, fractured an ankle, fractured a toe. He had a cartilage operation on his knee, developed a deep venous thrombosis in his leg and suffered numerous attacks of tonsilitis. Bill certainly had his share of illness and injury.'

Then, of course, there was the painful matter of that double jaw fracture at the hands of persons unknown. (Or if known full well, then not publicly acknowledged, anyway.)

His own somewhat fearsome reputation finally underwent a Damascene conversion on the road to Ayresome Park. 'He had a bad image,' said *Goal* magazine, paradoxically of a genuinely good guy. 'His crunching tackles, his flashes of indiscretion and his habit of giving away penalties had earned his bookings, early baths and official reprimands,' said the magazine beneath the headline 'Boro fans loved to hate Bill Gates.'

Vince Wilson supposed him 'an intellectual with a killer instinct,' wondered what made the 'quiet accountant' snap on a Saturday afternoon, added that Bill's worsening record meant his approach had to change; Shack, somewhat improbably, thought enthusiasm Bill's worst enemy.

'A rugged centre-half who wouldn't flinch at a head-on meeting with Cassius Clay if he was wearing a No 9 shirt,' said the *Sunday Mirror*. Raich Carter, manager in the mid-60s, thought him 'a model professional,' nonetheless.

The scrapbooks offer further evidence for the prosecution, not least in the form of a £10 fine — payment acknowledged by the FA Benevolent Fund with a receipt written over a twopenny stamp. (When did that stop, then?) By 28, in media eyes at any rate, the Boy Wonder had become a 'veteran'.

Ever honest, Bill accepted the charges both official and editorial. 'I knew I had to stay away from trouble,' he said. 'It would have been fatal to have carried on the same old way. In some cases I didn't deserve a booking, I will never deny my full blooded approach but I don't mind telling you I'd lost faith in myself.'

If officialdom suffered metaphorical headaches, however, his own had become blindingly, inescapably, real. Before his 30th birthday he announced his retirement, the testimonial between second and first division champions enthusiastically arranged — his final game for the club.

It ended 4–4 — 'fiesta football, sunshine soccer, golden goals, a match that will live long in the memory,' said the *Gazette,* rather ironically, the following evening. Alan Foggon scored a hat-trick for Boro and David Mills the fourth; Jordan, Yorath, Lorimer and Bremner replied for Leeds.

The crowd stood to salute the beneficiary, none doubting that he'd played in an efficient manner — and for William Lazenby Gates, an extraordinary new chapter was about to begin.

4.

'THERE ARE LOTS OF OPPORTUNITIES IN LIFE. SOME PEOPLE TAKE THEM AND SOME PEOPLE DON'T'

Len Shackleton, mentioned just a couple of pages back, was a Sunderland and England winger — Newcastle United, too, come to think — whose autobiography was called *Clown Prince of Soccer*. Most memorably, the chapter headed 'The average club director's knowledge of football' offered nothing more than a blank page.

The internet uncharacteristically offering almost nothing on Monument Sports, this chapter on how Bill Gates developed his sportswear empire from a small unit in Middlesbrough to a multi-million pound chain of ten stores across the north was in danger of similar vacuity.

It's resuscitated by Boro fan Simon Lee who provides extracts from several publications, including Harry Glasper's *Middlesbrough A-Z* and *Ayresome Angels: the Boys of '67* by Gordon Cox and Alastair Brownlie.

Glasper supposes Bill to have had a reputation as a football hard man. To have been a great all-rounder but to have enjoyed fluctuating fortunes. 'He often only had a first team place because of injuries to other players and was regarded as a utility player.' In football, 'utility', 'versatility' and 'all round ability' may be pretty much synonymous, though the first may have a pejorative sheen.

There's also a Middlesbrough year book from 1970–71 — 'At the crossroads when the season ended, Gates took the right turn for himself and for the club. Manager Stan Anderson forgot about his centre half search even when Gates was ruled out with a broken jaw (you remember that broken jaw) after the FA Cup tie with Manchester United. 'A brilliant reader of the game, he played with distinction at both full back and centre half, a very versatile player.'

With an almost reluctant irony, Cox and Brownlie claim that though he'd enjoyed his playing days, Bill's head was really screwed on away from the game — 'and that's how he made his fortune.'

During the last four or five years of his playing career, Bill reckoned, he'd visited sports shops all over Britain to gain understanding of how the business worked. Perhaps it just seemed a bit more exciting than accountancy. Bill wrote:

> Leisurewear was just coming in'. People had started wearing tracksuits and tennis shoes. Stan Smith was very popular. I could just see leisure taking off. I decided I would stop accountancy and open a sports shop in Middlesbrough. I'd only played a couple of games in the 1973–74 season and had options to move to Oldham or Hull but didn't fancy that. I thought I'd stop playing and open a sports shop, despite all the warnings not to.

> 'I was lucky to be in the right place at the right time and to spot an opportunity. Others had tried, but this was different. Leisure was taking off. Nike didn't have a shoe on the market at the time but the first year I was in business they had one blue training shoe out.

> 'Jack Hatfield [a long-established Middlesbrough sports retail business founded by a triple-Olympic swimming medallist whose father had been superintendent of the town's baths] wouldn't stock the white tennis shoes.

Chapter Four

His son didn't think they'd take off. We were good friends, but we saw things differently on the business front.

The first shop had been in the Dundas Arcade in Middlesbrough, a venture in which he unsuccessfully tried to persuade Neil Phillips, mentioned a little earlier, to become a partner. Dr Phillips admitted to wondering how differently his life would have turned out had he bought into the business.

At the Dundas Street shop in the mid-seventies Bill hit on the matchday wheeze of writing the Boro team on a blackboard in the window, updating the score as the afternoon went on. 'Shoppers didn't have little radios in those days and visiting my shop became a Saturday ritual,' said Bill.

He moved up the road to Hill Street, expanded to the fledgling Metro Centre where, even in 1980, the annual rent was £100,000 plus rates. Soon there were shops in Washington, Sunderland, Durham, Manchester, Liverpool and Nottingham and, crucially, a central warehouse in Washington to serve all of them.

'There are lots of opportunities in life, some people take them and some people don't,' he told Cox and Brownlie. 'Some people are lucky and some people aren't. I saw the opportunity and was lucky with the way things worked out. I started with one shop and finished up with ten.

'I knew that to move forward I would have to become a public limited company and I didn't fancy that, it was too time consuming. I'd built it up over the years and it was time to sell out and enjoy life. I discussed it with my wife and we agreed that the one thing you can't get back is time.'

Success may perhaps be explained with the adage, appropriated by many but authenticated by few, that the harder he worked the luckier he got, for there was no question that he worked all the hours. Judith thinks there was more to it.

'In any case that phrase has almost become a cliché. Bill was commit-ted to forward planning, professionally immaculate, absolutely dedicated

to the concept. He worked and worked and worked but there was a lot more than that.'

Dave Whelan, owner of J D Sports and a future chairman of Blackburn Rovers, took a close look at Monument but decided that (at the time) he couldn't afford it. Eventually the chain was sold to Blacks Leisure who traded as First Sport before they in turn sold out to J D.

Newspaper archives put the figure at £4.4 million, Judith supposes it to have been a couple of hundred thousand less. Had the Gates family stayed in Britain, says Ayresome Angels, they'd have been 'crucified' with tax.

'We had to leave the country. We looked at the Bahamas, Liechtenstein and Andorra but a good friend had been to the Cayman Islands so we had a look. I woke up there one morning — the sun was shining, the birds were singing, the sea was blue and it was lovely. Three months later we moved permanently, or for seven months of the year, anyway.'

For many years it did indeed prove to be pretty close to paradise, Judith in particular much involved in the Cayman community — but then, inexorably and inescapably, the island of dreams began to witness first stirrings of the stuff of nightmares.

In May 2023, amid a supposed High Street downturn, J D Sports announced that it expected to become just the fourth UK retailer — after Marks and Spencer, Tesco and B&Q owner Kingfisher — to record £1 billion annual profits. The top selling items, they added, were trainers and tracksuits.

5.

'THE AUTHORITIES DON'T SEEM PREPARED TO ADMIT THE SCALE OF THE PROBLEM. PEOPLE LIKE MY DAD LOVED FOOTBALL, AND IT'S KILLING THEM'

Always overpaid and usually underwhelming, former footballers on the sportsmen's dinner circuit like apocryphally to talk of a particularly fearsome opponent known as Exocet — 'You could see him coming but you couldn't do a thing about it.' Dementia's probably a bit like that.

Jimmy Robson's story is as indelible as it is incredible, perhaps summed up when appearing on television with his daughter Dany after his own Alzheimer's had been diagnosed in 2015. Several other players — Nobby Stiles, Bobby Charlton — had had the disease confirmed at much the same time. 'It makes me very sad,' said Jimmy. 'I know that one day I might get it, too.'

A free scoring forward, he was one of six or seven North-East men who helped take Burnley — one of those teams that folk like to term unfashionable — to the old first division title in 1959–60. Two years later, by then an England Under 23 international, he scored in the FA Cup final against Spurs — the 100th FA Cup final goal at Wembley — and had another disallowed.

He died, aged 82, on December 14th 2021, unable to remember or to articulate any of it — the seventh member of that vintage Clarets side to die with dementia.

Don't lots of people, especially older people, get dementia? Why point a finger at football? 'Seven out of 11 can't just be coincidence. There's no history of dementia in our family,' says Dany, now an accomplished campaigner and supporter of H4C.

She is also greatly questioning of the role of the Professional Footballers' Association, the players' trade union, who thus appear for the first time in the neurodegeneration narrative, but assuredly not for the last. Whether the PFA will themselves want to talk about the issues remains to be seen.'The authorities don't seem prepared to admit the scale of the problem,' says Dany. 'People like my dad loved football, and it's killing them like it killed him.'

Jimmy Robson was a miner's son from Pelton, near Chester-le-Street in Co Durham, always fiercely competitive and always pretty sharp at football. As a seven-year-old, so family folk-lore has it, he won a VE Day race and was invited onto the stage, then told that he'd to give them a song as well.

Having offered a rendition of *If You Were the Only Girl in the World*, doubtless tunefully though probably not romantically, he vowed never to win anything again and in that inverted ambition was unsuccessful.

Another family story records that Jimmy's grandfather, a boatman, would ferry workmen across the river from Byker to Gateshead, periodically able to fish misdirected footballs from the Tyne and thus to furnish the young'un's passion.

The then-coaly Tyne was rather less replete with good quality footwear. Shoes bashed to bits, Jimmy was obliged to wear his sister's.

At 15 he had unsuccessful trials with Sunderland, but was persuaded over the Pennines by ever-vigilant Burnley scout

Charlie Ferguson. Arriving by rail, it's said, he was so overawed by Burnley's mills — still dark and satanic back in the 1950s — that he wanted to cross the station bridge and catch the next train back again. Burnley insisted that he give it six months, a weekly letter the only permitted contact with the pit folk back in Pelton.

At 17, stand-in for the great Jimmy McIlroy — away on international duty — he scored on his debut in a 2–2 draw with Blackpool, only slightly miffed when another of the day's debutants, a kid called Bobby Charlton, scored twice for Manchester United and thus bagged the bigger of the banner headlines next morning. 'It didn't worry him, that sort of thing never did,' says Dany, now 51. 'Dad could never understand why people thought he was a hero.'

In 1961–62 he hit 37 goals, including five in an 8–0 win over Nottingham Forest and two other hat-tricks. The 100th Wembley goal, through Spurs' centre half Laurie Brown's legs, became subject of a painting which the FA gave to every member club. 'That didn't go to his head, either,' says Dany. 'Dad thought other people were legends, not him.'

Team mates recalled the great joker. 'If you'd just got into a hot bath,' said Trevor Meredith, 'it would be Jimmy who'd turn a cold hose on you.'

The first Burnley programme after his death carried Jimmy's photograph on the cover and devoted two pages to his memory — 'a footballing hero and a true gentleman. You couldn't hope to meet a nicer man.'

After 100 goals in 244 games for Burnley, he played for Blackpool, Barnsley and Bury — clearly a man for the B-teams — before becoming a coach. He also worked as a milkman — soon too many early mornings for Jimmy — and qualified as an electrician. 'We'd be driving through Nelson or somewhere and he'd point out houses that he'd rewired,' says Dany. 'Even when he was well, he'd talk about that much more than his goals.'

Jimmy had also been greatly proud of the medals he won for completing two marathons when in his late forties — 'far more than of his football medals' — though it's Dany, one of Beryl and Jimmy Robson's four children, who's the more enduring long-distance runner.

Veteran of more than 20 marathons and a couple of ultra-runs — athletics for the indomitable — she had also completed several London Marathons, Jimmy always proudly at the 25-mile mark to offer adrenaline for the last legs.

Recovered after contracting breast cancer, the disease which had killed her mother in 2005, Dany has won a place in the ballot — 'I'm sure it was my dad's doing' — for the 2022 event on October 2. 'It'll break my heart when I get to 25 miles and he's not there, but I know he'll be with me in spirit. I'm not really bothered about 26.2 miles, I just want to do 25. Then I know I'll be with Dad.'

In the event, she copped for Covid the day before the 2022 marathon. 'I'd trained really hard, I was absolutely gutted,' she said.

We meet in the Spring sunshine at Accrington Stanley, another renowned though historically less successful football club in east Lancashire. Wasn't it they who, many years ago, provided the punchline for a milk commercial? 'Accrington Stanley? Who are they?'

Dany's a part-time member of the club's media team and has used her contacts to help spread awareness of dementia among footballers, not least to the youngsters at Accrington. 'I've talked to them, of course I have, they're good lads but they're only youngsters. They don't want to think about it, they don't think it will affect them. They live for today.'

Back in November 2020, when with daily visits from carers her dad was still able to live at home, the Sky News website carried a piece — improbably by-lined Martha Kelner, US correspondent — about Jimmy. 'A gentle and endearing man with a soft North-East accent,' she wrote and had also spoken with Jimmy himself. 'Alzheimer's is a footballer's disease,' he'd said. 'I'd head the ball, pass out for a second, get my wits about us and carry on.'

Whatever her transatlantic inclination, Kelner understood the growing crisis. 'Football's institutions still cannot comprehend or do not want to acknowledge its magnitude,' she wrote.

John Coleman, Stanley's long serving manager, had in turn told Sky Sports that he thought heading the ball could be outlawed within ten years. 'Even now the Premier League is played mainly on the floor and you rarely see the ball in the air. I think it'll start with kids' football and develop into the professional game.'

Though it's a little over three months since Jimmy's death, Dany has frequently to wipe her eyes. Named after a French actress of whom her mother was particularly fond, she'd always been close to her father. 'My dad, my mate, my hero,' said the header on her Twitter feed, reporting his death.

She'd also written a piece for the *Burnley Express*. 'At first we thought it was forgetfulness, old age, any excuse. But then you realise the start of dementia and it's getting serious. Dad insisted it was from heading the ball.'

Though teetotal he was the life and soul of any party, loved fancy dress — always, always Deputy Dawg — loved playing games with the family but still hated losing. Wasn't it Jimmy who invented the Rootin' Tootin' Life, a sort of get-out-of-jail for any eventuality but available only to himself?

Wasn't it Jimmy who'd make up the rules, and the answers, in Trivial Pursuit? 'Don't even mention Trivial Pursuit' says his daughter, 'especially the one about Durham Jail. I never really knew him as a footballer, he was just my dad — cheeky, funny, capable of causing chaos but always loving, always kind.'

As with Bill Gates, an early sign of desperate days to come was that he'd forget where he'd parked his car in Burnley town centre. 'We'd spend hours walking round looking for it,' says Dany. Finally persuaded to give up driving, he took to the buses with similarly worrying results and ever more frequent falls.

When they took him to matches, the former star striker seemed more interested in the antics of Burnley Bee, the buzzword mascot, than in what was happening on the field.

Jimmy would put on weight because he might have two or three dinners — 'He'd forgotten he'd just had one' — took to wearing multiple wrist watches, the record about 20, tried vainly to dress himself. 'It could be a boiling hot day and he'd put on three jumpers, a gilet and a jacket and not in any order,' says Dany.

He was a stiff upper lip kind of guy. I'd never seen my dad cry until 2016 when Alzheimer's had been diagnosed and his emotions were all over the place. He really started go down fast when Covid began to spread. There was a lot of fear and he didn't understand, didn't know why they had to wear masks. In a way it had gone full circle. He looked after me in childhood and now he was like a baby and the roles were reversed. People would still ask him for an autograph, but Jimmy had forgotten how to write. At first we didn't want to go public because we thought it would make him vulnerable, living on his own, but I felt that the PFA was fobbing us off. It was only when we went on television that they got back in touch.

By 2020 he almost never left the house, looked after by family members and by a team of carers which the PFA helped to fund. 'I really only rang them to register that my dad had dementia,' says Dany. 'They sent me a booklet, mainly about knee replacements and things, and advice on how to fill in forms. As if we hadn't filled in enough forms....'

Early in summer of 2021 it became clear that he needed residential care — the same home as Scottish international Andy Lochhead, a former Burnley team mate, who died at the age of 81 three months after him.

'We thought it would be good for them to talk together and for a day or two they did,' says Dany. 'Andy then started trying to get my dad to book a taxi so they could "escape" and no matter that my dad couldn't even walk by then. Mercifully he never lost his cheeky smile or his ability to recognise his family.'

The last time she saw him alive he even (somehow) got a question right on Pointless. 'We told dad that it would only be temporary but it broke my heart because I knew it wasn't true,' says Dany. 'The staff were very kind to him, but he died when he went in there.'

The PFA, to which Jimmy had paid dues throughout his playing career, contributed nothing towards the £3,500 monthly care bill. 'In the North-East the miners' union really looked after their members who had an industrial disease,' adds Dany. 'We probably expected something similar from the PFA but (the charity arm) swatted us away like mosquitoes. We aren't going to be swatted away.'

Tony Parkes, long-serving Blackburn Rovers player, coach and manager mentioned in Chapter 1, was by that time also in residential care with dementia. With Tony's daughter Natalie, Dany asked the PFA for a joint £100,000 — the charitable arm was said to have £60 million — to help fund their care. The charity declined, propelling pundit and former England international Chris Sutton towards the asterisk key following Jimmy's death. 'The PFA used the usual delaying tactics. Another one less for them to worry about. Sorry, but this ******* stinks,' he wrote in the *Daily Mail*.

Football had already introduced a suggested limit of ten headers in a training session. Dany Robson doubts if it'll be respected. Nor does she believe that H4C will achieve its aim of limiting heading the ball during a match. 'It's the essence of the game, whether it's heading in soccer or the scrummage in rugby, That doesn't mean that I'll stop fighting for change, for greater awareness and for better care for people like my dad.

'He was a wonderful man, a lovely, lovely man. It seems brain injury in sport is now being talked about more, but nothing seems to happen. He was the perfect dad, never did anything malicious and everyone who knew him thought he was great. I want to do my bit for him; it's very the least I can try.'

6.

'WHEN IT ALL COMES OUT, WHAT HAS HAPPENED IN FOOTBALL WILL BE SEEN AS A SCANDAL WORSE THAN SAVILE, WORSE THAN GRENFELL TOWER, WORSE THAN WINDRUSH'

John Stiles awaits outside Doncaster railway station. 'You can't miss me, I look more like me dad every day,' he says, affectionately. Nobby — dear old Nobby — was both unmissable and pretty much unavoidable, too.

I've seen John twice before, within the space of a fortnight in 2016. Himself a former professional footballer, he's now a raconteur and comedian, given to the distinctly politically incorrect observation at sportsmen's dinners that he was so unlovely as a child that his football coach made him sleep in his own bed.

He also tells late night line-ups that the God-fearing Nobby, a former altar boy, was so anxious that his son inherit the hard man reputation that he sent him to a Roman Catholic school run by the Sacred Sisters of Saddam Hussein in the notorious Moss Side area of Manchester.

The first time I'd heard him was in Middlesbrough, the second at a dinner in Bishop Auckland at which, tears of a clown, he became unexpectedly emotional. By then it was becoming widely known that Nobby, the great folk hero of England's 1966 World Cup victory, was hopelessly struggling with dementia — almost certainly a legacy of his football career. Back then his son couldn't contain his feelings. 'My dad has been abandoned,' he said.

At much the same time, 2017, former Newcastle United and England striker Alan Shearer had spent a year researching and making a BBC documentary about footballers' dementia risk in which he recalled sometimes heading the ball 100 times a day in training.

In August 2022 I asked Shearer, who continues to be supportive of H4C, if we might have a chat. He replied, affably and courteously, that with the World Cup coming up his diary was 'rammed'. The programme, however, had been promoted with an interview on the BBC website: some extracts might further help colour a greatly disturbing picture.

> It made me realise that this is an horrific disease which doesn't just affect those who have it but the people around them, too. We hear a lot about footballers having problems with drink, drugs or gambling and the football authorities have put measures in place to help them.
>
> Similarly, after Bolton midfielder Fabrice Muamba almost died after a cardiac arrest on the pitch in 2012, defibrillators were put at every ground within a matter of months.
>
> All of that has helped to save lives, but very little has been done to investigate the effects of heading a ball. I find that staggering. There is a lot of anger out there because people feel that the football authorities have ignored them and they have not had any support. I've every sympathy for them.

Norbert Peter Stiles was the jigging, joyous, jingoistic symbol of that wonderful afternoon when we thought it was all over, patriotically prancing with the Jules Rimet Trophy still gleaming in one hand and false teeth, hard-bitten, in the other.

He was 24, stood just 5ft 6ins in his Umbro socks, had a comb-over once described as 'dramatic' — certainly it was breath-taking — and wore the optical equivalent of beer bottle bottom contact lenses compared to which Bill Gates's were 20–20 visionary.

He'd been born in a cellar in Manchester in 1942 — his parents feared air raids — observing in his autobiography in 2003 that he was a half-blind dwarf who'd been bombed by the Germans and then hit by a trolley bus when he was one.

What was that post-prandial line about Exocet missiles? Nobby probably wouldn't even have seen one of those, much less a Manchester Corporation trolley.

The previous year, after an England v Scotland match at Wembley, he'd attended the post-match banquet at the Café Royal but became disoriented in the maze of corridors, walking into a function and shyly sitting himself at the nearest table. All seemed to be going well, he liked to recount in his own post-pudding reminiscences, until someone asked if he were a friend of the bride or the groom.

Yet there he was back at Wembley for English football's finest hour, a red-shirted roast beef, a peering personification of national pride. 5ft 6ins notwithstanding, all England looked up to Nobby.

He played 28 times for his country, made 311 Football League appearances for Manchester United and helped them win the European Cup, played also for Middlesbrough and Preston North End, managed a couple of sides but seemed ever-oblivious to the great avalanche of affection beneath which England eagerly engulfed him. Perhaps it just went over his head.

Back at his own home in the Doncaster suburbs, John tells the extraordinary story of how, two days before the World Cup final, senior FA officials summoned team manager Alf Ramsey to the board room at Arsenal's Highbury stadium and told him that Stiles, the No 4, should be dropped.

Aware of concerns over one of Nobby's more robust tackles in an earlier round, about which he himself had tackled (and exonerated) the player, the future Sir Alf had (like that ineluctable Exocet) seen it coming and further defended his midfielder.

Like that of John the Baptist, another iconoclast, the FA demanded Nobby's head on a platter — though it's unclear who played the part of Salome. 'If he doesn't play,' said Alf, 'then you are looking for a new manager.'

Stiles remained insecure, concerned about fans' reaction. 'They were on the coach on the way to Wembley when Alan Ball told him to look out of the window,' John recalls. 'There were about 100 Cockneys with a banner reading "Nobby for Lord Mayor". It helped him no end.'

In his own after-dinner speeches, however, he continued to portray himself (as the *Daily Mail* once memorably put it) as a kind of accident-prone Mr Magoo.

Soon after his 60th birthday, Nobby had begun to show signs of forgetfulness. By 2013 he was seriously ill, much of his time thereafter spent either in care homes or in hospital.

So what happened next? Beneath the headline 'Betrayal of a true English hero' the *Mail* claimed: 'The way that Nobby Stiles has been treated by the sport he loved speaks volumes about the cesspit that is modern football.'

His son vigorously takes up the story over coffee and sandwiches. 'It eats away at me inside, it really does. When it all comes out, what has happened in football will be seen as a scandal worse than Savile, worse than Grenfell Tower, worse than Windrush. I'm not going to give up on it; I've only just begun.'

John had been a two-year-old at his grandparents' home in Dublin when the Three Lions so thunderously roared. 'When Geoff (Hurst) scored the fourth goal they threw me up in the air, I'm told. I'm not sure where I landed.'

He played in the Football League for Leeds United and Doncaster Rovers and further afield for Shamrock Rovers and

Vancouver Whitecaps. He worked as a football agent — 'hated it' — before joining the veg-in-season circuit.

Sometimes, as his dad's illness progressed, he'd also provide him with a sort of after-dinner autocue. 'He'd learn his speech parrot fashion but sometimes still forget. He loved speaking so I'd sit alongside him, just saying things like 'Bobby Charlton, dad' or 'George Best, dad.' It would trigger something and then he'd be away again.'

When finally it seemed inevitable that his dad needed residential care, John heard that the PFA — here again — had found a suitable place for former Manchester City manager Malcolm Allison and rang to ask for details. 'The first thing the guy said was that they weren't going to pay for anything. I hadn't even expected them to, but it's all they seemed to be bothered about.'

Following the death of former England international Jeff Astle in 2002, the cause recorded by the coroner as 'industrial disease', it was increasingly assumed that Nobby's illness had been caused by repeatedly heading a football, particularly in training, over many years.

After his death, on October 30th 2020 at the age of 78, his wife Kay agreed, with the support of her family, that Nobby's brain should be donated for medical research. Dr Willie Stewart, a Glasgow-based neuropathologist with a speciality in football-related illness, looked particularly for chronic traumatic encephalopathy, CTE, the neurodegenerative disease the existence of which can only (as we were saying) be confirmed after death.

Dr Stewart talked medically: 'With Nobby CTE was widespread throughout and at a late stage. His brain presented a story which was entirely typical of someone with CTE. All the pathologies you would expect to see were there.' John Stiles puts it more bluntly. 'His brain was raddled with CTE. Football killed my dad.'

Though long perturbed by the evidence of his father's decline, and angered by football's apparent indifference towards the gathering grey mist, John abided by his mother's wish not over-sensationally to involve Nobby so long as he were alive.

Things changed after his death. 'When he passed away, I thought of how much he had suffered,' said Kay, sister of Republic of Ireland international and Leeds United legend Johnny Giles. 'If by donating his brain it could save one person from suffering as he did, then I knew that we must do it.'

Such was his determination, John secured a meeting with FA chief executive Mark Bullingham. 'He seemed pretty genuine,' he says.

He also cites another well known ex-player, a former England international central defender not yet 60, with problems remembering where he left his car. It's an improbable but potent symptom of an insistent and pernicious problem.

John agrees that his father, public image notwithstanding, had been a 'very private' person. 'You could walk into his house and never know that he'd been a footballer, much less a World Cup winner. There was one photograph on his desk, a lovely picture of the World Cup team all dressed up in suits, and that was it.

'His attitude never altered, he thought that he'd been the luckiest man alive. He played the game that he loved for the country that he loved. He married the woman that he loved and it all took place in the swinging sixties, but when he came home, football went out of the window really.'

Kay might never have given it house room in the first place. 'For all that she was Johnny Giles's sister and Nobby Stiles's wife she had no interest in football and claimed that she didn't understand it. They were a brilliant couple even so.

'He was also a brilliant dad, never shouty, always supportive and always fair. If we stepped out of line, he might remind us about it, but never in a bad way. I don't think even we realised how much he was loved until after his death.'

Seeking to provide financial security for his family, Nobby had in 2010 sanctioned the auction of all his medals and mementoes, including the Wembley shirt from 1966. The sale raised more than £400,000, Manchester United believed to have contributed around half.

By 2013, however, the man with the gap-toothed smile had become anxious and aggressive. 'For a year or two we could never really settle him,' says John. 'We knew what it was, we just didn't know the answer.' A call from Dawn Astle, Jeff's daughter, helped strengthen his determination to learn more. 'Morally,' says Nobby's lad, 'I don't think that I had any alternative.'

Caitlin Stiles, Nobby's granddaughter — John's niece — devoted a 12,000-word dissertation in the last year of her law degree to neurodegenerative disease in sport. It was a passion project, she said, proposing both a no-fault compensation scheme run by governing bodies, and an injury surveillance initiative across football which could allow clubs and governing bodies to track risk.

'The stories of those affected by neurodegenerative diseases paint a vivid picture of the need to access social care and yet currently the social care system is difficult and expensive to navigate,' she wrote.

'As a sports fan myself the benefits of sport are clear,' she added, 'but myths such as "heavier balls used in the 1970s" or beliefs that the older generation of footballers "smoked and went down to the pub" illustrate the need for awareness and education.'

Similar to Head for Change, John's focus has also been on education, on trying to show young footballers the dangers of repetitively heading a ball — especially in training. 'Many of them are just starting out. I understand that they don't think it can affect them because they're only young, but they need to know.'

Bearing a pile of self-financed leaflets, intending to hand them out to the players, he'd gone to Doncaster Rovers' training ground and was escorted from the premises. The club blamed Covid restrictions, suggested he make a more formal approach.

A few months later he was featured — Rover of the Day, described as a 'classy midfielder' — on the club's website. They couldn't even spell Stiles. It probably didn't help.

He then wrote to each of the 92 senior clubs in English football, and to those in the Women's Super League, offering at his own expense to front a players' presentation on the risk of constantly and forcefully heading a football. Dr Stewart, the neuropathologist, agreed to accompany him.

There were 'a few polite letters,' he supposes, but at the point in April 2022 when we meet not a single acceptance. 'It struck me that, since Jeff Astle's death, there hadn't been one piece of literature sent to players warning of the risks. There are young, innocent lads who have no idea what might lie ahead. You're not talking about sore knees — you can replace a sore knee, you can't replace a brain.'

A few days before we meet, he'd done an ITV News interview alongside Tom Charlton, Bobby's brother. 'Football's absolutely swimming in money and yet you have players who've given their lives and been heroes to the fans without any form of help,' said Tom, a lovely man who'll crop up later in the book.

'I think it put the shits up them,' says John. 'We're gaining momentum but we need a lot more from the FA and the PFA. Footballers should know the risks and there's still a long way to go. It's an industrial disease and in any other walk of life the union would be all over it. It's an absolute scandal and the biggest scandal of all is that the football authorities knew about it and did nothing. It has to stop, this is a deadly epidemic.'

John also admits to being 'terrified' of himself becoming a victim. 'I set myself little exercises each day, try to finish the crossword. I've spoken with loads of players and many of them are scared stiff, too. What I want to see is heading drastically reduced in training. I just don't think it's necessary and I think that's where the damage comes.'

He's also finishing a novel about three young footballers in Manchester who became involved, not with medical issues but with a paedophile coach.

He'd attended the match at Spennymoor Town in September 2021 in which heading the ball was restricted to the penalty area in one half and outlawed altogether in the other and about which much more will be written ere long. The crowd of 250 was far outnumbered by the worldwide avalanche of media reports.

'The impact was massive, it didn't really matter about the number of spectators. It was about getting the message across and in that respect it was very successful,' he says. 'Something ignited there, we won't let the light go out.'

Thoughts return to that dinner in Bishop Auckland, to the man billed as the comedian and to the poignant moment that he'd not laughed but cried.

By whom had Nobby Stiles been let down? The answer comes at once. 'By everyone,' says his son.

7.

'MY MUM KNOWS NOTHING ABOUT FOOTBALL BUT SHE IS THE MOST DANGEROUS WOMAN IN THE GAME'

S pring is in the air; sadness, too. 'I'd almost forgotten how lovely the changing seasons are in England,' says Judith Gates, back in Castle Eden. 'I'm falling in love with this house all over again.'

It's mid-April now. Bill's still looking at football on television in another room, watched diligently in turn by Sam, his latest carer, and with his right arm raised, as if perpetually appealing for offside.

When she sits next to him some lunchtimes, Judith might instead suggest that they watch *Judge Judy,* that addictive American import about an adversarial attorney. 'You can get a bit too much football,' says Judith, judgmentally. Bill's thoughts on the subject are unknown.

These days, unlike the Anfield faithful, she usually walks alone, too. 'The Durham coast is so lovely, so silent. The moment you get out of the car and onto the cliff path you can feel the tension flowing out of your fingertips and you remember that many of our ancestors worked in the pits here.'

In the evening she'll spend more time alongside Bill on the sofa –'side-by-side, companionable' — with a bit of a soft spot for *Dragons' Den*. No guesses what her husband would rather have on the 56-inch screen.

If there is a less melancholy side to these gatherings between author and principal it's to ponder their impact on the Gates family's caramel wafer mountain, before finally the conversations are concluded. Already the mountain may merely be a munro.

Two days later it's the 60th birthday of David, born when — even then — the press pack would wait outside the Spennymoor school gates salaciously seeking thoughts of the new dad. 'My little boy 60,' says Judith, almost incredulously but in the manner of mothers everywhere. A couple of days after that, David's due in from the United States on his first return visit since Covid cramped the world.

Already they've looked at specialist care homes in the expectation that, even with live-in care, it may soon be impossible to meet Bill's needs and to keep him safe. 'I dread the day,' says Judith, 'that he has to leave our house.'

Today's catch-up is more formally to talk about Head for Change, its aims, arguments and the reasons for its existence. She talks of speaking truth to power, a phrase which I suggest has become cliched. Judith doesn't agree and talks truth to power — talks it powerfully — anyway.

'Our goal is to create a safe space for our sporting heroes — past, present and future — who suffer from sports-related brain injuries and to connect with the best brains in science and research to make positive change,' says the H4C website by way of summary. The constant feeling, adds the website, is of being abandoned. 'It is of families receiving a diagnosis and being left to get on with it.'

Judith says again that they aim to be part of the solution. 'It's become a bit like a spider's web, very time consuming, but the central tenet is always to honour Bill. I think I'd have done this even if I hadn't had an academic background because it affects someone I love and it affects my family. My grief was channelled into action. Whenever a door opens I put my foot in it, literally and the other way. I have to have total immersion, I want answers, I want to rattle cages.

'Both sons have been supportive, Nick particularly so. None of us thinks that anything is impossible; we don't close things down.'

Nick, five years the younger, heads the global Coaches Across Continents charity which uses football to nurture children in the Third World, mainly Africa. But for Bill's illness, says Judith, she and her husband would still be travelling the world to help.

'My mum,' Nick once said, 'knows nothing about football but is the most dangerous woman in the game.'

'It's not a journey that's going to have a good ending. It's a journey where you watch someone you love melting away, but it's a journey, nonetheless,' says Judith, as she had earlier. 'You almost don't know what your brain can do until it can do it no more.'

She also wants to talk about the international Concussion in Sport Group and the curious imbalance of its membership towards organised sport's vested interests, about the Professional Footballers' Association and how sluggishly it seems to have dragged its affluently shod feet, about the need to educate young sports players — particularly those seeking a full-time career — on the inherent dangers of their Lorelei calling and about where sport's duty of care should lie.

Chiefly the focus to date has been on football and rugby, the latter more self-evidently brutal, though it takes little imagination to suppose that other sports, sometimes on other continents, and in particular American football, may every bit as fundamentally gravely endanger their participants.

The PFA had previously denied that the players' union had been asleep at the wheel. A Digital, Culture, Media and Sport committee on concussion in sport, chaired by Julian Knight MP, had declared it 'astounding' that when it came to the risk of brain injury in sport, governing bodies and the Concussion in Sport Group — chiefly comprising representatives of those global governing bodies — had been 'allowed to mark its own homework.'

It was July 2021 and a tipping point, says Judith. The committee also concluded that more should have been done to protect sport participants from brain injury. Though the Health and Safety Executive was responsible by law, the report added, the role seemed to have been delegated to national bodies such as the FA.

'That is a dereliction of duty which must change. The failure of these sporting organisations to address the issue of acquired brain injury is compounded by a lack of action from government. Too often it has failed to take action on player welfare and instead relied on unaccountable sporting bodies.'

Litigation looms heavily, not least among top-level rugby players in both codes claiming that the game's governing bodies failed in their duty of care. In the United States, the NFL has paid out hundreds of millions of dollars in similar cases. Judith's 'at once' insistent that she won't be following that route on her husband's behalf but knows ever-increasing numbers who will.

Other organisations, not least the Jeff Astle Foundation, have similar aims to H4C. Many already work collaboratively — as H4C seeks to do — with sport's governing bodies. H4C has also coordinated the Repercussion Group, a team of researchers working in sports-related neurodegenerative disease 'to examine the scientific basis for taking a player-centred approach towards brain injury in sport.'

The door, Judith concedes, has in recent times been pushed slightly further ajar, the pressure for change and wellbeing grows, though she regards the word 'momentum' as warily as might a matador approach a bull that's only had a slice of toast for breakfast. Ever-updated, the calendar on the kitchen wall overflows. She's doing it, she repeats, for Bill.

Only occasionally is discourse distracted. 'Oh, look' she says, reacquainted with the rites and the delights of an English spring, 'just look at that lovely bird.'

Bill, once that Titan, is still elsewhere, not watching the birds which once he also loved but looking at football on television.

Neurological tests in 2014 had suggested that he might merely be suffering from amnesia mild cognitive impairment, they called it — though that was the time, homeward by train from a London clinic, that he forgot where in Durham he'd left the car.

Three years later they attended a specialist clinic in Toronto where probable chronic traumatic encephalopathy — devastating in life but clinically only able to be diagnosed after death — was overwhelmingly suggested. The only cause is repeated forceful impacts to the head.

In the good old bad old days it was called *dementia pugilistica,* an affliction among beaten-up boxers. Roughly translated, it meant punch drunk.

Though her doctorate is non-medical, an education-related PhD, Judith determined academically and assiduously to learn more. After jumping through endless Charity Commission hoops, Head for Change was formally launched in January 2021.

'In a very sad way the timing was right. Jack Charlton had just died, Nobby Stiles had just died, Bobby Charlton announced that he had dementia and there were a lot of rugby issues coming to the surface. We had to optimise it; if there was a time, however lamentably, it had come.'

The media, not least the *Daily Mail, Mail on Sunday* and the *Guardian,* have been supportive. 'I don't think we've used the media as a battering ram,' says Judith, carefully, 'but we have been quite strategic.'

In a compelling piece she wrote for the *Guardian* in 2021, she talked of 'a well known passion for asking questions and a lifetime of activism against injustice,' an activism which had also manifested itself in campaign for reform of the domestic violence laws in the Cayman Islands.

'As a former academic I did what academics do, I threw myself into research on sports related head injuries,' she wrote. 'My readings were eclectic. Nothing was too trivial for me to consider. Nothing was too complicated for me that I did not strive to understand.

'Research projects had been commenced and discontinued, reactions were minimal or expedient. It seemed as if emerging knowledge highlighting the fragility of the brain, knowledge that was clamouring to be heard, was falling on deaf ears.'

Vested economic interests were evident, she added. 'I wondered who was profiting and how. Potential conflicts of interest were pervasive. Predominant themes were sports-friendly viewpoints which minimised the risk of concussion and head injuries whilst simultaneously downplaying connections between sport and neurodegenerative disease.'

Her academic scepticism (she said) recognised an old but perhaps less debatable adage: he who pays the piper calls the tune.

She's H4C's chair, her two fellow trustees Dr Sally Tucker — a London hospital doctor and an ethics expert — and Mel Bramwell-Popham, wife of former Welsh rugby union international Alix Popham, capped 33 times and a member of the 2008 Grand Slam team. 'We just found one another' says Judith, in the slightly disingenuous manner of a mutual game of hide-and-seek.

Billy Tucker, Dr Tucker's father, was a central defender — another central defender — with Swindon Town, Bury, Hereford and others and himself suffers from a neurodegenerative disease strongly thought to be football-related. He was born in 1948. 'The last ten years have been an unexpected and frightening journey down a lonely and darkening path,' she writes on the H4C website.

Alix Popham, still in his early 40s, suffers early-onset dementia almost certainly caused by a passion for a perilous sport. 'My life's ambition is to find a miracle,' says his wife.

Head for Change also quickly recruited a team of 'ambassadors,' many of them Welsh, ranging from Jamie Baulch, a Welsh international sprinter and television presenter to (Welsh) cricketer Simon Jones and (Welsh) MP and former priest Chris Bryant.

Another is familiarly rotund Welsh tenor Wynne Evans, never much of a sportsman, whose contribution may be supposed incomparable. It's unlikely that cyclist Geraint Thomas OBE, active involvement detailed in the final chapter, is a son of Hibernia, either.

Very many familiar footballers have also offered support, ranging alphabetically from John Aldridge to Dean Windass and otherwise embracing Bruce Grobbelaar and Kevin Keegan, Gary Lineker and Alan Shearer.

'I think we have come a very long way in 15 months in establishing ourselves as key players in this arena,' says Judith. 'We have a serious purpose and a solid structure and we've definitely raised awareness. There's still a very long way to go and I can't imagine myself sitting back any day soon. I very much hope to be around when we have real progress, real results, to report. For everyone's sake, there needs to be systemic change in football.'

Formed in 2001, the Concussion in Sport Group comprises around 36 world experts on the subject, meeting in conference every four years and issuing a 'consensus' statement thereafter. The lead author of four of the five statements was associate professor Paul McCrory, an Australian neurologist.

That the group was heavily sponsored by global sports bodies like the International Olympic Association, World Rugby and FIFA has long (shall we say) raised eyebrows. Could it be sufficiently, transparently, independent?

In 2016, the last time they'd met because of Covid, the consensus statement said: 'A cause-and-effect relationship has not yet been demonstrated between CTE and sports-related concussions and exposure to contact sport. As such, the notion that repeated concussion and sub-concussive impacts cause CTE remain unproven.' Its views, said the CISG, had been reached after the 'expert panel' read 60,000 published articles before the conference began.

The Guardian thought the argument conservative and controversial. 'While it may have been the consensus among the panel of 36 experts, it certainly isn't the consensus among the wider scientific community and the athletes and families affected by the disease.'

Nor was it the view of Judith Gates and others in H4C, echoing the parliamentary assertion that the CISG's constitution and funding represented sport marking its own homework and marking it much too generously. They may not have realised that there'd been cribbing, too.

Visibly, if nothing else, American football seemed yet more likely to impact its players' future wellbeing. Autopsies on III former NFL participants showed that all but one had some degree of CTE. A similar study in Australia found that 12 of 21 top level AFL players had had CTE.

Hana Walker-Brown, in her meticulously researched 2022 publication *A Delicate Game,* cites former Harvard player Chris Nowinski in his own book, *Head Games.* 'I was told if it ain't bleeding, it ain't hurt. Suck it up.'

In 2016, and again with acknowledgment to Hana Walker-Brown, McCrory, of the Concussion in Sport Group, had said in a lecture that the problem in the NFL had been grossly overblown, accusing the media of 'over-simplified views'. The CTE thing, he had somewhat bizarrely observed, was not all it was cracked up to be.

In October 2021, Judith Gates and Sally Tucker were signatories to a paper rather breathlessly called 'Towards complete, candid and unbiased international consensus statement on concussion in sport' which accused the CISG of 'consistently underplaying risks' and demanding its overhaul.

The group's four-yearly reports, it added, had been part of a process that was narrow, compromised and flawed. 'A careful reading of these studies suggests that the authors have adhered to a libertarian framing of casualty, risk and intervention rather than considering a precautionary public health and patient-centred point of view.' The CISG, says Judith, has consistently sought to emphasise all that medical science doesn't know as opposed to all that it does.

Then in March 2022, sensation. Dr McCrory, the CISG's chairman, resigned over allegations of plagiarising another neurologist's work. It prompted an extraordinary statement from the Australian Football League, among the CISG's principal backers — and Aussie Rules football, it should perhaps be explained, makes soccer look like sand castles for sissies by comparison.

The AFL said that it had launched a 'comprehensive and independent' review into the work and advice of concussion doctor Paul McCrory. Dr McCrory, it added, was understood by the AFL to be 'a pre-eminent expert' in the field.

'The AFL believes that it is important as a matter of integrity to ascertain the status and reliability of past research activities and outcomes and clinical work for which Dr MrCrory has been involved for the AFL.

The Guardian (again) was also quickly on the ball. 'Dr McCrory has been a prolific public spokesman about concussion in sport globally. He has also on multiple occasions expressed personal doubts over the relationship between concussion and CTE.'

InSight, an Australian website, thought that the McCrory case had sent 'shockwaves' through international sport. 'Currently' it stated, 'Australia's international reputation with regard to CTE could arguably be likened to our reputation for acknowledging and acting upon climate change.'

Alan Pearce, another associate professor, thought it a 'major credibility issue' within the AFL. 'It dents confidence,' he added, 'in all concussion science conducted by the CISG.'

Judith Gates had formed similar reservations pretty soon after starting her own research. 'The CISG in its present form cannot continue. Who can have confidence now?' She's being diplomatic, she adds, and will attend the latest CISG symposium in Amsterdam in October. More of that later.

Jeff Astle, West Bromwich Albion and England and one of very few strikers to have scored more goals with head than feet, was just 59 when he died in November 2002. The cause of death was listed as industrial disease, the reality that his dementia had been caused by repeatedly and forcefully heading a football.

It didn't change much. 'Football authorities should have taken a stronger and more sustained interest in the matter of brain injuries in sport following Jeff Astle's inquest in 2002,' concluded the DCMS report following the 'homework' comments.

After his retirement, Astle also become well known for appearances on the *Fantasy Football* programme and, in their neck of the Derbyshire woods, as a window cleaner. 'Jeff Astle never misses the corners,' it said on the side of his van.

West Brom fans began carrying 'Justice for Jeff' banners. In 2014, after the family donated his brain to Dr Willie Stewart's research programme, he became the first former professional football to have CTE confirmed as the cause of death, resulting from repeated low level brain trauma. The following year the family — led by Dawn, one of his three daughters — launched the Jeff Astle Foundation, a 'fitting and lasting legacy' to promote education and awareness about brain injury in sport.

'We have thought for a long time that every hit on the head can harm,' says the Foundation website, which talks also of 'the struggle with football's authorities.'

In November 2020 the website reprinted in full a *Mail Online* piece, written by Kieran Gill — who was to play in the 'no heading' match at Spennymoor and subsequently write a compelling book on the brain health issue — following PFA assistant chief executive Simon Barker's claim that the union cared for 'each and every former player struggling with dementia.'

Players' families demurred, talked about being sent forms or leaflets but of little further action. 'The PFA have shown complete disregard and cowardice...I hope they are brought to task....They have shown no compassion,' said Eileen Hasleden, widow of former Doncaster Rovers and Rotherham United player John Hasleden, another for whom a form proved the norm.

'I went to the PFA about this in the year 2000 so there were people 20 years ago bringing the problem to their attention,' said Adrienne Fearis, daughter of former Irish international Tommy Carroll.

Jane Beresford, former player Graham Barrett's daughter, had also rung the PFA to report her dad's illness. 'I gave them Dad's name but didn't really get much joy there. It was like 'Well, you know, lots of people get dementia.' I never bothered ringing again and they never rang me back.'

The PFA, however, asserts on its own website that it is the only football organisation which solely prioritises players' needs. 'Throughout our history, the PFA has been instrumental in supporting. ...and pushing for research into links between neurodegenerative conditions and playing football.

'Our team are passionate in helping footballers navigate personal and professional challenges. We are here to partner and support you.'

Much media attention was focused on the chief executive's reportedly large salary and on the £62 million funds said to be controlled by the PFA Charity, a separate company potentially responsible for helping in cases like those above.

Some might have seen it as a surprise, therefore, others as a masterstroke, that when in February 2022 the PFA announced the creation of a care department for former players with neurodegenerative disease — a 'hugely important' development said PFA chief executive Maheta Molango — the 'project lead' was named as Dawn Astle.

Judith Gates employs the old adage about it being better in the tent peeing out than outside peeing in — or is it the other way round? — remains greatly censorious of the players' union but declines to criticise Dawn Astle. 'She's done a wonderful job since her dad died. It'll be interesting to see what happens next.'

Frustration was also voiced at the PFA decision to restrict help to those with assets of less than £23,250. John Stiles called it a disgrace.

Head for Change has written to the Charity Commissioners expressing concerns about the PFA Charity 'The PFA Charity has lost the credibility any charity should have,' says Judith. 'The FA should form a new charity, very much based on making the game safer.'

Judith also insists that they want to collaborate. 'We want to work with the FA, the PFA, the Premier League and the English Football League to develop a cohesive strategic plan which includes working together to take constructive action. I want to do all in my power to protect others from the devastating consequences of sport-related neurodegenerative disease.'

So how might success for H4C ultimately be assessed? 'It's not really like the ironing where you've done it and you can look at the results. I'd love to have neurodegenerative disorders classed as an industrial disease among sport players, that really would be like the ironing.

'I'd love to have funded residential care for ex-players. Some may be managing the situation but they're living with something that will get worse day by day and families may have to sell their homes to pay for care. We have peace of mind in that sense because we can afford to look after Bill with the resources at our disposal. Others can't.

'There are former footballers absolutely living in fear, scared to death. The news that Chris Chilton had to set up a Gofundme page appalled me.' Chilton, Hull City's all-time record scorer with 222 goals in all competitions, died in 2021, aged 77. He had dementia.

'Sometimes you have to do the right thing and that means challenging blinkered views and self-serving perspectives,' says Judith. 'Unfairness and the abuse of power affects me deeply. Power can be a force for good but it's open to that abuse. On a personal note, as I've said, I'd just like the corrupt to lose.

'It's a thundercloud that's getting darker.'

8.

'JUDITH'S FORMIDABLE, THAT'S THE WORD. SHE'S DRIVEN, AND SHE'S NOT GOING TO LET IT GO NOW'

Sunday May 1st, May Day. Judith Gates emails: 'It has been a busy week,' she says, unsurprisingly, and reels off a list of engagements, high powered meetings, throughout the land. To me it feels ever more that this initiative has momentum, wheels, the wind beneath its wings.

Dr Willie Stewart, too, has announced a further three projects closely related to H4C. When Dr Stewart's demanding diary allows, a session with him appears imperative.

Even the popular prints have in the past few days turned attention to CTE. The coroner at the inquest into the death of former Welsh international and Cardiff City footballer Keith Pontin unequivocally concluded that the cause of death was chronic traumatic encephalopathy caused by repeated head impact.

Back in 2019, his wife had told the Welsh papers that she was proud of his career but wondered if it had been worth it. Former players, she said, were being 'forgotten' by football's authorities.

This week's inquest heard that Pontin was a big, strong, old fashioned centre half (what else?) dominant in the air. 'Combative' someone said, admiringly not euphemistically. It wouldn't have taken a neurological scientist to conclude that an awful lot of CTE victims seem to have been central defenders.

Is there really progress, greater awareness at least? Judith's greatly cautious, talks of years of procrastination and of yet more years before real change. Besides, she has yet more on her mind right now. The following Sunday, May 8th, will be Bill's 78th birthday.

Four of them had been close friends at Spennymoor Grammar School — Bill, John Davison, Bob Hunter and Ken Foster, who's flown back from Alberta, Canada, for the birthday lunch. For Covid reasons, it's his first return to Blighty for three years, when he attended Bill's 75th.

'There were people he didn't recognise or remember even then,' says Ken. 'What's happened to Bill is very harsh, very emotional. There's no other way to put it.'

We meet for lunch at the village pub in Bolam, Co Durham, round the corner from the cottage where Ken and his wife Ann are staying. Fifty years earlier, when it was called the Shoulder of Mutton, the pub's outside toilets attracted the biggest horse flies, positively thoroughbred horse flies, in entomological history.

Like Dr Gates, Ann has a PhD — hers related to counselling. 'When they start talking, Bill and I leave the room,' says Ken, with undue modesty.

Small world, it further transpires that Ken's brother Geoff and Geoff's wife Jean were until their retirement my long-suffering and ever-patient opticians. 'Ah,' Jean had said after one test, 'so you're colour blind as well.' 'As well as what, Jean?' It was a real bolt from the green.

The quartet had been friends since first form days — 'almost inseparable' says Ken. All married Spennymoor girls, each a year younger than themselves. All but Bob — on a long-planned holiday in Spain — would again be together for the birthday bash in Castle Eden two days later.

Ken's anticipated the question about the common spark. 'It's quite hard to say. We just had the same sense of humour, the same lack of discipline, We kind of struck a balance, enjoyed each other's company, had a lot of fun. We were in the headmaster's study quite a lot, probably me more than most because my father was also a headmaster and for some reason the Spennymoor head didn't like that.'

On one occasion the quartet had offered to strike a deal with the religious education teacher. 'We were always a bit boisterous in RE because it wasn't a GCE subject for us, but on this occasion we hadn't done our homework for other subjects so asked him if we could just sit quietly at the back and get on with it. 'He said he couldn't possibly agree to it but after another couple of weeks he did. That's how we got our homework done.'

He and Bill also played in the same school and district football teams, Ken up front until Bill left for the Boro and his mate moved back to take his place. 'I remember coming off the field and my head was ringing from heading the ball, and that was maybe just five times once a week. What must it have been like for full-time players?'

Had he been envious of Bill's football success? 'You don't get envious of your friends. Besides, he was better than I was, anyway,' says Ken, though friendship couldn't make him a Middlesbrough fan. 'I think I was only at Ayresome Park once in my life. I support Sunderland.'

He'd also been on the Rome trip, remembered Pauline Blanch, the Shildon lass — 'Ah yes, the blonde' — who'd first caught his mate's eye, recalls that (somewhat improbably) the boys had been boarded in a convent, been allowed a glass of wine with their dinner and that the girls, yet more surprisingly, stayed elsewhere.

'I remember getting a ticket to watch Cassius Clay, as then he was, still only about 18 but you could tell how good he was going to be. I can't remember if Bill was there. We also became friendly with a couple of young Italian boxers who hadn't quite made the

Olympic squad. If there was any problem with the locals, they'd straighten it out.'

Spennymoor Grammar School seems to have had some awfully good (and doubtless educational) jaunts, on another occasion visiting the Guinness brewery. 'I can't remember if we were allowed to sample it,' says Ken, judiciously, over a new-laid bottle of Old Speckled Hen.

What of the unscripted pregnancy? 'There seemed to be quite a few,' says Ken. 'We had a Friday night club and I think the deputy head stopped Bill going, goodness only knows what he thought Bill was going to do. Most people just accepted it but some of the snootier kids thought it was the best thing since sliced bread.'

Eventually the school divided the playing field, one half for boys and one for girls. It seemed a classic case of closing the stable door after the horse had bolted, and not very firmly at that.

Ken was a civil engineering graduate, aged 26 when he and Ann emigrated to Canada with no job and little money. 'The Canadian economy was growing, you can always get a job if the economy's growing,' he reasons.

He found a job, ultimately bought the company, remained a global consultant after retirement and coached the Alberta Cougars Under 18s football team to the national championship. Regularly they saw Bill and Judith on their travels. Particularly, he says, his friend made a great sliced fruit breakfast and loved strawberry rhubarb pie, a favourite at parties.

Until his illness he'd never changed, always a smile on his face, always full of fun. Same old Bill. You could tell in 2014 that his memory was starting to go but we never imagined anything like this. He was a bright lad at school but he was always going to be a footballer and did well to keep up with the accountancy.

He got into sports shops at the right time, before there were megastores and he got out at the right time, too. The accountancy background must

have helped a lot but obviously he had a flair for it, too. I remember him
telling me that he sold the chain for a lot more than he thought he'd get.
To have seen him deteriorate is just awful. We've had lots of evidence of
brain damage in American football, too, but it's just met with platitudes.

And Judith? 'Judith's formidable, that's the word. She's driven and she's not going to let it go now. My wife says it's a method of coping; whatever it is, she's amazing.'

From the pub, we stroll round to the cottage to say hello to Ann. It's recalled that, in the different days of 1961, Judith had been advised to call the expected baby Honor — perhaps a nod to the nubile Ms Blackman, then black-clad and popular — on the oblique, paradoxical and uniquely offensive grounds that she most certainly wasn't. 'I think she was incredibly brave,' says Ann. 'She still is,' says her husband.

Unaccompanied by strawberry rhubarb pie but lubricated with champagne, the birthday lunch goes very well — an afternoon of moments, Judith reports. 'The one that brought a lump to my throat was when Ken, gently but thoroughly, embraced Bill in a bear hug on arrival. Bill's face was a picture.'

They'd also spent much time debating what brought, and kept, the faithful four together. The men considered that they were definitely unique, prompting their hostess to quote the infamously celebrated courtesan Mandy Rice Davies. 'They would say that, wouldn't they?'

Ken Foster, headed back across the Atlantic the following day, had also much enjoyed the reunion — 'in a way it's tragic but it was lovely to see him. I very much hope to be back again next year.'

9.

'I KNEW THERE WOULDN'T BE CONVERSATIONS, I'D NO ILLUSIONS ABOUT THAT, BUT IN MANY WAYS HE WASN'T MY DAD'

David Gates has landed back in Britain two days earlier, for Covid-related reasons — like Ken Foster in the previous chapter — a first return from the United States since Bill's 75th three years earlier. He knew what to expect, of course.

'My dad's gone now,' he says at once. 'I walked into the room, put my hand on his shoulder and said 'Hi dad, I'm home.' He looked up, said nothing and went back to the soccer. He's never once mentioned my name.'

On the Saturday of the father-son reunion, *The Times* magazine had carried a lengthy interview with Steve Thompson, a rugby World Cup winner with England in 2003, who suffers from early-onset dementia. Pretty inarguably, it supposed CTE, persistently bashing brains about.

Thompson is 6ft 3ins tall, weighs 18 stones, and is built (as again they sometimes say in North-East England) like a brick outhouse. He is just 43. Unable to remember anything of the World Cup final, or the birth of his children, he has written — had ghost written

— an autobiography called *Unforgettable: Rugby, Dementia and the Fight of my Life* in which he details suicidal thoughts and talks of watching the 2003 final on television. 'All I see is a fat lad, round head, big arse. Knowing what I do know now, I 100 per cent wish that it had never happened.'

In October 2022, as top level rugby faced what the *Daily Telegraph* deemed an 'existential crisis' — both financially and as the head impact debate and its legal ramifications grew ever more forceful — BBC2 showed a powerful, hour-long programme about the Thompson case and the truly existential issues that it raised. There'd be strong language, it warned. Rugger buggers, see.

Thompson reminisced at the start about how much he'd enjoyed rugby. 'I loved everything about the game, the physicality was a major part of it. You enjoyed knocking each other about, but nothing was said about head injuries.'

He talked subsequently about forgetting his children's names — Steph Thompson tells them that their dad has a 'poorly head' — about thoughts of self harm and worse. 'Every week a little bit more slips away,' he said, and revealed the online abuse he'd received for a high-profile campaign to make the game safer. 'The rugby community that took me in as a kid is now turning against me.'

The programme also talked with Sam Peters, a *Mail on Sunday* journalist who has long campaigned for improved safety protocols in rugby. 'Suddenly in almost every press release we were being told that player welfare was the game's No 1 priority,' said Peters. 'In rugby union? Really?'

World Rugby had issued 'guidance' — guidance, nothing more — that full contact training should be restricted to 15 minutes a week. 'It feels like a bit of a joke,' said Thompson. 'It's not mandatory and can easily be ignored. It's an empty gesture really, there's always an excuse for not doing it.'

He'd insisted throughout that his chief aim was to prevent present and future players suffering as he now is — and here, perhaps, the strong language. 'I don't want them going through what I'm going through. It's shit. There's no other word for it, it's shit.'

David Gates lives in Shrewsbury near Boston, Massachusetts, and had weekly kept in touch with his family through the imperfect medium of modern technology. Though long in America, he retains a marked English accent save for the frequent use of the word 'piece' to mean 'set-up' or 'situation'.

In Co Durham a piece was what the bairns used to perform at Sunday School anniversaries, in Scotland it remains a jam sandwich.

'Most of the time dad will just stare blankly at the television but then he'll say something quite surprising' says David. "That's Alex Ferguson,' he said, and it was, but then he went blank again.'

Covid had driven Bill and Judith from their swish home overlooking a Florida golf course to their swish home on a Cayman beach. Suspected and damn-near certain, chronic traumatic encephalopathy compelled them back to England, and to Castle Eden, a mile or two from the Durham coast. 'When they were still in Florida we'd go down every couple of weeks' David recalls. 'Dad was still really active, still playing tennis. That was just three years ago.

'I knew what was happening, of course, so I wasn't shocked in that respect, but not to mention my name — nothing like that. I knew there wouldn't be conversation, I have no illusions about what dementia is, but in many ways he's no longer my dad.'

David, of course, was the natal product of that bright Olympic flame back in 1960. Mother and son have called at our house en route — a rather elliptical route — to watch the bank holiday match between Spennymoor Town and Blyth Spartans before which she will present a shirt from the 'no heading' match to Alan Iceton, a friend and team mate from Bill's formative football days with the Moors.

Chapter Nine

David recalls watching his dad play for Middlesbrough at the echoing old Ayresome Park ground, working as a 14-year-old Saturday lad at his dad's sports shop in the Boro, becoming Monument Sports' North-East general manager.

At the match, with other players' children, he might wander into the dressing rooms after the teams had gone — 'I remember how basic they were, physio table in the corner and great big baths' — or dribble plastic cups along the corridor outside. Sometimes they'd even go onto the pitch, perhaps chased by a grass-rooted groundsman.

'I don't think we thought of ourselves as special in any way. We lived in Marske but after a term mum sent me to a school in Saltburn. I'd sometimes come home past a group of lads outside Bydales School (Marske) and would worry a bit if Boro had lost that weekend, but I don't think they cared less.'

The relationship with his father, he says — and for several seconds he weighs the word — was weird, more gaffer and worker than father and son. 'Nick also worked for Monument. We were quite bright, it wasn't as if we were nuggets, but I was treated as an employee. My dad has had an exceptional life, given us all sorts of possibilities. We owe him a great deal.'

Perhaps because of the circumstances of conception and birth, however, he is much closer to his mother. 'It was quite difficult for dad because he was still just 17 and a football player. I get all that. Mum and I are just an entity really; we're on the same wavelength, we think in the same way.

'We can sit and not talk for an hour and that's fine or sit and talk for a couple of hours. It doesn't have to be about anything important. We have great conversations, we enjoy being with one another.'

Judith, I tell him, has already been described in the embryonic book as formidable (and quite likely will be again.) 'I don't think of her as formidable,' he says. 'I just think of her as mum.'

With Nick he'd started a coaching company called Play Soccer, which ran until 2010. He now works in special needs education but still plays football. 'Centre midfield, more the Eric Gates role. I don't have to run around so much,' he says, recalling the international uncle who now looks after chickens on a smallholding ten miles away, For all the overlying sadness of the return to Blighty, he's happy to be back.

'I love America, I love my wife and my girls but I still think of the North-East as at the centre of the piece. Mum and I went for a walk along the cliffs yesterday and it was just so good to hear the accent again, to say hello to people you didn't know and to look at the sea.'

What of Head for Change? He doubts that football will ever outlaw heading. 'Football is mainly a working class game and you have to remember the excitement it brings and besides, there's big money involved.'

It concerns him, nonetheless. 'You don't head a football and become ill the next day, you head a football and become ill 30 or 40 years later. Players need to be educated.'

His mum, coming up 77, is chatting over tea and biscuits in the next room. Might she one day take up knitting, or crochet or — you know — bingo? David doubts it. 'The females in my family are all phenomenal — my mum's phenomenal, my daughters are phenomenal. They're just a force, which is great.

'She can't catch a ball, she can't ride a bike and she can't knit but, believe me, my mum really is phenomenal.'

10.

'HE DIDN'T NEED MUCH PERSUADING. I THINK THE QUID PRO QUO WAS A SMALL BOX OF MILK TRAY'

The Brewery Field, its origins perhaps needing little explanation, is home to Spennymoor Town, a football club which plays in the National League North — two steps below the English Football League. The stadium's impressive, its people greatly welcoming.

In former times it was also home each spring to hundreds of amorous amphibians essaying courtship rituals with the frogs resident in the pond behind the bottom goal, but these days there'd probably be an FA rule, or an online petition, against it.

It was at the Co Durham ground, on September 26th 2021, that the pioneering Head for Change charity match took place in which heading the ball during the first half was restricted to the penalty area and in the second was outlawed altogether — a first in adult football and a game-changer for public awareness.

'With the media it was just a feeding frenzy, a tsunami,' says Judith Gates, who — ever replete with ideas, ever good with words — likes to talk of the kick-off that bounced around the world. 'I was there from 12.30pm and literally running around the ground between camera crews. It was intended as a conversation starter and its success was phenomenal.'

The organisers counted 422 media reports worldwide, read by an estimated 47 million people. The match, said the BBC website, was 'an historic moment for British sport.'

'The entire sport of football, worldwide, could be fundamentally affected by what went on in those 90 minutes at the Brewery Field,' said *Soccer America*. 'My husband will enjoy today,' said Judith, 'but he won't remember it tomorrow.'

The Athletic also quoted Dr Gates and might equally have been talking to Steve Thompson. 'Bill wished that no other player in the future, and no other families in the future, would have to face what he was facing and have to suffer what we were suffering.'

Amid such global interest, particularly on social media, not everyone was going to stand on his feet and holler. A critic suggested that they'd soon be taking the field in crash helmets, another that they should play with balloons. 'I think,' says Mark Solan, one of the organisers, gently, 'that they probably missed the point.'

The game was a partnership between Head for Change and the Solan Connor Fawcett Family Cancer Trust, a Spennymoor-based charity set up by Mark Solan in 2015 after both his mother and grandmother had died from the disease. Usually it's shortened to Team Solan.

Credit for the idea of a charity match is given to Town groundsman Mark Sleightholme, though with the accustomed admonition about keeping off the grass.

The game started with local lad and former Leeds United midfielder Mark Tinkler penalised in the opening minutes, a footballer not thinking outside the box but ironic because the last Premier League goal scored with a header from outside the penalty area had been by Alan Smith, his former Leeds team mate, back in 2003.

The Spennymoor game ended 5–5 after Mark Solan's late equaliser. 'It was a worldy,' he insists. 'I went to do a swan dive but unfortunately got stuck.'

'Every time I hear about that goal it gets better' says Janice, the cancer charity's office manager. She hears about it quite a lot, she adds. A worldy? Debra Swinburn, Spennymoor Town director and local solicitor, considers her verdict as carefully as a good lawyer might. 'It was a worldy for Mark,' she says.

The match had also to be approved by Moors chairman and successful businessman Brad Groves who, small world, had once worked for Bill Gates in the Monument Sports warehouse. 'He didn't take much persuading,' says Debra. 'I think the quid pro quo was a small box of Milk Tray. I don't think anyone ever dreamed that it would grab worldwide attention the way it did.'

Cadbury's Milk Tray, it transpires, is a familiar currency in those quarters.

The only disappointment — 'insane' says Mark — was that after all the publicity the Sunday afternoon crowd barely reached 250. 'I just couldn't comprehend it, we'd had publicity all over the world,' says Judith. 'I remember looking out of the window and asking when people would be coming. They said they always left it late. It wasn't about the money though, of course, it was nice to raise some, but we did expect a lot more people.'

Debra Swinburn grew up in the village of Kirk Merrington, a mile or so from Spennymoor, has practised in the town for 30 years, got to know Bill and Judith Gates when, early in the 21st Century, they took control of the Whitworth Hall Hotel on the edge of the town — former home of Bonny Bobby Shafto, fabled in song and in the Spennymoor school magazine. She acted for them in both England and in the Cayman Islands, particularly taken with Bill's frequent aphorism that the harder he worked the luckier he got, though Bill would be unlikely to claim it as an original.

'We worked together professionally but soon became really good friends,' she recalls over coffee back at the Brewery Field.

'Bill was still very fit and fiercely competitive — tennis, five-a-side football, anything he could play — and was clearly still a man on a mission. He was very charismatic, very engaging, still followed the Boro, clearly had looked after himself.

'Bill and Judith had different skill sets but were brilliant working together, really complemented one another. Judith was very aware of sport but I wouldn't say at the same level. She's one of the most amazing people I've met — like another mother, or an aunt anyway. I feel very lucky to have known them both.' Now? 'It's just heart breaking, isn't it.'

Mark Solan, a 48-year-old former retail manager, launched his charity with one of those 'white collar' boxing bouts. He raised £21,000. Now it has two big shops in Spennymoor town centre — 'boutiques' he likes to call them — with facilities behind the scenes for everything from counselling to crafting. There's a wig room, too.

They exist, he says, for anyone who suffers from cancer or has ever been affected by it. The logo's an amalgam of Superman and Rocky — his two favourite films, Mark insists.

He'd already organised several fund raising football matches. A photograph on the wall, another boxing bout, shows him making a haymaker at former Sunderland footballer Julio Arca and looking like he didn't want to come second. He became involved with Head for Change after being approached by Debra, a Team Solan trustee.

'To be honest I'd never even heard of Bill Gates the footballer, just the Microsoft one,' he admits. 'I could see that Head for Change was really going to take off. We're similar charities and I wanted to help — it wasn't just so that I could get another game of football.

'The media coverage was amazing — I don't suppose I'll get on Sky Sports again. I've even got a clip from Australian TV somewhere. I'm so glad I was persuaded to do it. I don't know if you'll ever change what happens on Saturday afternoons but you can change an awful lot in training, especially in youth football. People are just focusing on 90 minutes, but there's much more to it than that.'

Bill Gates kicked off but (of course) took no further part. Squads representing Spennymoor Town and a Bill Gates XI were mostly made up of former professional footballers from the North-East.

'I saw a lot of ill-informed comments but the game was just about raising awareness, starting conversations, and we were having them in the dressing room among ourselves,' said Mickey Barron, with over 300 games for Hartlepool United. 'The coaches would give us long balls and we'd head them for 15-20 minutes three or four times a week. I think you could get more chances to score if there was less heading in the game.'

'It was a bit like five-a-side in training, short and sharp,' said former England international and Everton and Sunderland player Gavin McCann. 'You have to be a bit brighter with your positioning.'

'At the time you're playing you don't think about it, but how can you know that it's not a possibility?' said former Middlesbrough and Birmingham City player Stuart Parnaby, then 39.

Its report headed 'Small town Spennymoor...hosts a major moment in world soccer,' *Soccer America* supposed the point that football without heading could work to have been made. 'The game, of course, *proved* nothing. It was not a scientifically planned exercise,' wrote Paul Gardner.

What it did do, one hopes, was to embarrass the soccer powers — in England the, FA — into at least taking serious action to reduce the amount of heading in the game. The requirement that the number of headers be reduced in practice sessions is both a feeble move and one that seems, at the very least, laughably unenforceable.

'The call for more research is a blatant time-wasting manoeuvre, one that was cleverly and successfully used for years by the tobacco industry as it stonewalled accusations that its product caused lung cancer. There is absolutely no excuse for not acting now.

Another game, perhaps an annual event, is planned. After publicity surrounding the first, a former Spennymoor resident — 'second cousin, it turns out' says Judith — got in touch from Australia. They hope soon to have a H4C group Down Under, where brain injury from contact sport is also a major concern.

As a salute to Bill Gates, they'd love to stage a match at Middlesbrough FC's Riverside Stadium but the next will again be at the Brewery Field. Among Judith's 'visual impact' ideas, a nod to the FA's 'Football should be unforgettable' initiative, is that the teams emerge through two lines of life-size cardboard cut-outs of players who've suffered or are suffering from neurodegenerative disease.

It's also whispered that a familiarly rotund Welsh tenor may be doing a turn, as they say up north. Go compare.

'It will be a way of continuing the conversation, we have to keep it going,' says Judith.

11.

'I SPENT THE NIGHT IN MIDDLESBROUGH HOSPITAL. IT WENT ON LIKE THAT FOR TWO DAYS AND THEY HAD ME TRAINING AGAIN ON THE THIRD'

Head for Change has 15 ambassadors, many of them rugby men and one (as we have noted) an incomparable opera singer. It also has around 65 'football supporters,' all well known in the game and including former Middlesbrough, Manchester United and England player Gary Pallister.

At the beginning of May 2022 H4C sent an update to the group, advising of recent developments. 'The more we learn,' said the letter, 'the more we know that we are facing an epidemic. We need to prevent brain injuries in current and future players, preserve the brain health of past players and protect those who are already victims of dementia.'

The letter also gave details of a new three-point strategy for education, research and care and support developed in Glasgow by Dr Willie Stewart and of a meeting at Wembley with football's governing bodies at which Judith Gates and Sally Tucker had 'strongly represented the lived experience of past players and family members.

'We asked for the views of family members to be paramount in research going forward. We requested greater urgency with research results being translated into preventative measures in a timely fashion. We queried the ethics of using current players as research subjects, knowing that this could be exposing them to already known dangers. Overall we represented the need for a precautionary approach that promotes protection for players.'

The previous October, the man known to football as Pally had told the *Sunday Telegraph* — an interview which subsequently appeared everywhere from the *New York Times* to the *Knutsford Chronicle* — of his worries that he, too, could become a victim.

Worse than that, he'd long experienced migraines. More worrying yet, he'd been a central defender. 'I was probably one of those who shoved their head in the sand and said it wouldn't happen to me,' he said. 'I've suffered awful migraines. I've been knocked clean out, woke up on the pitch and not known where I was. You put it all together and think "Crikey, I'm a prime candidate for dementia."'

It's both coincidental and a bit ironic that Pally should feature in one of football's better known concussion-related stories, after accidentally banging heads with Liverpool's Neil Ruddock towards the end of a match at Anfield in January 1994 between Liverpool and Manchester United.

That Ruddock was known universally as Razor, it should for the uninitiated be explained, was not because he was particularly close shaven. He scored despite the clash of heads. Anfield was exuberant but Ruddock dazed, unaware and unable to answer basic questions from Liverpool physio Phil Boersma who sent word to team manager Graeme Souness that the player not only didn't know he'd scored but had no idea who he was.

The story's re-told in Ruddock's neatly named autobiography, *Hell Razor*. 'If he's no idea who he is,' said the manager, expletives deleted, 'get him back out there and tell him he's Pele.'

Souness, it should perhaps be added, has himself no recollection of the comment. It's one of those apocryphal anecdotes oft trotted out by after-dinner speakers at sportsman's evenings in which only the names change — see also pulled off at half-time, happy 30th birthday grandma, we called him Exocet etcetera, etcetera, etcetera.

Pally's fine about an interview for the book, the only slightly unusual proviso that I ring the evening before just to remind him. Probably it was just because he didn't have a pen and paper to hand.

It's 8.30 on a bright May morning when he walks — brisk, bright, grey bearded — into the Mocking Bird deli in Yarm, *Sun* and *Daily Mail* under his arm. One of the newspapers leads on the death of Dennis Waterman, the other on Boris. 'I like to sit here and watch the world go by,' he says.

Yarm's a footballers' haven just south of the Tees, the North-East equivalent of one of these affluent Cheshire villages — thought by the tabloids to be 'leafy' all year round — in which half the Premier League seems to lay their heads. The Mocking Bird is an agreeable little bolt hole for former players. It's owned by Helen Camsell whose grandfather George Camsell was a former Co Durham miner who played in the Northern League before scoring 20 goals in 21 appearances for Durham City — Football League members in the 1920s. Frying pan and fire, he then swapped the perils of the pit for the dangers of professional football, joining Middlesbrough for £500.

Just 5ft 6ins tall, all that they say about good stuff and little bundles, Camsell hit 325 goals in 419 Football League appearances for the Boro and in just nine England games scored 18, including four against Belgium in 1929 — 'the best England centre forward you've never heard of,' says a piece on the BBC website. Nothing records how many of his goals were headers but goodness knows he rose often enough to the occasion. He died, aged just 63. Cause unknown.

Pally's 56, looks physically fine, insists that he's not. 'My back's shot, arthritis, my legs and feet are shot. That's football, but I still try to do my 10,000 steps each day and to get around the golf course.' He also does hosting and in-house television work for Man United but admits to being 'a bit bored at other times.'

His mother herself suffers from dementia and is in a care home. 'She's struggling,' he says.

Conversationally he seems equally fine — friendly by nickname and nature — though that may not, of course, be supposed a specialist opinion. There've been few worries, he says, save for the time a few months earlier after another breakfast at the Mocking Bird. He'd almost completed the 20-minute walk home when he felt the car keys in his pocket. 'I just thought "Shit," is it going to be me next?' he says. He'd driven down in the car.

He was born in Kent, returned to Teesside with his parents, began work as a wages clerk while playing in the Northern League for Billingham Town. From Middlesbrough he joined Manchester United for £2.3 million — 'a pacy defender with excellent aerial ability and terrific ball control, part of arguably the greatest central defensive partnership the club has known,' says the Manchester United Legends website. Between 1992 and 1995 he missed just one game.

The other centre half was fellow England international Steve Bruce, from Corbridge. 'There was always a bit of bravado, a lot of testosterone about, particularly with me and Brucey because we were North-East lads and it was expected of us somehow. It was the old invincible thing again, wasn't it.'

Appreciative fans knew them, slightly strangely, as Daisy and Dolly. He insists he doesn't know which was which. When finally he returned to Middlesbrough, the fee was £2.5 million — 'typical United, made a profit even after all those years.'

He suffered several serious head injuries, not least in a match against Everton when Welsh international goalkeeper Neville

Southall — familiarly a former binman — made to punch the ball and punched the centre half's head instead.

Just before half-time in a game at Newcastle he again took a fearful blow to the head and was carried off. 'I had to sit in a darkened room. I started throwing up, I was losing my speech and had tingling in my arms. It felt like my head was full of sea shells.'

The manager looked him over, said he should be OK for the second half. 'I told him I couldn't even see other players, never mind the ball,' says Pally. 'It was a really weird feeling, any movement caused pain. I spent the night in Middlesbrough hospital and it went on like that for two days and they had me training again on the third. It's the kind of mentality you were dealing with at the time.

'I was brought up heading the ball, it was a big part of my game and I was very proficient at it. Maybe not 100 times a day in training but a lot and I never once had a conversation about what the long-term effects might be. You're fit, you're reasonably happy and you just get on with it. It was probably only after Jeff Astle died that I started to think about brain damage but it was a bit late for me, my career was over by then.'

The death within three months in 2020 of England World Cup winners Nobby Stiles and Jack Charlton, both of whom had been suffering from dementia, was also a 'seminal moment' says Pally. 'It brought things out more into the open. I saw Nobby — wonderful character, everyone loved him — go through it and I'm seeing (former Middlesbrough central defender) Gordon McQueen going through it. You're hearing about more ex-professional players all the time.'

His own 'debilitating' headaches started again two or three years ago. 'The chances are I probably will get the illness, given the position I played almost all my life. I've always been hopeless at names, people pull my leg about it, but there may be a lot worse than that.

'Players like me need to take a look at themselves in the mirror and wonder if they could have done more, but the PFA should probably have been more aware, too. Things may be changing now but there still seem to be people dragging their feet. I know that players like me are supposed to be fearless, but they need to be made aware of the dangers. Everyone needs to know.'

He'd at once accepted the invitation to be part of H4C. 'You haven't just to answer for yourself but for the people who come after you. There are still a lot more questions than answers, but if I can do just a small bit to help provide them, I'll be happy.'

12.

'THIS DISEASE TESTS YOUR KINDNESS. IT TESTS YOUR PATIENCE. IT TESTS YOUR FAMILY. IT TESTS EVERYTHING EXCEPT YOUR LOVE. BUT THE MORE YOU LOVE, THE MORE YOUR HEART BREAKS'

Back in February 2021, Nick Gates wrote a piece for the Head for Change website about his stricken father's uncontrollable compulsion to walk. He called it 'The Lonely Walk' and it warrants reproduction.

> A 'voice' in my dad's head tells him to walk. So we walk. Sometimes we walk ten times a day. Six weeks ago we walked so much that he ended the day in hospital and we feared he had suffered a stroke. So now we have to find ways to divert 'the voice.' Within a few minutes of finishing one walk 'the voice' asks: 'Do you fancy going for a walk?' He doesn't know how many times he walks in a day. He doesn't remember. I remember every step.

> For those who don't know about sports-related neurodegenerative disease (CTE) it is a brutal disease. My dad is scared, confused and bewildered.

But he is strong and proud and dignified. He knows that he is confused. We have moments of understanding and connection but, increasingly, my role is to provide care and support. Whilst we recognise his patterns, each day his brain is different and establishing a routine is very hard.

This disease tests your kindness. It tests your patience. It tests your family. It tests everything except your love. But the more you love, the more your heart breaks.

I am proud to be part of Head for Change, supporting families like mine through their difficult journey. I'm working with football to try to find ways to educate young players and coaches so that they can make the necessary changes to protect the future of the game and their own futures. And we are all working together to re-imagine research to support change.

Two months ago I accepted that we could no longer create memories for my dad, but we could create moments. So now we have moments. While we walk we have moments of laughter, moments to remember playing in big games at huge stadiums, and some moments of peace. But most of the time he walks a lonely walk to nowhere. And I walk by his side. And my heart breaks.

Nick, Bill and Judith Gates's younger son, drives down to our house after taking his dad for a routine medical appointment. It's early May 2022 and that momentum — it may not be called reverse momentum, that would be oxymoronic, but perhaps it is a perverse momentum — seems, however melancholily, to be maintained.

In the past few days former Everton and England B player Mick Lyons, 70, and ex-Everton and Manchester United man Colin Gibson, who's 62, have both announced that they're suffering with what's believed to be football-related dementia. Both were defenders. The word 'toll' seems in every sense appropriate, and football wonders for whom the bell will toll next.

'Sometimes you get yourself into a slightly embarrassing position where you completely forget something and you haven't got the answer and can't find the words,' Gibson told the *Daily Mail*. 'People think "Oh, look at that thick footballer." I'm not going to go down without a fight.'

The Premier League has announced a study — involving technologically advanced mouthguards — to try to establish how many headers in a game may be 'safe' and the PFA has launched an initiative to attempt to discover how many former footballers are living with neurodegenerative disease. We shall with luck hear more of both.

So how's his dad doing? 'I wish I had his heart rate, I wish I had his blood pressure. He'd be very fit if he wasn't so unwell,' says Nick, not quite paradoxically.

He brings with him a great scree of scrapbooks, meticulously maintained by his dad to memorialise an outstanding football career. Doubtless they will add nostalgia to the narrative, doubtless they'll recall something of Bill's testimonial against Leeds United when a friend's son carried the old first division championship trophy — won by United — and both his sons carried the second division trophy, lifted by the Boro.

Nick, 55, is the founder and head of Coaches Across Continents, a charity set up in 2008 to harness football as a force for good — and for change — especially in the Third World. It has won 29 global awards. Last year, he says, they had influence in 132 countries across six continents — and always they've had friends.

After Newcastle United's St James' Park ground became a supporters' shrine to the uniquely charismatic Sir Bobby Robson, the club gave 1,500 of the shirts and scarves left in his memory to Coaches Across Continents — and the RAF (friends in high places) flew them to Africa. Suddenly there were an awful lot of Magpies in the Third World.

Formally CAC talks of sustainability and social development, of HIV education and of female empowerment. Among the best bits, says Nick, is the simple pleasure of making kids laugh. 'It's challenging but it's a lot of fun. I don't think there are many bad days.'

CAC partners with H4C with CAC's education programme, Head Safe, an initiative supported by former England manager Kevin Keegan, switching as easily and as effortlessly between the two as a 1950s pedal cyclist going through the gears on his three-speed Sturmey Archer. Head Safe's 'innovative' educational programme' — 'the first of its kind in the world' — had by 2023 worked with 35 clubs, across all departments, and within their communities. Eighty-six per cent of football people to whom Nick spoke had never heard of CTE.

Most also erroneously believed that modern footballs were lighter than the sodden, sodding balls of former times. 'That widely held misconception highlights the urgent need for education,' says Nick.

So how had his dad changed in the 15 months since he wrote that poignantly agonised account?

'As a positive he's safer and he's calmer. As a negative he's worse. It was a frightening time because whatever was telling him always to walk was just dominant in his brain.

> I'd be getting up at four o'clock, working till ten o'clock on Coaches Across Continents and then my dad would get up and want to go for a walk. He might talk about getting fit for the new season, about whether he'd get a game, about what time kick-off was. Then we'd finally get back and I'd start on CAC again.

> I think everyone needs to know that it's horrific. Footballers need to know it and their families need to know that it affects them, too. We absolutely need to do this for future generations because it's also incredibly scary for families. It's a monster and it's stalking us now.

We'd first spoken on the telephone in 2009 when Nick was somewhere in Malawi and it was as instantaneous as chatting to a neighbour over the garden fence, discussing the state of the vegetable patch. Ever the innocent, I'd expressed incredulity.

'They don't have wires any more,' said Nick, cheeky beggar. He supposed that he, too, had been wrongly wired. 'I have my mother's football ability and my father's brains.' However humorous, and his mother's physical coordination is said to be at the very opposite extreme to her formidable mental dexterity, it was only half true.

For the same *Northern Echo* column, I'd also had lunch with Bill and Judith, a couple of years off their golden wedding and still holding hands like kids at a funfair (or, perhaps, at the Rome Olympics).

Bill — 'he's not a soft touch but he's got a soft heart,' his wife had said — had also become a frequent visitor to Africa, helping Coaches Across Continents and improbably supposing the dark continent to be a bit like Dean Bank, Ferryhill, the Co Durham pit village where he grew up. 'Very few people have much but they're lovely folk and they're happy, just as we were in Dean Bank. It sounds almost pretentious, but I'm seeing the difference that football is making, the way that it changes lives.'

In 2011, when we met again, Bill and Judith had returned from another African safari, Bill scoring four in a five-a-side match — and no matter that three of the opposing team were 10-year-old boys, the other two were ten-year-old girls and he was also the referee. 'I told him to be careful because the nearest hospital was ten hours away and within a few seconds he was on his backside. He'll soon be saying it was six goals,' said Nick.

It was a greatly happy occasion. Bill seemed fine then. 'Too young?' Judith had echoed. 'Of course we were too young, but I'm awfully glad that we did it.' Soon, however, there'd be health questions, and there'd be growing doubts. Ultimately, unconquerably, there'd be darkness.

Nick had also been a central defender, good enough to play for England Under-18s and narrowly to miss out on selection for the Under-15s. Ultimately he decided on further education, attended Millfield — the sports-oriented public school in Somerset — and then Harvard University, despite trials with several Football League clubs and offers from some of them.

He worked in business development with Middlesbrough FC, began Coaches Across Continents, discussed with his father seven years ago the formation of a charity to address issues around brain injury in sport — brain injury like Bill's own.

Though not formally launched until January 2021, H4C was born from that conversation. 'It's his legacy, a way of giving something to the next generation,' says Nick. 'We aren't in the blame game, we want to be part of the solution. There's much more awareness but there's still a long way to go. People think, or claim to think, that it's an old people's problem, not theirs, but it's a problem for nine-year-olds, it's for everyone.'

Don't know or don't want to know? 'A bit of both, I think. Thousands and thousands of players and their families are going to be affected by this and there's a danger that football is sitting on its hands. The dream of having proper education in clubs is a bit tricky because it's labour intensive but the pay-off is huge and it has to be done.

'Even now there's a focus on the first team squad but it affects all levels, including what they call the non-league game. People don't properly understand dementia. It's not just about forgetting where you left your car keys. We still operate under a dark cloud.'

He also cites several misconceptions — 'cool misconceptions' he says, the American influence — not least the notion that the danger is dissipated because modern footballs are lighter. The regulation weight, he says, has been the same for more than a century.

Another is that the number of headers in a game is decreasing — 'it's actually the opposite' — a third that there's a 'safe' way to head a football. 'It's like saying there's a safe way to be punched in the face,' says Nick.

The week previously he'd led a Head Safe delegation with a group of 32 English Football League clubs at Swindon, further discussing player safety and care. The chief concern remains the number of times a ball can be headed in training — 'if you're going to do that, use a softer ball,' says Nick, though he doubts that heading could ever be redundant.

> *People say that football can't change but you only have to look at the 1980s when characters like Vinnie Jones were playing. Now it's all 90mph stuff.*
>
> *If you banned heading completely you'd need to look at cycling, and then there's rugby. In Bill Beaumont's generation they were big guys who trained maybe twice a week and played on a Saturday. Then it became professional, the guys got even bigger and stronger and the impacts became harder.*

There's a danger, truth to tell, that the book — though not H4C — could be taking its eye off the oval-shaped ball. Needs must, we will return to the rugby field ere long — and before 2022 is out, the professional game's very existence will be called into question.

If not to the same degree, her younger son shares Judith Gates's well-informed caution. It wouldn't do to call it scepticism. 'They talk about ten-year studies but there've been a lot of studies already and I'm not sure how much more we can learn from research,' says Nick. 'It's very clear that there's a connection between repeatedly heading a football and neurodegenerative disease.

'Success would be drastically reducing the numbers of headers in a player's career, that would be an incredible step forward. For there to be real progress, the true momentum needs to start now. The next three years will be crucial.'

Then he's off back to Castle Eden, perhaps even for a short spring evening walk with his dad, ahead of trips to America and to Zanzibar. 'I still walk with him, talk with him, try to take away some of the anxiety. Sometimes he'll have little flashes — the other day he remembered (former Sunderland centre half) Charlie Hurley but obviously he's deteriorating. Football did that to my dad.'

13.

'THE BRUTAL TRUTH IS THAT THERE AREN'T ENOUGH PEOPLE SUFFERING FROM MND TO MAKE RESEARCH A GOOD INVESTMENT FOR DRUG COMPANIES'

It's not just CTE, not just dementia, which may particularly affect sportsmen (and, it's to be expected, sportswomen, too.) Studies with increasing confidence suggest a link between strenuous exercise and the incurable and ultimately hideous motor neurone disease. They talk, too, of increased risk from repeatedly heading the ball.

'We have suspected for some time that exercise was a risk factor in MND but until now the link was considered controversial,' said Dr Jonathan Cooper-Knoc in 2021, following further research. 'This study confirms that in some people frequent strenuous exercise leads to an increase in the risk of MND.'

Dr Willie Stewart's study in 2019 concluded that while former footballers were 3.5 times more likely to die from any neurodegenerative disease they were, specifically, 4.33 times more likely to die from motor neurone disease. The risk is thought to be greater among those sports players genetically disposed towards the disease.

MND is brutal, fearful. Footballers like former England manager Don Revie and Scottish international Jimmy Johnstone have succumbed to its predations, others like Lennie Johnrose and former Liverpool man Stephen Darby — whose wife is the England women's captain Steph Houghton — battle the disease. Marcus Stewart, who scored 250 goals in 650 appearances for clubs across the English leagues, was 50 when diagnosed in 2022.

Johnrose, once with Hartlepool United and affectionately remembered at Lancashire's 'B' teams — Burnley, Bury, Blackburn — had been diagnosed in 2017, went public the following year, had no doubt that a career embracing 430 senior games had provoked his illness and campaigned for greater awareness of the dangers,

'That increased risk should cause massive shockwaves but it's hardly made a ripple,' he said after the publication of Dr Stewart's findings. He also expressed himself 'sickened' at the absence of heading restrictions — at the time — in children's football and accused governing bodies of 'taking risks with people's lives'.

Though his health precipitously deteriorated, he'd for a time continued working as a primary school teacher, visited football clubs to talk about MND and its risk factors, worked to raise both funds and awareness of the disease and wrote an autobiography using voice recognition technology. 'I can't count the number of times he's come home with concussion after he's bashed heads with someone,' said Nadine, his wife. 'You just can't know what damage that does.'

Len Johnrose was just 52 when he died in August 2022 — 'a real gentleman and an incredibly popular character,' said the Professional Footballers' Association, which had helped support him and his family.

Among the disease's earlier and higher profile victims was former Middlesbrough player and manager Willie Maddren — 'one of the Boro's finest ever players' says the club's official website.

In the early 1970s, ironically, it was often he who kept his friend Bill Gates out of the side.

Scottish rugby union international Doddie Weir and England rugby league man Rob Burrow — just 5ft 5ins tall, barely 11 stones — were also relatively youthful victims, both of whom used their status to raise awareness and funds in the yet-unequal and ever-unfair struggle.

Doddie Weir died in November 2022. Rob Burrow's stricken situation was marvellously magnified by his former Leeds Rhinos team mate Kevin Sinfield, whose extraordinary fund raising efforts for MND research had raised getting on £10m.

In July 2022 Gloucester and England Saxons lock Ed Slater announced his retirement at 33 after also being diagnosed with MND, prompting accusations that the government had 'blood on its hands' after the failure to deliver £50 million worth of promised research funding. Willie Maddren, of course, had written much the same thing.

Willie was a Billingham boy, born in 1951, made his Middlesbrough Reserves debut as a substitute after Gates had taken a fearsome kick in what euphemistically is termed the midriff. It was among the less graphically chronicled of Bill's many injuries.

Willie scored, broke his nose and chipped an ankle bone on his first team debut, went on to make 341 appearances and won England Under-23 honours before a knee injury ended his playing career when he was just 26. 'One of the best uncapped defenders of his time, one of the greatest players ever to pull on a red shirt' says *The Who's Who of Middlesbrough.*

Diagnosed with MND in 1995, magnificently supported thereafter by his wife Hilary, he completed an autobiography, *Extra Time,* and was just 49 when he died in August 2000. 'I will fight this illness to the bitter end,' he'd written, 'though I know the odds are not stacked in my favour.'

Back then, relatively little was known about MND. 'The brutal truth,' Willie wrote, 'is that there just aren't enough people suffering from the disease to make research a sound investment for drug companies.'

The book was one of numerous fund raising efforts, continued by Hilary after his death, to raise funds and awareness for the Motor Neurone Disease Association. She also wrote a moving final chapter, after her husband's passing, for a second edition. 'I was besotted with Willie but I don't think I realised how special he was until I saw how he coped with his illness.'

In 1996, Middlesbrough FC had organised a benefit game against Inter Milan — proceeds again went towards MND research — and have since named the education centre at the Riverside Stadium in his memory.

Joined by Judith Gates, her friend since those red roaring days, we take lunch at the Shoulder of Mutton. Her Majesty's platinum jubilee celebrations will be waved off the following day.

Hilary was a florist, nine years Willie's junior, his second wife. They'd met when she was a barmaid in Stockton when he thought her 'a bit stuck up.' Nor was the course of true love straightforward thereafter. 'How we ever got married is a wonder,' Hilary wrote. 'Willie nobly asked my father for his daughter's hand in marriage but, sadly, forgot to ask me.' Oversight acknowledged, he proposed that the wedding day should be May 12th — that being the only free Saturday he had that year.

John, her second husband, is a nephew of the late and greatly lamented Sir Bobby Robson, the former Newcastle United and England manager. She still uses the surname Maddren when on MND business, though we swap Bobby Robson stories, of which there are a great many, over the fish pie.

The grittiest, least appropriate and quite likely apocryphal — though one which Sir Bobby loved to tell — may concern his time as manager of Ipswich Town, when he bumped into one or other of the Cobbold family, the club's patrician owners, in the gent's at the Great Eastern Hotel near Liverpool Street station.

The chairman eyed him disdainfully. 'Where I come from, Robert, we wash our hands after using the lavatory.' 'Where I come from Mr Chairman,' said Bob, 'we don't pee on them in the first place.'

Hilary estimates that she and Willie together have raised around £350,000 for the Motor Neurone Disease Association with which for more than 20 years she's been a volunteer — all sorts of roles, she says, but often just a shoulder to cry on.

'MND sufferers are always such kind people, always patient, so often smiling. Willie himself did a lot of fund raising and took part in clinical trials but like everyone else he hoped there'd be a cure in his lifetime. Sadly it hasn't yet happened.'

As a player he'd frequently suffered migraines, never complained, got on with it. 'There was a lot of bravado, a lot of macho about at the time,' says Hilary, that theme becoming familiar.

His retirement fund was boosted by a testimonial against the Scottish national team helping him emulate his friend and open a sports shop. The business grew to four Teesside outlets, Willie worked and worried endlessly. 'He wasn't as successful as Bill,' says his widow.

For 18 stressful months between mid-1984 and early in 1986 he'd become Middlesbrough's manager at a time when the club was on its uppers, struggling on and off the field. His £12,500 annual salary was thought to be the Football League's lowest. 'To this day I'm convinced that that 12-month period (when the sports shops were struggling) coupled with the pressures of football management, were the onset of my MND,' he wrote.

For a year after his diagnosis he and Hilary kept the terrible news to themselves. 'At first the symptoms were quite mild. His daughter was doing A-levels and he thought she had enough on her plate' says Hilary — and nor was he very keen on Boro fans finding out. 'He knew what was going to happen and he didn't want them to see him in a wheelchair.'

As signs and symptoms of serious illness became harder to hide, Willie asked long-serving Teesside journalist Ray Robertson to handle the story — front page news in the first edition of the *Evening Gazette,* March 13th 1996. By the time the second edition hit the streets he'd been relegated to page three by news of the Dunblane massacre. 'In a strange sense he was quite relieved to have it out in the open, but he was still quite embarrassed about it all, particularly about being on page one,' says Hilary.

The following year, Middlesbrough played Chelsea in the FA Cup final at Wembley. 'He didn't want to go. He wanted supporters to see him walking down Wembley Way, not being pushed down it in a wheelchair. He was persuaded to attend and the crowds parted like the Red Sea to applaud him. It was a turning point, he was more accepting of it after that.'

Convinced of a causal link between football and MND, she accepts that it may not just be heading the ball which is responsible. 'There are many occasions when he'd be bashing with someone else's head, even in training. Visually he'd be quite badly affected — he talks in the book about running towards red (the colour of Middlesbrough's shirts) because that's all he could see.

'The MND symptoms came on slowly. There'd be tingling pains, loss of dexterity in his fingers, those headaches. He was always accepting of it but he was a big, strong man, thought he could cope and become quite frustrated when he couldn't. It was especially hard because he'd been so fit but he still battled, still smiled.'

For years he'd been an enthusiastic member of Eaglescliffe Golf Club — the days when golf clubs had waiting lists, smiles Hilary. When he told them there was no point in renewing his annual subscription, it suggested further evidence that the game was up. 'He realised he'd never again complete a round — a very sad day, but he still raised money and still kept cheerful.

'A lot of people had never heard of motor neurone disease until Willie was struck by it. He was never bitter, never resentful. He realised he'd had an amazing life, even if he never left Teesside and it was only with Middlesbrough. Willie never asked "Why me?" It was always "Why not me." He was incredible.'

Judith Gates agrees. 'Willie was always grateful for all the things he'd done, all that he'd been able to achieve. He was never sorry for himself, that wasn't Willie at all. The way that Hilary looked after him was magnificent — an inspiration to me, an inspiration to us all.'

In 2005, an Italian study of 7,325 former professional footballers found eight with MND. The average figure would have been 1.2. A 2007 study suggested increased risk to those who'd suffered multiple head injuries — 'including heading a ball.'

The Motor Neurone Disease Association remains properly cautious, insisting that there could be other causes — at one point a footballer's repeated contact with grass treated with pesticides was thought a possible factor — and that more research is needed.

Hilary Maddren accepts the caveats. 'MND isn't like cancer, where there's often the chance of a cure. MND is always terminal. We know that. A cure may still be a long way off but one day, I believe, it'll happen.'

14.

'IF YOU GOT A BAD CONCUSSION, STUMBLING AROUND A BIT, IT WAS REGARDED AS A JOKE AND PLAYED AFTERWARDS ON THE VIDEOTAPE, SO EVERYONE COULD HAVE A GOOD LAUGH'

Alix Popham played top level professional rugby for 13 years, was capped 33 times by Wales and was a member of the team which in 2008 claimed the Grand Slam. 'Known for his physicality and aggressiveness, he put his body on the line week after week,' says the BBC website.

'A hard-charging back-rower with a shock of bright blond hair who hit every tackle like it was the last he'd ever make,' says *The Guardian,* perhaps prophetically. 'Well known for his blockbusting tackles,' sums up his Wikipedia page.

Mel, his wife, had put it rather differently. 'Alix gave his heart, body and soul to rugby, he really did, but he didn't know he was going to give his brain as well.'

In 2011 a shoulder injury compelled Alix's retirement. In April 2020 he was diagnosed with early onset dementia and with probable chronic traumatic encephalopathy (which, it will be remembered, can only be confirmed at post-mortem), aged just 40.

A week later he met Judith Gates, ultimately helped co-found Head for Change, but it was Mel who became a trustee alongside Dr Gates and Dr Sally Tucker (to whom we hope in time to return.) 'I couldn't have been a trustee,' says Alix, 'not with my diagnosis.'

Alix says that they didn't know Judith had all those degrees, 'She was just a very nice woman and she's been incredibly supportive to us and to a lot of other players and their families. I can't speak too highly of her, her energy is amazing, she doesn't let go of anything.'

I'd read interviews with him, watched post-diagnosis videos setting out his straitened circumstances, noted that he always had Mel by his side or in the room as both comfort blanket and, if necessary, interpreter. 'She used to call me The Politician because I'd never answer a straight question,' Alix tells me. 'It wasn't really my fault, after ten seconds I couldn't remember what the question had been in the first place.'

If not frail — femmer, as in North-East England they would say — he'd seemed diminished, somehow anxious, forever blinking at the camera or referring the question to his wife. 'It's watching the light gradually fading in him,' Mel had said, almost tearfully, in another interview.

Dementia was inexorable, wasn't it, a one-way street which always had a dead ending?

Our chat at his home near Newport in south Wales has been arranged by email. It's therefore something of a surprise that Alix himself rings when the train's somewhere between Birmingham and Chepstow to check the time of arrival and a yet bigger surprise when, alone, he pulls up at the station in a black Discovery with the Head for Change logo brightly emblazoned across the side. The sub-text 'Be part of the solution' is beneath.

The biggest surprise of all, however, is that he seamlessly completes the 15-mile journey back to Newport whilst holding a jauntily informed conversation about everything from jurisprudence to jelly babies. Goodness knows how we got onto jelly babies.

It seems sensible at once to remark upon his lucidity, his memory and his apparent cognitive clarity. Though the story is properly hedged about with caution, by great leylandii of medical caveats and by a formal non-disclosure agreement, and while the crucial role of exercise and diet cannot too greatly be stressed, what's happening medically is potentially sensational, nonetheless.

'A game changer,' says Alix on several occasions. It could, in truth, be the biggest game changer since William Webb Ellis picked up the ball and (it's reputed) ran like billy-o with it.

Discovery? The evidence of the next couple of hours will confirm that you really do learn something every day. 'I feel like I'm getting my life back,' he says. For how long might sport, medical science, mankind run with this one. and for how long might the momentum be maintained?

Alix Popham was born in Newport in October 1979, played rugby from the age of four, knew no other but the red-blooded sort, the brutish encounters which prompted someone once to suppose rugby union to be a game for hooligans played by gentlemen and soccer, of course, the ungentlemanly opposite.

By the time he was six — 'at the latest' — it was head-on. 'You didn't think of it in any other way,' says Alix. 'We played an awful lot of rugby and were pretty good at it. I think we lost twice in 13 years. I didn't really grow between 12 or 13 and 16 or 17 but I was always an aggressive player.'

Top grade club rugby, traditionally if speciously amateur, had become a professional sport in 1995, bringing with it more training, more strength, more speed and more risk. From 1998 Alix played in turn for Newport, Leeds Tykes, Llanelli Scarlets and Brive, in France. In the UK they trained three days a week with a match on Saturdays, in France they trained four days a week.

When push came to shove, maul to mayhem and head to head, doctors estimated that he had suffered more than 100,000 sub-concussive impacts — blows to the head up to 50 times a match and every one of them inflicting a little more trauma damage to the brain.

A neurologist suggested he look at it like a leaking tap. 'If it drips once or twice onto a patch of mud there'll be no mark but if it drips for 13 or 14 years then there'll be a lot of damage and there's a lot of damage showing up on your scans.'

Nor, Alix insists, had they ever been warned of the danger, though the Rugby Football Union had formally launched studies into possible brain damage in the sport as long since as 1975.

'Never once,' says Alix, back at home. 'We were told right from the start, when we were four, that to go into a tackle with only 99 per cent was the way to get hurt. We went into everything 110 per cent. There was no education, no guidance from coaches or the RFU. That's what upsets me. No one told us anything.'

Now he and an anxiously growing number of others — including former England internationals Steve Thompson and Michael Lipman — seek legal comeuppance from World Rugby, the RFU, Welsh Rugby and others. The youngest is 32. The action is ongoing and inevitably complex, thought to involve several hundred former players both professional and amateur, the legal waters potentially treacherous for those seeking to write about what might happen next. An earlier quote is irresistible, however:

'If someone was getting a kicking on the side of the street, I'd pull up and try to stop what was going on,' Alix had said. 'It feels like the governing bodies are driving past that person being beaten up.'

Then in an extraordinary few days early in 2023, it seemed like the Rugby Football Union had remembered the story of the Good Samaritan, or at least what might be supposed the best bits. On January 19th — the day that it was also reported that 55 'amateur' players were joining the legal action against the authorities — the RFU announced that in an attempt to reduce the number of concussions, tackling above the waist would be banned in the community game, below the top two English tiers, from July 1st. Hitherto the high point had been across the shoulders.

Not least because the executive seemed hardly to have consulted the 66-member RFU Council, and because no one at all had consulted community clubs and their players, the reaction was largely aghast. Clever folk cried existential crisis, others just said it would kill an already endangered game.

Owen Slot, informed and articulate rugby correspondent of *The Times,* was among the questioning pack. 'Among the many recent challenges set out for English rugby by their nebulous leaders at Twickenham has been the need to discover where exactly the waist is located,' he wrote. 'Is it where your teenage son's jeans are hanging? Or is it where Simon Cowell hitches his belt?'

What folk formerly termed the popular prints were probably blunter yet. Given the anatomical area under debate, you'd not have bet a twopence ha'penny stamp against headlines about Twickers in a twist.

The Welsh Rugby Union held back, said (sensibly) that it would need to consult. Besides, there were other dogs at the door of the Principality Stadium in Cardiff — the WRU had announced that the great Welsh anthem *Delilah* would no longer be broadcast before and during matches. Cacophony ensued, a critical chorus of which we shall hear a little more later.

Eight days after the first waist-not announcement, and amid talk of votes of no confidence, something yet more earth shattering occurred: the RFU abjectly apologised, said it had got the whole thing wrong — 'a huge embarrassment' said *The Times* — and promised widespread consultation on what should happen next.

'We agree that we need to do something about the tackle height for future-proofing the game, but the wording will be an experimental law to lower the tackle height with consultation from the game,' a 'source' told the paper. The likelihood, it was supposed, was that the new tackle threshold would be the sternum, though where Simon Cowell kept his sternum was, sadly, unexplained.

With the help of a voice synthesiser and of a ghost writer, Steve Thompson — who'd announced his early onset dementia diagnosis at the same time as Alix and after being urged by Alix to seek medical help — has produced a book, called *Unforgettable,* about his seemingly losing battle in which he admits contemplating suicide.

'I look down upon myself and think why am I here? I'm broken. It would be a lot easier for everyone if I just did myself in. I start to think that the pain, the trauma, it could be gone for everyone in the blinking of an eye. I could end this now. It's me who's the problem so if I go, the problem goes with me.'

In the book he also confesses that he'd never really loved rugby as a sport. 'What I loved was the companionship, the togetherness, the feeling of belonging but if I could hitch a ride on the Tardis and return to my teenage years, I would much rather never have seen a rugby ball.'

In October 2022 Thompson expressed similar sentiments in an hour-long television documentary telling his story. 'I feel like a phoney. It feels like I haven't done these things. I can't remember it.'

Much has also been written about Ben Robinson, a 14-year-old Irish schoolboy who died as the result of head injuries sustained in rugby. World Rugby has consistently claimed that it takes player safety very seriously.

Though he still describes his mid-term recollection as 'raggy' — a meeting with Nelson Mandela before an international in South Africa is half-remembered only because he's seen a photograph of it — Alix's general impressions remain.

'When we trained it was from nine-to-five, three or four days a week and it was like the Wild West. People were going down left, right and centre and that was just training. What went on was crazy, we almost never stopped. One time they hired an Olympic judo athlete who taught us a judo technique for pulling people out of a ruck. We called it a crocodile roll because it was like when a crocodile has a victim and turns them. Finally it was banned.

Most of the time there was only one physio or medic and they were in the clubhouse treating someone. If you got a bad concussion, stumbling around a bit, it was regarded as a joke and played afterwards on the videotape so everyone could have a good laugh. You'd be given sniffing salts and that was it, get on with it.

You'd be taken off with a knee injury but if it was your head, you were expected to carry on. No one was guaranteed a game on the Saturday; if you were fit enough, still standing, you played.

It never occurred to us what was happening. Looking back it was bloody obvious, wasn't it?

It became bloody obvious, anyway. At first it just seemed absent-mindedness, perhaps familiar in the dementia narrative, which affected him. He might nip out to the shop and forget why he'd gone, might forget his pin number. Probably there was a car keys story, too, there often seems to be. 'We knew our bodies were going to be buggered by the time we retired,' Alix once said, 'but no one told us our brains would be as well.'

Then his anger and frustration increased, on one occasion slamming a door until it broke and on another ripping out the banister. He was a big, big man — 6ft 3ins, 17 stones — the stair rails didn't stand a chance.

Another time he almost set the house on fire while Mel was out after forgetting that he'd left the grill on and, most crucially, phoned his wife in the middle of a familiar 25-mile bike ride to report that he'd no idea where he was or how he could get home again. That's when Mel persuaded him to visit the doctor and when the dark hours of the neurological nightmare became ever more satanic. 'It's not really that he was reluctant to go to the doctor, it was like he just couldn't believe it was happening,' says Mel.

Alix went public on his dementia diagnosis in December 2020, the month before Head for Change was formally launched. He also helped found Progressive Rugby, a not-for-profit lobby group drawn from both the amateur and professional game which campaigns for greater protection for players 'to ensure the game continues to thrive.'

Though the group professes itself 'supportive of the core physicality of the game' it argues that much more should be done to protect players from 'brain trauma and broken bodies,' calling in an open letter to Sir Bill Beaumont, chair of World Rugby, for changes across contact in training, workload, health care and insurance.

The UK Rugby Health Project, another independent body and affiliated to the Global Rugby Health Research Network, conducted a study of 189 retired rugby players — 83 professional, 106 amateur, 145 from union and 44 from rugby league.

Depression was frequently encountered, thought to be a result of repeated concussions. Ten per cent of former professionals thought that life was often or always 'hardly worth living.' Many were said to struggle, and to suffer, in silence.

Leading writers like Owen Slot have suggested that rugby faces an existential crisis, that unless far-reaching change is achieved then its future is at stake. While the game is studied and bloodied, the potentially lethal impacts legitimately continue.

Alix reels off several of their requests — demands? — with barely a pause; for two or three others he checks his phone. His latest scans support the suggestion, however tentatively, that something quite remarkable may be happening.

Progressive Rugby, H4C and others have also welcomed a guideline that full contact among professional rugby players in training should be restricted to 15 minutes a week — but why, Alix wonders, isn't it mandatory? Why don't concussion protocols demand an automatic 28-day step-down — 'that's the safe time it takes to recover.' Why the pussyfooting?

Within 10–15 years, he forecasts, junior and amateur rugby will effectively be a non-contact sport.

At H4C his candour and high profile meant that he became a sort of agony aunt — rugby would doubtless use a different phrase — for many other former players. Probably more than 50 per cent are struggling, often with depression, he says. 'Some struggle even to get off the settee. 'It's a very dark place. I know players and their family members who've had serious suicidal thoughts. For this generation and the coming ones, something has to drastically change.'

Alix changed, too. The diet now excludes alcohol — 'three big cups of coffee a day, though' — and includes an exercise regime which embraces strenuous running, swimming and cycling across six days a week — Sundays, like a Valleys tabernacle, off for good behaviour — usually early in the morning so he can spend more time with his family.

In September 2022 he aimed to contest an Ironman triathlon — 2.4 mile swim, 112-mile cycle ride and a marathon run, in that order — as an H4C fund raiser. 'There were two possible venues, northern Italy or Bolton,' he says, grinning. 'For some reason we chose northern Italy.'

In the autumn of 2023 he was hoping to be part of a five-man rugby union relay team taking part in a cross-Channel swim against rugby league contemporaries, an event in which Sky TV had shown much interest and which he hoped could raise a great deal of money for H4C. 'I'll be the one walking like a penguin,' he says.

Though swimming's still affected by that shoulder injury — 'it's a sort of adapted breast stroke' — he's confident of happy landings and of a positive future. 'Possibly everything happens for a reason and I'm trying to work out what the reason might be. Maybe I was quite physical on the pitch but I was never a fighter. I want to be this fit for as long as possible. I'm fighting now and I really hope we can win.'

The house is decorated with the inflatable ephemera of their daughter Darcey's fourth birthday the day before, four excitable shih tzus bristle briefly outside. Alix offers a large slice of birthday cake, made by mother and daughter, says he won't have any himself. 'I had a piece last night, that's enough for one week.'

Probably it was a mistake to leave all the balloons and stuff up, he says. 'Darcey thinks it's her birthday today as well.'

Interviewer and subject sit a yard apart on high kitchen chairs, one more confidently than the other (and one not trying to write shorthand, either). 'A year, 18 months ago I could never have done this without Mel being here,' says Alix.

Darcey's elsewhere, Mel at a hospital appointment to discuss long-Covid symptoms. There are two older daughters from Alix's first marriage. 'Mel and I knew one another when we were 11, went our separate ways and then somehow got together again,' he says.

While the familiar blond mop has gone, the no-less familiar tattoos indelibly remain. He wears shorts, T-shirt and baseball cap — always the baseball cap — looks tanned and fit, talks effortlessly and articulately, appears wholly at ease. He is calm.

Though diet and exercise are thought to have been crucial, he is also undergoing revolutionary medical assessment and treatment — abroad, let's say — which the neurologist involved hopes will form the basis of a paper for the *Lancet* medical journal, Alix at its guardedly optimistic centre.

Other former rugby players — 'the boys' he calls them — have also been part of the programme. 'I'd a message from one just this morning,' says Alix. 'He'd been in a really bad place, said he couldn't thank me enough.'

Mel, successful director of an A-list recruitment company in London, returns half way through and is greeted affectionately. 'The new treatment's mind blowing, it makes my head spin,' she says. 'People talk of wonderful breakthroughs of people like Henry Ford, Albert Einstein or Louis Pasteur but if this comes good the doctor could be up there with all of them. The initial signs are very promising.'

Alix enthusiastically agrees. 'I've always tried to visualise things, to try to see how things will work out, but I could never have visualised this. You learn to be cautious but it's like everything I could have prayed for, and more.'

Though impossible not to feel the excitement, and to share it, it would be both unwise and inappropriate to offer further detail, not least in the light of that non-disclosure agreement. Suffice that not for a moment in those two-and-a-half absorbing hours has he seemed lost for words or in any other cognitive difficulty, rather that his memory — 'Oh, you mean Paul McCrory' — appears on occasion better than mine.

After returning me to Chepstow, he heads — on his own — for Cardiff city centre, where (he says) they do a great Thai curry. In the opposite direction, I return north on a ham and chutney sandwich and, buzzing, on a high.

For 55 years I wrote stuff which, by and large, appeared in print hours later. A book's much different, its accustomed gestation making a full-term woolly mammoth seem premature, publication — if at all — at some indeterminate distant date. Numerous changes are likely, potentially endless blips between cup and lip. How will Alix get on in the Ironman event, if not the Channel swim? What will have happened with the legal challenge to rugby's governing bodies, and at what consequence? Might more be disclosed about Alix's experimental treatment, NDA notwithstanding?

Can Head for Change move man mountains? Might Progressive Rugby proceed apace? Whither — wither? — the game?

Not a fortnight after the visit to Newport, it's revealed that Alix's former Welsh team mate and captain Ryan Jones, capped 73 times and three times a Grand Slam winner, has also been diagnosed with early onset dementia and probable CTE and has joined the legal action. Anxiety, depression, mood swings — all the now-accustomed concomitants are manifest. He's 41 and, like Alix Popham, had retired because of a shoulder injury.

'I feel like my world is falling apart,' he tells *Sunday Times* sports writer David Walsh, who has devoted many column inches to the subject. 'I'm really scared because I've got three children and three step children and I want to be a fantastic dad.

'We don't know where to go, where to find support. It terrifies me because we don't know if in two years time we'll be sitting here and these episodes will be a week long.' Two pages in the sports section are headlined with another of Jones's quotes: 'Rugby is walking eyes closed into a catastrophe.'

Alix Popham agrees. 'We need to draw a line in the sand, realise the mistakes that were made and move forward. Otherwise the sport is going to die.'

Back between Chepstow and Birmingham, I'd found myself earnestly hoping, perhaps even praying, alongside the Pophams, that things will continue to change, perhaps almost miraculously, for the better. Alix and Mel, this generation and the next, could yet be part of the solution.

15.

'MY DAD WAS ALWAYS VERY SUPPORTIVE OF THE PFA, BUT I THINK THEY'VE FAILED FAMILIES AND FOOTBALL PARTICIPANTS IN GENERAL'

There's a video on YouTube of Billy Tucker, a former centre half with Hereford United, Bury and Swindon Town, returning to Hereford in 2016 to share his memories. Though already diagnosed with dementia, at least he still had some.

Bill appears engaging and engaged, if perhaps a little distanced, talks of happy days — 'Hereford really looked after me' — of a still-celebrated FA Cup defeat of Newcastle United and of his former team mate and Welsh international John Charles. 'one of the best players in the world.'

Charles, appointed CBE for services to football, died in 2004, aged 72. Though it was cancer which killed him, he was living with dementia — the result, his widow Glenda believed, of excessively heading a ball either as centre half or centre forward.

A BBC interview with her in 2018 included the claim by Dr Don Williams, a psychiatrist in Charles's home city of Swansea, that possible links between football and dementia were being 'swept under the carpet.' He wasn't the first, and would certainly not be the last, to suppose so.

Bill Tucker still lives with dementia, confirmed in 2014, though his decline is as inexorable as it is inescapable. 'The last years of his life have been an unexpected and frightening journey down a long and darkening path,' says Dr Sally Tucker, his daughter, on the Head for Change website. He is 74. she 38.

Sally, to whom fleeting reference has already been made, is one of three co-founding trustees of Head for Change, a surgical registrar at Charing Cross Hospital in London, a committed feminist and (it transpires) a friendly, forthright and accommodating interviewee.

She'd been introduced to Judith Gates through a mutual acquaintance, candidly supposes that having two trustees entitled to the title 'Dr' can be useful — Judith's doctorate is non-medical, of course — acknowledges that the colleague more than twice her age is at the heart of the action. 'Judith and I have a shared philosophy but Judith's very much at the centre of it, making connections, having meetings. She's the brains behind it, to be honest.'

Since Charing Cross Hospital is nowhere near Charing Cross — it's in Hammersmith, they do these things to perplex us provincials — we meet over a couple of Diet Cokes outside a nearby café in the course of an eventful summer week in the crusade to address brain trauma issues in football and other sports. 'There's a growing body of scientific knowledge,' she says. 'I don't think that sport can just carry on the way that it is. We need to remember that the brain is fragile.'

Three days earlier, July 18th 2022, the Football Association had announced a complete ban on heading in all under-12s football in the forthcoming season, an experiment approved at international level and which the FA hopes will become permanent thereafter. Already it's banned in training for under-10s.

In *The Times,* former Republic of Ireland international Tony Cascarino supposed it to be the precursor of yet greater change.

'This is the first step of what I believe will be a number over the next decade or so to take heading out of the game. This is only going in one direction and I can't see football surviving in the long term with heading.'

For five days thereafter the letters page continued the ever-widening debate, one reader suggesting that striking the ball with the fist — above head height — be legalised instead. A reply suggested that they'd been doing that in Ireland for ages — 'it's called Gaelic football' — another, from a gentleman in Devon, that the handless Diego Maradona had clearly been ahead of his time.

Three days later, July 24th 2022, it's confirmed that 185 former rugby union players — Alix Popham and Steve Thompson head-lined among them — are joining to sue the sport's governing bodies. Their principal aim, they insist, is not financial but to secure a safer sport. The *Daily Mail's* headline is 'Rugby in the dock.'

The week's back pages again report on more cases of neurode-generative illness among well-known former football and rugby players, raising concern but simultaneously heightening aware-ness. They include 70-year-old former Leeds and Manchester United centre half — centre half! — Gordon McQueen, capped 30 times by Scotland and recalled earlier, who may soon have to move into full-time care.

Gordon, a former coach with Middlesbrough, has long lived a few miles from Teesside at Hutton Rudby. 'I'd do anything for my country except live there,' he'd told me a few years earlier.

Though not perhaps momentous, to the layman (and to the jobbing journalist) there appears once again to be momentum.

Sally Tucker's professionally cautious — 'probably a bit more optimistic than Judith' she admits — while the indefatigable Judith Gates herself goes on North-East regional television on the evening of the Hammersmith consultation to discuss the under-12s prohibition and, of course, to talk about Bill. 'He's paying dearly for his strength in the air,' she says, also expressing the view that good men plant trees so that those who follow might enjoy the shade.

However guarded in turn, however world-wary, she concedes that it's good news. 'There's tacit recognition that this decision by the governing bodies means that heading a football is dangerous.'

Dr Tucker has had a working morning of what might be termed a cadaverous nature — 'I'll probably smell of formaldehyde' she'd forecast — but arrives fresh and fragrant, a keen runner and cross-fit trainer. 'I've watched my dad unravel from a kind, sharp, generous, hilarious hero of mine,' she says, in no doubt that the cause is repeatedly heading a football — 'perhaps 70,000 times' — over a lengthy career.

'There's no family history of dementia, nothing in the genes, both my father's parents were playing competitive Scrabble into their nineties. There can be no other explanation.'

As a sports-mad child she'd had a soft spot for Liverpool, photograph of Michael Owen on the bedroom wall, but now sticks her neck out for Swindon Town. Bill, she says over the first of the Diet Cokes, had been an amazing father. 'I know all about the father and daughter thing, but we were incredibly close.

'We were both very active, had the same sense of humour, went on bike rides with my brother and played a lot together. He introduced me to all sorts of sports, told me there was no real difference between what men and women could achieve.'

Maybe there is. Two years previously she'd tweeted that the countries with the best coronavirus response records had one thing in common — 'they're all led by women.'

Like Bill Gates, Bill Tucker had trained in accountancy while still playing. When his wife went to university in her forties, Bill Tucker took a professional step back to help look after the family. 'He demonstrated to me that men and women should always have equal opportunities,' says Sally. 'I think the message was that I could do anything I wanted to do, that no different rules applied.

'I had an amazing, really lovely childhood, my dad gave up lots of time for me and my brother. When I was growing up he'd happily come out to wherever we might be to pick up me and my friends in the early hours of the morning, never complaining, always with a laugh and a joke. We shared some wonderful times.'

At one point she'd contemplated becoming a journalist, still thought she might try the inky trade after a couple of years medical experience, discovered how much she enjoyed being a doctor but these days works a four-day week. The fifth, she says, is given to Head for Change.

Her social media profiles suggest that she has four degrees including graduate qualifications in medical ethics and law and nutrition and medicine. Four? 'Something like that,' says Sally, so probably it's five.

Enshrined in the Hippocratic oath, her guiding principle in campaigning for the greater protection and welfare of sportsmen and women is 'First do no harm.' Players, she believes, are effectively being used as guinea pigs, put directly and almost deliberately in harm's way even as amber warnings flash red.

'We've had conferences and meetings where I've asked if it's acceptable to expose players to these impacts. They don't answer those questions. There's need for a huge overhaul of the way that sport works, much more emphasis on education and on welfare.'

She'd also spent two years working in Australia, noticed changes in her father when her parents visited and on her return in 2013. 'There was just something different. Previously he'd been so sharp and so witty, a great ability to read a room and he seemed to have lost that. He became increasingly confused. When we were small he'd test our times tables on a Saturday morning, sometimes with a little prize. Now he couldn't even remember them himself.'

Not long previously she'd gone for a walk with her dad and discovered they were in a field full of cows. 'There was no gate at the other end and I thought we might be cornered by them. When I wondered what we should do I realised that he wasn't looking after me, as he had all those years, I was in charge of him.'

An added agony, if not quite along the scriptural torment of 'physician heal thyself,' is the personal frustration of being unable medically to ameliorate. 'Sometimes I feel so strangely inadequate because there seems to be nothing I can do and it feels like the futility and inability of medicine. I have all these qualifications and want to help, but I can't.

> *Occasionally there are little glimpses of his old self, perhaps a wry smile, but they become fewer. It's a tragedy I can't do anything about and a lot of the time now it's very difficult, very dark, my main sadness on how it's impacted my mum.*

> *They'd postponed so much to bring up me and my brother, hoping to do all those things when they retired, but mum's become an institutional carer. She wants him to be comfortable and happy but she's lost most of her retirement. She wanted to see the world and it makes me sad there's nothing I can do.*

> *He's in steady decline. The thing you don't really realise is that every day's an enigma. You never really know how it's going to be. Sometimes there are little glimpses of the old dad but you just don't know.*

> *Loss is part of the human experience but when suffering can be averted, or prevented, that's when it feels important to create change. Any preventable loss of that future is tragic.*

Sally had been able to arrange a meeting with Gordon Taylor, the long-time chief executive of the Professional Footballers' Association and team mate of her dad's, at Bury. 'Gordon Taylor was very sad, very concerned, but I think he worried about getting the PFA into a situation he didn't want them to be in.

'My dad was always very supportive of the PFA, but I think they've failed families and football participants in general. It wasn't an easy meeting.'

Research continues, as it must. While a second major study might validate Dr Stewart's — and while she would welcome one — Dr Tucker and H4C urge immediate action to educate and protect participants, formally to warn them of the risks of their sport and fundamentally to change the head-first approach.

'If you were doing a drug trial you would halt giving the drug until you had information that it was safe. The ethos of football is "We'll carry on with what we're doing and wait to see what the research tells us." Unless we change the approach now, then we're exposing players to harm.'

The proposed under-12s ban is undoubtedly a positive step. 'It hurts to head a football, that's why children don't naturally do it, If they don't head a football until 12, the natural thing is not to do it after that. Football could market itself as a safe sport and most people would appreciate that, football could get away with it. I don't know how to change rugby to make it safe.'

'We don't know how much, if any, heading is safe but banning it completely is probably the better option. You could make a strong argument that it wouldn't have a significant impact on the enjoyment of the game.'

They press also for head trauma among sports players to be classed as an industrial disease, opening channels for compensation and putting greater pressure upon those who hold the purse strings.

Might H4C become a commitment for life? 'You're never going completely to eliminate the risk from anything but certainly you can prevent a lot of what happens. The governing bodies owe it to their players to do that.'

Another cautious ending. 'I'd like to think there's momentum, I really would, but change doesn't happen quickly. There's a very long way to go yet.'

16.

'PEOPLE WOULD CROSS THE ROAD TO AVOID YOU, EVEN IN MIDDLESBROUGH'

Pat Harvey was a 22-year-old unmarried mother, her son just past his first birthday, when first she met Bill Gates. It was 1974.

Illegitimacy still a stigma? 'Oh, stigma with a great big capital S,' she recalls. 'People would cross the road to avoid you, even in Middlesbrough.' Perhaps drawing on personal experience, Bill was wholly different.

Pat had previously worked in an office, took time out to have the baby, needed to return to work, as she puts it, to keep them both fed. 'The employment agency sent me to a new sports shop in the Dundas Arcade — the arcade didn't even have a roof back then — where they wanted an assistant. Bill interviewed me — I wasn't sporty, I'd never worked in a shop and I hadn't even heard of him.' Mind, she adds gallantly, her dad had.

First impressions? 'He was just a very nice man, none of the airs and graces you might expect from a former professional footballer, He said we should maybe give one another a trial, suss each other out. I started the same week. One of our jobs every evening was to put a grille, like prison bars really, across the windows. The area had a bit of a reputation.'

She progressed to become the manager; almost half a century later she remains friends with Bill and Judith, still lives in the Boro, still talks with undimmed affection of happy days in sportswear. 'It was a wonderful experience, an education that opened all kinds of doors for me. Bill was just so kind.'

It becomes noticeable, however, that over coffee at her home near the James Cook hospital in Middlesbrough we're both talking about her old employer in the past tense, not the way he is — though the way he is frequently brings Kleenex to her eyes — but the way he was. Perhaps, who knows, it's inevitable.

Among other footballers of whom Pat had hitherto never heard was Alex Smith, described in the *Middlesbrough Who's Who* as 'an honest full back' and his team mate Frank Spraggon, 'a model of dependability.' After retirement, both worked in the shop.

There was me, Olivia, Lucy, Glenys, Betty, a Saturday girl called Lynn. We had no staff turnover, no one left, queues for Saturday jobs. There was another shop we were associated with in Redcar that was like something from Are You Being Served, everything in great rows of little drawers.

Bill moved everything into the 1970s but we still sold footballs with laces in those days. Alex would blow the bladders up, I couldn't, but Bill did teach me how properly to lace a football boot which wasn't quite as easy as it looked.

The sportswear industry had changed little over the decades, plimsolls — a bit like Henry Ford's motor cars — in any colour so long as they were black or white, shorts seemingly made trendy by two red stripes down the side. By the mid-1970s it was ready to accelerate and Bill, chronically gammy knee notwithstanding, primed to stay ahead of the game. Sports goods were about to make a fashion statement, though Bill Gates could never be said to be a dedicated follower. He led.

'There'd be loads of reps in their posh estate cars, always something new, Pat recalls. 'Bill would get everyone involved, always sought our opinion, treated his staff with respect, wanted to know how you and your family were getting along.'

Soon the business moved to new two-storey premises in the nearby Hill Street Centre, soon afterwards he was eyeing opportunities elsewhere, not least in the massive new Metro Centre near Gateshead, developed by future Newcastle United chairman Sir John Hall.

Soon afterwards the young mum became the shop manager. Nearly half a century later she still talks of the business as 'we'. 'It was a different world back then but we were totally, totally dedicated to that business. There'd really only been one sportswear shop in Middlesbrough, Jack Hatfield's, the area was ready for someone like Bill.'

The Hill Street shop had officially been opened by Birmingham City and England centre forward Trevor Francis — 'the country's first £1 million footballer' says Pat, clearly having swotted up by then, though again her dad needed no introduction. 'You can imagine the interest it created, huge crowds, lots of press and television, brilliant move.

'Bill would hold little training sessions with us — darts, rackets, whatever it might be so that everyone knew what they were talking about. I still wasn't much of a sports person myself; I did take up badminton but it was short-lived. We were taught that our uniforms and appearance had always to be clean and tidy, that we had to speak to every customer, to appreciate that if we didn't know the answer to a question, we knew someone who did. Bill had mystery shoppers before almost anyone else had heard of them.'

Then there was the Saturday afternoon scores service, at least during the football season. 'It was long before the internet or even much coverage on television, people would flood to the shop just to see how Middlesbrough were getting on and, of course, they might be tempted to buy something while they were standing outside, looking in the window.'

Though less visible as the business expanded across northern England, the boss changed little. 'He was so even tempered, so caring, so nurturing, just a lovely, lovely man. I don't think we ever really had a cross word.'

Sometimes cross words may have come cryptically close, not least on the not infrequent occasions that Teesside's finest exhibited their athleticism by making off without paying. Pat recalls one afternoon when she spotted a larcenous hand around the door. 'Bill was in his office upstairs and I just screamed for him. The guy made off over The Border (at the time the town's less-salubrious dockland area, a place for frontiersmen) with Bill in vigorous if slightly middle-aged pursuit.

The thief got away. Ever-loyal, Pat supposes that must have been down to the boss's bad knee, an' all.

On another occasion he'd rather ironically been to a crime prevention panel meeting, returned to the shop the following morning and asked if they'd had a quiet day. Pat thought that they had had.

'Then what about the chap caught with 20-odd stolen sports shirts?' asked the gaffer. 'Oh, where did they come from?' said Pat. 'Here' said Bill.

Part of the reason for the success, she believes, is that Bill and Judith really looked after their workforce. 'There was always a party, everything paid for, at Christmas. As the business got bigger he'd lay on buses so everyone from the different shops could get together. After they sold up and went to the Cayman Islands we didn't just get a Christmas card, we were taken out for a meal every time they came home.

'I think he was a bit of a romantic, too. On a big wedding anniversary he not only took Judith back to the Trevi Fountain in Rome, where they'd been all those years before, but had secretly arranged to fly friends out to meet them for a celebration. That was Bill, he was lovely.'

And now? 'It's not that I don't know people in a similar position. I know they've lived the dream but what's happened is still so sad. All that vibrancy, all that talent. What a terrible thing to have happened.'

17.

'I'VE BEEN IN BOARD ROOMS FULL OF PEOPLE FROM OXFORD AND CAMBRIDGE AND ALWAYS HAD THE ADVANTAGE OF THEM, BECAUSE I WAS FROM CO DURHAM'

Brad Groves worked for Bill Gates when he had nowt, which is to say that Brad had nowt and Bill still had a fair few noughts to add to his burgeoning bank balance.

These days Brad runs Great Annual Savings, appropriately and acronymically GAS, a greatly successful company advising around 15,000 businesses on energy and other economies and based at the Sea View HQ in Seaham Harbour, a wondrously transformed former pit town on the Durham coast.

Successive Marquesses of Londonderry mined coal here, Lord Byron (more improbably) wrote poetry here, in 1962 nine people died in a lifeboat disaster here and still are mourned. More recently Seaham seafront has become known for Tommy, Ray Lonsdale's 9ft 5in statue of a First World War soldier bought by the community for £102,000.

Though there's more chance of a marine panorama than from the sort of Blackpool boarding house where proclaimed sea views might only have been obtained by standing on the chimney pot with a good pair of binoculars, it probably helps if there's no sea fret to worry about. This morning, the August heat wave at last receding, there is.

The Spectrum Business Park, on which GAS is based, stands on the site of the former Dawdon Colliery which at its 1920s peak employed almost 4,000 miners. The Durham Mining Museum website records 101 accidental deaths during the pit's 90 indiscriminate years — the youngest aged just 11, many more 14 and the oldest 63.

Casualties also included a miner who cut his finger on Christmas Eve 1934 and a few days later died of bronchial pneumonia, septicaemia, cellulitis and heart failure. The list, adds the Mining Museum with the customarily incredulous exclamation mark, is likely by no means to be complete.

Great Annual Savings and its associated companies now offer work to around 350 — by some way Seaham's biggest employer — in a building enthusiastically described on the company website as 'stunning' (though not, it must be assumed, concussive).

In the GAS reception area, the usual collection of image-building business magazines reveals further evidence of what happened when finally the coalhouse door slammed shut. Where once Seaham dug deep, and paid a lugubrious price for its coal, now there's a factory making spare parts for Bugatti and a logistics company approaching a £100 million annual turnover. None of the magazine articles is about Great Annual Savings or its founder. 'Brad's fiercely private,' says a colleague, though that's a claim to which we shall return.

In the boardroom, half the size of a football pitch, all is forward thinking, too. Today's the initial formal team meeting to plan the second 'no headers' football match — next to none, anyway — at Spennymoor Town FC on Sunday September 25th. Brad's chairman and owner of the Moors, too. It's also hoped that he'll formally kick the match off. 'Bill won't be well enough,' says Judith Gates.

Among the other differences from the east Durham of two or three generations ago is that at 60 the menfolk were either dead or dying — if not crushed by a tub then victims of what coroners called pneumoconiosis but pitmen knew simply as 'dust' and not even included in the formal casualty figures. The women, victim in turn, were content to sit alone by the concessionary coal fire, consoled by memories of what absurdly were supposed the good old days.

Dr Gates informally takes the chair. She is a 77-year-old great grandmother, indefatigable, indomitable and damn near incredible, driven like a top of the range Bugatti. Already this morning she's had an hour-long meeting with Brad Groves and afterwards there'll be further gatherings. 'I'm not stand-offish,' she says. 'I'm one of those who figures that if you think you can do it, then you just might.'

A couple of days earlier she'd forwarded a video of a talk by neurologist Dr Emer McSweeney called 'The silent killer in contact sport' in which Dr McSweeney had described chronic traumatic encephalopathy as 'the most fearsome risk for millions of amateur and professional athletes across the globe' and warned that many experts downplayed its reality.

Dr McSweeney also told of the dangers of sub-concussive injury, repeated lower force impacts — 20 per cent of those found to have CTE had never had a single recorded concussion — and that effective brain, as opposed to skull, protection was 'desperately needed.' That CTE couldn't be diagnosed until after death was no longer true, she added.

Among others at today's meeting are Mark Solan — mentioned earlier — whose Spennymoor-based cancer charity works closely with H4C on match arrangements, Adam Brown who's the GAS head of marketing, Lisa Hopkins — Brad Groves's group executive assistant — and Paul Frost, him off the telly, whose media company is charged with making a film about the upcoming Billion Pound game. They hope to launch it in the autumn at a dinner — who knows, maybe even a gala dinner, roast beef and balloons — at Middlesbrough's Riverside Stadium. There's also been preliminary interest from Netflix.

The teams on September 25th will again represent Spennymoor and Middlesbrough, Mark busy recruiting former professionals with North-East connections. The name of Superkev is mentioned, though whether Keegan or Phillips — football folk would understand — is unclear. 'The Middlesbrough team's much stronger on paper,' says Mark, inevitably inviting the observation that football isn't played on paper, not even in 2022, but for the most part still on grass.

One side or the other is likely to include the neuropathologist Professor Willie Stewart, Glasgow based but globally renowned, invited to give an 'educational' talk at the Brewery Field on the morning of the match and happy to do so on condition that he gets a hurl in goal. 'I'm going to buy him some gloves,' says Judith.

Welsh rugby international Alix Popham, featured in an earlier chapter amid optimism guarded like a federal penitentiary, also hopes to play and to bring with him opera singer Wynne Evans, otherwise Gio Compario. They hope he'll sing *Memories* — what else? — from the centre circle, the only debate over whether he'll need a microphone. Maybe not, they conclude.

'I want it to be goose bumpy, I want it to be emotional and I want it to be remembered,' says Judith, fizzing like a bottle of Jones's pop. They also hope to screen recorded messages of support from dozens of former players.

Before the main match they hope to have walking football — no headers in that pedestrian pursuit, either — featuring England walking football international Tommy Charlton, perhaps the least well known of a celebrated Ashington fraternity, and also to have input from Spennymoor's academy and women players.

Last year's game attracted more than 60 million media hits around the world but a crowd of little over 300. 'I was looking out of the window wondering where everyone was,' Judith recalls.

'They said that people always came at the last minute. I told them it was the last minute.'

Kieran Gill, the *Daily Mail* journalist who played in the 2021 match — 'potentially the most significant trial in football history' he wrote subsequently in his compelling book *The Beautiful Game and the Ugly Truth,* sub-titled 'Football's tragic link with dementia' — will notably be absent. He'll be on honeymoon, one or other of the Disneylands, which seems a pretty reasonable explanation.

Adam Brown nonetheless talks of a 'VIP super-list,' warns that they're unlikely to attract the same global interest this time — but they're hoping for an awful lot more from Spennymoor.

It'll be billed as The Billion Pound Game, that being the estimated cost of dementia care for footballers over the next generation. The teams, it's hoped, will enter the field through an avenue of up to 100 cardboard silhouettes held by children — that's the outline, anyway — each representing a professional footballer who has died with or is suffering from dementia.

The idea's from the Cayman Islands, where Judith was an activist in the crusade against domestic abuse towards women. The 'Silent Witness' march adopted a similar approach. 'I can't tell you how effective it was,' she says.

Rather a lot of affected players have been named? 'I've thought of 100 without trying. I'm sure that John Stiles will have a lot more,' she says. 'I lie awake at night thinking about all this and when I finally go to sleep, I dream of hundreds of footballers.'

Her style's collaborative — 'I'm inviting you to tell me when I'm talking rubbish,' she says. None does. She's also quick to praise. 'With Great Annual Savings it can't be quid pro quo because you give me a quid and I might give you fivepence back. You people have been wonderful.'

The meeting overflows its allotted hour, resultant responsibilities threatening total immersion. Ever upbeat, Judith displays just the occasional tremor: 'Less than six weeks to go...' she says, slightly apprehensively, and returns to the fray.

The following day Judith emails about communication with former Blackburn and Bolton Wanderers player Paul Fletcher, later Burnley's chief executive.

Fletcher, now 71, is helping organise a dinner next year to remember Burnley's promotion to the old first division half a century ago, wants to give profits to Head for Change, recalls Bill Gates as 'a dirty bugger'. 'I think they maybe kicked each other,' says Judith emolliently, acknowledging a 'lovely' gesture.

Fletcher, a proud Lancastrian and member of the George Formby Society — the two may be synonymous — had also eloquently addressed the Northern League's annual dinner in 2011, as had leading international referee Howard Webb, at the time still a police sergeant in south Yorkshire.

After accepting the invitation, singing unpaid for his supper, Webb had also been asked to officiate a fans' game the following day ahead of the Champions League Cup final at Wembley — a VIP match ticket and two nights in a five-star hotel among the incentives. He still attended the Northern League function, in Durham. He spoke, smiled and signed autographs and then, as if wary of being turned into a pumpkin, left on the stroke of midnight to drive the 250 miles to London.

His finest moment may have come when someone at the dinner asked about his alleged bias towards Manchester United. 'It becomes tiresome' said Howard, 'and my son Cristiano is fed up of it, too.'

If Google is to be believed, and who might ever question the oracle, Brad Groves has only once given a media interview. It was in 2015, when GAS employed 60 people. Now the 350 is boosted by indirect employment for a further 150.

Four days after the planning meeting, I'm back at Sea View HQ on a blousy, breezy August morning, a busy market day in Seaham's pedestrianised main street, queues outside the sea front ice cream parlour and the promenade atmosphere not fretful in the least.

The 53-year-old chairman, dressed casually and wearing train-ers — doubtless top of the range trainers — couldn't be more affable or more helpful, if only he didn't talk so fast. The notebook glows red hot, the coffee goes stone cold. (Note to self: buy a record-ing machine.)

'We don't go in for awards or media promotion. We are a private entrepreneurial company not in the public domain,' says Brad, though it should not be assumed that the GAS light is hidden under a bushel. A huge social media presence suggests otherwise.

The chat's down to the Bill Gates connection. 'I owe him so much,' says Brad. 'He and his partner Tom Knight taught me to be honest, respectful and humble and to work hard. Bill told it as it was, took no bullshit, kept things simple, passionate about the business, never forgot where he came from or that his dad had been down the pit. They were men of their word, supported me in everything I did. 'I've been in boardrooms full of people from Oxford and Cambridge but always had the advantage of them, because I was from County Durham.'

Though by no means the first to employ the adage, Bill was also given to the observation that the harder he worked the luckier he seemed to get.

Brad was a miner's son from Easington Lane, a few miles inland. Though undoubtedly part of the former County Palatine, what the tourism industry now likes to call the Land of the Prince Bishops, the village was heretically hijacked by the 1974 local government reorganisation and awoke, emasculated, in Tyne and Wear. Appropriately, it was April 1st .'We still have a Durham postcode,' insists Brad.

It was a tough neighbourhood. 'I was pretty street-wise' he sup-poses. 'You soon learned to look after yourself nearly 50 years ago in Easington Lane, especially if your first name was Bradley.

He was a talented and coveted footballer, hoped to turn profes-sional, joined Monument Sports at 16 as a retail trainee. Further reason to be grateful to the man at the top, they switched him to the warehouse — which worked Monday to Friday — so that he might be free to play football on Saturday. Another employer, he says, would have sacked him.

'Bill would have the whiteboard out on a Monday morning, going through the orders, but the first 20 minutes we'd spend talking football. He was into everything, no matter how small — your dubbin, your whitener, your studs — but knew all about the bigger stuff, too. We sold a lot of top-of-the-range leisure wear, back then we were dressing football hooligans.'

The boss also taught him, or tried to teach him, to restring a tennis racquet. 'I wasn't particularly academic, that was Trudy my sister, and in putting things together, building things, electronics, I was utterly useless, the least technical guy in the world and the last person on earth he should have trusted to restring a tennis racquet.'

Like Pat Harvey in the previous chapter, he also recalls an incident of shoplifting — this one at Monument's Grainger Street shop in Newcastle. 'We were all there. The guy took off and we took off after him. Tom Knight had been a top class sprinter and was trying to restrain him, Bill sat on him and was thumping him in the face. I can see it, he was wearing a Lyle and Scott jumper, like a golfer.'

Ten years after joining, football aspirations annexed by injury, he was a board member of Blacks plc, the company to which Monument had been sold, thereafter spending a decade in senior management positions across the country before formally starting GAS in 2012. 'The plan was always to come back to the North-East and create jobs and wealth,' says Brad. 'It was always my base, even when I didn't live here.

'We'd known nothing about the sale until Bill gave me a box of Milk Tray one day and said they were off to the Cayman Islands. It wasn't much and I probably thought "greedy bastard" until I learned later that I was the only one who'd got anything.'

Remember that fruitful meeting at Spennymoor Town when Debra Swinburn had reintroduced Judith Gates to Brad Groves?

She carried a box of Milk Tray that day, too. He got both the choc-
olates and the joke.

Externally striking, the Sea View HQ is wondrous (if not necessarily stunning) within. 'Nothing like this outside of London,' says
Brad, a man not given to bragging.

A large screen in reception proclaims GAS 'officially' Britain's
No 1 business-to-business costs comparison company; around it
are large photographic murals of Seaham structures among which
Tommy, contemplative, is prominent. All taken by a staff member,
says Lisa Hopkins, guiding the tour.

There's a subsidised staff restaurant called Gastro, a games
room, a 'snug' — where folk can just sit and chill, lights out if they
want, says Lisa — and, best sea view of all, a top floor gym that
a Premier League football club might envy. Gavin Cogdon, the
group's 38-year-old health and wellbeing manager, is Spennymoor
Town's record goal scorer and has a degree in sport and exercise.
You can at once tell who he is: if Brad's the one who wears the trou-
sers, Gav's the one who wears the shorts.

In the chairman's office there's a photograph of Seaham Hall —
'not because it's a five-star hotel but because it's where my grand-
dad died of cancer when it was a hospital' — while elsewhere are
images of Eppleton Colliery, where his father had toiled. 'That was
the wages office,' Brad indicates. 'They didn't get paid much, mind.'

Easington Lane, a community that even its own mother might
have struggled to call beautiful, was a haven for Sunderland football followers. 'There were only four of us in the village supported
Newcastle, that made you street-wise, too,' says the boy named
Bradley. 'Not even my boys support Newcastle.'

Corporate acumen trumping personal allegiance, GAS is
Sunderland's chief shirt sponsor. 'Newcastle have enough backing,
I thought Sunderland deserved it more,' he says. 'Everyone remem-
bers Jimmy Montgomery's save (against Leeds United in the 1973
FA Cup final) but they've been to Wembley twice in the last two

years and won promotion. They'll remember those shirts too. It was good business, a massive opportunity.'

Like Newcastle United, Spennymoor Town play in black and white. 'If Sunderland fans come they wear the second or third choice shirts,' he says.

He'd become involved with Hetton Lyons, a greatly successful Sabbath side — 'four FA Sunday Cups in eight seasons, Durham Sunday Cup seven years running' — before joining Spennymoor Town, struggling at the time for survival in the Northern League, in 2009.

'To put it bluntly the place was a shithole,' says Brad. 'The ground was horrific, the pitch was horrific, it was all burned out Portakabins. The club was very close to packing up, it was an absolute eyesore and I thought it could change.'

They won four Northern League titles — 'just the second club to gain more than 100 points in a season' — lifted the FA Vase at Wembley in 2013 and now, three rungs further up the football pyramid, have a magnificent stadium, over 100 volunteers, 450 youngsters in the academy set-up, an average 1,300 gate in a town of 20,000 people and annually attract 35,000–40,000 visitors to the town. Further promotion? 'Only if it's sustainable' he says.

The football club is also a base for the GF (Groves Family) Community Foundation, formed in 2021 to address socio-economic problems in Co Durham and Sunderland — 'delivering hope to all' says the strapline — and involved in everything from food banks to walking football to mental health support. 'We galvanise people and assets, execute key delivery strands in disadvantaged communities,' the website adds.

Judith Gates and Debra Swinburn are old friends. When a 'no headers' match was mooted, Spennymoor Town — where Debra's a director — seemed the ideal location, Even without the chocolate box, the sweet talk, it's likely they'd have been pushing at an open door, though Brad questions whether a heading ban is feasible.

It's part of the game. Much could be done to raise awareness of the risks, to educate players of all ages, to curtail heading among younger age groups. It's hard to get change, too many people at the top of football are dinosaurs. That first game raised awareness massively but players need to make informed decisions and at the moment they still aren't. I'm a great believer in giving people choices.

There's a lot of money flushing about football these days and too much of it's at the top of the game. It should be filtered down to the lower levels and to support people like Bill.

Unalone, he marvels at Dr Gates's energy, enthusiasm and commitment. 'She's an amazing lady, incredibly bright and intelligent. You'd never think she was nearly 80, would you?'

Bill had gone with her to the first meeting. 'He'd declined a lot then but to see him now, it's horrendous. If that's the result of football, then we all need to think how we can help.'

18.

'I REALLY CARE ABOUT FINDING THE ANSWER, BUT I DON'T WANT TO COME ACROSS AS A SAINT'

The Queen is dead, her state funeral still four days away when Dr Michael Hornberger gives up two of his crowded hours for an interview about dementia, particularly among sports players, and how the risk and rigours might ultimately be addressed.

He is Professor of Applied Dementia Research at Norwich Medical School, part of the University of East Anglia, its work described by the Norwich-based *Eastern Daily Press* as 'life changing'. Though his optimism is as close-guarded as that majestic catafalque in Westminster Hall, he is optimistic, nonetheless. 'A diagnostics breakthrough within five years, therapeutics within ten,' he ventures. 'In five years a blood test from your GP which can diagnose the disorder even if symptoms are years away.'

Positive lifestyle change can already decrease the risk by 40 per cent, he believes. Among much else he has spoken of the benefit of kippers which, life enhancement notwithstanding, must remain an acquired taste.

A cure? 'You have to be cautious but I can see many positive changes on the horizon. I think one day there will be a cure, but I don't know when.'

Born in Germany 46 years ago, he was persuaded to work alongside Head for Change by Judith Gates, as irrepressible as she is irrefusable. Judith, he says, is a force of nature. 'She is an extremely independent woman, where she gets the energy from I don't know, but her heart is certainly in the right place. It's not just about Bill, she gets the big picture. I sometimes wonder if we support her enough.

'It's a pincer movement. Judith is brilliant at lobbying and I'm trying to provide the scientific validation. I'm really positive that things can change for the better.'

Since the dementia field appears chiefly to be approached down Acronym Avenue, he is also much involved with SCORES — Securing Cognitive Outcomes after Repetitive head impact Exposure in Sport — an independent study which over ten years' regular testing seeks to compare the rate of cognitive decline among former footballers with that of the general public. Much more of that in the next-but-one chapter but for now he's happy to wrap a protective professorial arm around his acronyms. 'The funders love them. It's about maintaining a high profile. Judith's very good at acronyms and slogans,' he says.

It's wholly coincidental that, on the day before the state funeral, the *Sunday Times* should interleave its many pages of national mourning with a lengthy piece by the science editor headed 'World's drug firms optimistic about Alzheimer's breakthrough' and that the piece should begin with a 'slightly grim' joke said to be popular among dementia specialists.

'I've been in this field for 30 years,' said Robert Howard, professor of old age psychiatry at University College London, 'and during those 30 years we've always been five years away from a life-changing treatment.'

Professor Hornberger has doubtless heard it before, unlikely to have fallen off his chair even at first hearing, but those to whom the *Sunday Times* has spoken assert reason to be hopeful, too. One hundred and forty three treatments are in late-stage trials, a real breakthrough murmured at a time when 152 million people world-wide, a million in Britain, will have Alzheimer's by 2025.

'A positive result would be incredible,' Dr Susan Kohlhaus, director of research at Alzheimer's Research UK, tells the paper, adding that while a first-generation drug couldn't be expected to do all they need to cure the disease, they can build on the discoveries.

Nor, of course, is Alzheimer's akin to CTE, perhaps not even a neurological first cousin, and in any case CTE's the specialist subject of Professor Willie Stewart in Glasgow, to whom previous chapters have alluded and who, at last, we hope to meet, and to watch keep goal, in the next one.

For Michael Hornberger, however, there's a sting in the tail — or possibly the tale — but that must wait until this chapter's concluding sentence.

We meet over coffee and curiosity in the spacious foyer of Norwich Research Park, racks around the walls offering maga-zines with arcane titles, much less contents, that a jobbing journal-ist might struggle to comprehend. He is as accommodating as he is erudite, as patient as he is positive, enthusiastic — zealous might be a better word — about explaining dementia and reducing the risk of developing it. Chiefly he calls it a disorder, not an illness.

As a youngster in Germany he was passionate about both sport and science, though his football ability was limited. 'As in England, football is part of the culture in Germany but I was useless, always the last one to be picked, one of those,' he laments.

He was a child, he says, who forever would ask why — 'my mother thought me a pain in the backside — I was.' A little domes-tic research had thrown up the fact that he'd read every science book in the local public library — 'very small town, very small library' self-effacingly he insists.

His parents were both GPs, 'desperate' that he join their practice and thus disappointed. 'Even now my mother calls me half a medic,' says Michael, cheerfully. That his grandmother developed dementia — 'every day I watched her change' — may have sharpened his speciality. Is he fuelled by empathy, perhaps by compassion?

You have to have empathy, put yourself in somebody else's shoes. I always tell my students that it's very important to understand people who have the disorder. It's very easy as scientists to fall into the trap of not doing that. It's extremely complicated and I have to simplify things, downplay the complexity. I really care about trying to find the answer but I don't want to come across as a saint. I believe that research is absolutely vital and that people underestimate the grit and determination of what we do.

Most scientists care deeply about the situation they're facing. I love what I do but you can't just go home at five o'clock. I'm passionate about the public education side, telling people what the score is. I love working with older people, they have a wonderful perspective on life. Norfolk also has one of the oldest populations in the country, which is important for my research.

Compassion, perhaps even an almost biblical compassion? 'I really do want to help them,' he says and is also a regular fund raiser for Alzheimer's Research UK. In 2021, until Covid constrained, he planned a sponsored cycle ride from Land's End to John o'Groats. Instead he sat on a tough-exercise bike in his sitting room, a total of 874 miles over 14 successive days of what might reasonably be termed going nowhere fast. 'A lot of fun,' he'd told the *Eastern Daily Press* though the grimace suggests that it was a pain in the backside, too. His children — 'my girls' — made him a crown, a medal and a certificate of commendation.

In 2022, after a family holiday in Germany, his wife and children returned by car while he, further sponsored, cycled the 350 homeward miles in two-and-a-half days. 'The last bit was easy, just 70 miles,' he insists. In 2023 he plans another effort for Alzheimer's Research. 'I can't tell you yet,' he says, 'but that might be quite fun, too.'

In March 2023 he and a friend cycled from Norwich to Aberdeen, where the Alzheimer's Research UK annual conference was being held, 500 miles over four days. Whether it was quite fun is, sadly, not recorded.

The day before we meet he'd travelled by train to a meeting in Cambridge, bike in the vestibule, and then cycled the 70 miles back. 'When I got home,' says Michael, 'I had to make the dinner.'

His first degree was from Osnabruck University, his masters from Vienna, his doctorate from University College London — where he developed an enduring allegiance to Arsenal FC but insists that his English was at first so poor that he'd little idea what his academic peers were talking about.

These days it's impeccable, though just briefly he seems to sound like legendary Arsenal manager Arsene Wenger, who was French. 'You mean from the Invincibles era or the later years?' he asks, mischievously.

After six years in Australia he and his wife, herself active in the dementia field but working under her maiden name, returned to England. He led research in Cambridge — 'I worked with some fantastic people, it just fascinated me, it still does' — before moving to East Anglia University, where he also holds the title associate dean of innovation, in November 2015. He cycles, listens to jazz or plays the violin. 'I don't get much time, these days it's more like fiddling,' he says.

His 308-page book, *Tangled Up: the Science and History of Alzheimer's Disease*, addresses questions like what caused Alzheimer's, whether it can genetically be inherited ('very low risk') and why those with the disorder seem to 'live in the past.' On Amazon the paperback's £9.99, has unanimously gained five stars.

These days he's also a Norwich City season ticket holder, the capricious Canaries with six straight wins when we meet (and rather fewer in the months thereafter). Does he cringe a little when head and ball make full-impact contact? Yes, he says, he does. 'You watch the header, maybe from a goal kick, you see the spray flying, it's a mighty impact.'

It's perhaps coincidental that, just this autumn, the Norwich City Community Sports Foundation has launched Duncan's Club, a weekly gathering for people with dementia named after former City captain Duncan Forbes of whom it was said that if he shouted in Norwich you'd hear him in Great Yarmouth.

Forbes, almost inevitably a central defender, developed dementia, dying in 2019 after six years in a care home. A mural the height of the main stand at the Carrow Road stadium remembers him: 'Six feet two, eyes of blue, Duncan Forbes is after you.' Duncan's Club gatherings were almost immediately oversubscribed. A second weekly session was planned.

It's another little coincidence that the *Spectator* magazine, out on the day of our meeting and also eulogising the dear departed monarch, should recount the story of Her Majesty chatting to a 100-year-old recipient at a Maundy Money service, inquiring the reason for his good health. 'I'm a Norwich City fan,' he (allegedly) replied. 'I only smoke and drink when they win.' Times change, too.

Perhaps Michael Hornberger's greatest passion, coupled with a degree of academic ownership, is to address the risk of cognitive disorder and to promote diagnosis often many years before symptoms appear. A week after our meeting, a study from the University of Birmingham Centre for Human Brain Health claimed 'conclusively' that regular bad dreams, particularly among men, could themselves be a symptom of higher dementia risk. 'This is important because there are very few risk indicators that can be identified as early as middle age,' said Dr Abademi Otaiku.

Michael Hornberger identifies what might non-medically be termed the usual suspects –'modifiable risk factors' — smoking, drinking alcohol ('a societal disease'), excessive salt, lack of physical fitness and obesity. Sixty-three per cent of Britons are said to be overweight or obese. A diet which might dip a toe into the Mediterranean would help, he supposes. In a Football League Managers Association talk in January 2001, he'd also smoked out those kippers, insisted that what was good for the heart was good for the brain and urged increased brain activity.

The brain was positively galactic he added — 'an incredible resource' — as many cells as there are stars in the Milky Way. 'It's a classic case of use it or lose it.'

Footballers, of course, ride without helmets and often without regard to the unremitting wall of death already outlined. What of the rugger blokes? We're sitting across a table about a yard apart. Myopia notwithstanding. I swear I see him shudder.

'I don't want to drive people away from physical activity, that's the last thing I want to do, but it's about making people consider how they play sport, about decision making, about understanding the risks. You look at how often a player might head the ball during the game, you should clearly reduce it or get rid of it completely. The science can only give you the evidence, and I think we need more evidence, you have to make your own decision.'

And the rugger beggars (who, goodness knows, had plenty of other problems piling one upon another in September 2022). 'There needs to be a different approach to rugby, players aren't protected. They shouldn't just be checked if they suffer a head impact, they should be going home or to the hospital and they shouldn't play again for weeks. It needs to change massively.'

For football at least, he and Judith Gates are discussing education for players, to underline the dangers of their meretriciously glamorous but patently risky career. Women, it's said, are even more at risk than men. 'If they were properly made aware of the importance of brain health it could make a huge difference. It's something I'm passionate about, I'd love to make a real difference, to explain how they might live healthier lives.'

A continuing problem is funding. 'I don't take anything from their importance but cancer and heart disease is much better funded than dementia research. We're 20-30 years behind cancer and that's some amount of funding. It can be extremely frustrating.'

While doubtful that heading can completely be removed from football — 'for one thing it would effectively do away with corners' — he'll campaign with Head for Change for its reduction, particularly among younger players. It's important, he says, that change comes from the players themselves. 'It's like Formula One where the drivers wanted haloes. If the players want it no one will argue, players are critical to the story. Maybe in 20 years they'll look back and wonder how it was all allowed to happen.'

At the end, however, he's convinced that the key player will be politics. 'There's a lot of money in football. I don't want to come across as a complete cynic, but you know how it is.'

Is he saying that money talks (or, as Bob Dylan sang, that it doesn't talk, it swears?) Professor Hornberger pauses but momentarily. 'The short answer to that is "yes".'

19.

'I REMEMBER (DOWN THE PIT) THEY USED TO CALL THE DAFT LADS THE HEEDYBAALS. A BIT LATE, BUT IT ALL STARTS TO MAKE SENSE'

It's 11 o'clock on Sunday morning, a bit backend-ish as they say in North-East England, and outside a red brick building at the back of Spennymoor High Street a patient queue stretches for getting on 100 yards.

Our first guess, that it must be one of those newer and rather hip-happy churches, is wrong. It proves to be a medical centre and these are people awaiting one or other of the jabs which in the autumn of 2022 are deemed necessary for the body if not necessarily for the soul.

Half a mile away, though with still four hours until kick-off, there's a bit of a buzz around Spennymoor Town's football ground, too. Handsomely and imaginatively repurposed, the Brewery Field sits amid streets of pre-war housing and may have had to take a deep breath in order somehow to squeeze between them.

It's the day of the Billion Pound Game, the second awareness-raising match organised by Head for Change and by the Spennymoor-based Solan Connor Fawcett Family Cancer Trust.

Already the media are encamped and incorrigibly cadging coffee. Most early arrivals wear purple lanyards, denoting high status, if not quite the 'VIP super-list' anticipated by Adam Brown.

A French television company wants to mic-up both Judith and the referee throughout the event. It's perhaps fortunate that they weren't similarly wired a few minutes earlier when Judith takes a call from another broadcast organisation requesting that she re-send the press release she'd issued two weeks earlier.

There, too, is *Daily Telegraph* chief sports reporter Jeremy Wilson who the previous day had written a piece recalling record scorer Alan Shearer's television documentary on the heading debate and outlining the Head for Change attempts to influence it.

'It's the game we all love, the game I've been involved with all my life,' said Shearer. 'I know it comes with risks, in terms of breaking your legs or breaking your ankles. You go into the game knowing you could have a serious injury but you don't go into the game thinking you could get dementia. We need it to be as safe as possible in terms of brain injuries.'

On the *Telegraph* website, it provokes the mixed messages to which H4C may be accustomed, though by no means resigned. 'Eventually all of us will die, life would be boring without taking some risks,' says one. 'Obviously a well-intended campaign but 50 years or so too late,' claims another.

A third's more jokey. 'Who knew that Bill Gates played for Middlesbrough before founding Microsoft?' it asks. Time was that the former sports shop millionaire left behind with his carer in Castle Eden might have appreciated that one.

Former Tyne Tees Television front man Paul Frost, his company making a documentary about the game, reveals also that he's writing a book to be called *Grumpiness,* as befits a feet-beneath-the-table member of the Teesside Grumpy Old Men's Breakfast Club. 'There are so many things you get grumpy about when you're our age,' says Paul, cheerfully.

Outwardly chipper, clad in Spennymoor black and white, Judith seems a little anxious. She is a 77-year-old great grandmother, after all, but today is still very much her baby.

Since it's primarily a Judith Gates Production, there are also copious little catchphrases: 'Protect the players of today from becoming the victims of tomorrow'; 'Protect the players, protect the game' and, perhaps most poignantly, 'They can no longer remember. We will never forget.'

Like others, she's also committed to what might be termed further education. 'You can't have an informed discussion without being fully informed.'

The billion pounds refers to the estimated cost over the next 30 years of dementia care for former footballers. The match is immediately to be preceded by a parade of youngsters carrying 66 labelled life size silhouettes — with over 100 names read out — representing some of the ex-professionals who've died with dementia since England's win in the 1966 World Cup final or who are known to be living with it. Five of the victorious team fall into that terrible category.

Two of the cut-outs, representing Jack Charlton and Nobby Stiles, stand almost cheek-by-jowl in the players' tunnel, as so often they were beneath the banner of the Three Lions. John Stiles, Nobby's lad, is busy with passionate interviews as many weeks earlier he had been for the book; Tommy Charlton, Bobby and Jack's younger brother, talks cogently and compellingly, too.

Lovely man, Tommy watched the 1966 final on a girlfriend's television in Ashington. 'I was just an apprentice down the pit, I couldn't afford to go to London and Bob and Jack had enough on their minds without me bothering them,' he says.

He'd also been in the studio audience the night that Jack revealed on live television the existence of his now-infamous Little Black Book (and nor was it, for the benefit of the uninitiated, a Gideon Bible.) 'I remember thinking 'Jack lad, you shouldn't have said that, they'll crucify you' says Tommy. 'They did.'

Paul Frost relates one of many stories about Jack's absent mindedness, long before illness was suspected, telling of the night he dropped the f-bomb (as media folk like to call it) on live television. 'We were talking about when he was manager of Middlesbrough, that great promotion side of 1973-74. I asked him who the outstanding players were. He said he couldn't remember any of their ******* names. There was nothing I could do.'

In 2020, Bobby Charlton's family announced he had been diagnosed with dementia. . Though Big Jack died with the disorder, his immediate family are reluctant to support a direct link with football. Tommy's more forthright. 'We were very close. You can't imagine how horrible it is to watch one brother die with the disease and the other one fade away with it. Bob and Jack were rich men, but what good has that done them now, poor lads?'

Though his brothers saw the world, Tommy remained closer to home, an apprentice at Lynemouth Colliery in Northumberland, little football ambition beyond the Ashington Welfare League and even that ended by a knee injury when he was 23. 'I was never much good, anyway,' he says with a little smile, 'and compared to my two brothers I was pathetic.'

He later moved with the mines rescue service to Rotherham, in his sixties taking up walking football with a team called the Mature Millers — 'the Millers' being Rotherham FC's nickname — and in 2018 becoming the third Charlton brother to represent England, albeit with the ambulant Over-60s.

That walking football outlaws anything above head height proved no panacea, however. A few months earlier Tommy had fallen backwards while playing, landed on his head, spent a day in hospital and can still remember nothing about it.

> 'After that I spent ages wondering if I was going to be next with dementia. My wife tells me never to head the ball and I tell my grandsons the same thing. I think they take it in.

I'm very pleased to be involved with Head for Change, really getting quite passionate about it. I'm just an ordinary chap but I've personally seen what dementia does and I'm starting to put things together. We want the man in the street to understand, too.

Press and television have a lot to answer for, they don't put it across the right way. I want to put across the reality of dementia. It's an awful, awful thing. I'd like it so that professional footballers weren't pressurised into heading the ball. It's difficult to put into words but I've seen the suffering, and it's awful.'

We talk again a bit later in the day. Tommy's been having a think, particularly recalling those early days down Lynemouth pit. 'I remember they used to call the daft lads the heedy baals. At the time I thought nowt about it. A bit late, but now it's all starting to make sense.'

As his wife had forecast, Bill Gates is too unwell to kick the match off or to attend at all. 'He grows frailer,' reports Nick, their younger son, still greatly active with Coaches Across Continents and with their Head Safe initiative, returned from Japan to address first team and academy coaches at several Football League clubs on brain injury-related issues. 'Only four per cent had even heard of CTE. I find that offensive,' he says. 'They're very receptive, they just don't understand.'

Nick's the manager of the Head for Change team, former Middlesbrough player and Darlington manager David Hodgson marshalling the opposition.Former Welsh rugby international Alix Popham, featured in an earlier chapter, has driven from Wales with his H4C trustee wife Melanie and their four-year-old daughter, seems in great good fettle and despite his early onset dementia diagnosis is looking forward to his first game of soccer for getting on 30 years.

He's just back from Italy where the ironman athletics challenge for which he'd trained was called off after torrential storms. Much closer to home, though maybe no more clement, he plans to try again at Tenby next year. Sadly, they haven't been accompanied from south Wales by the incomparable opera singer, he who they'd hoped would sing *Memories* in the centre circle. 'We just couldn't pull it off,' says Mel.

Mark Solan, chief executive of the cancer charity, is literally running around, trying to fill late gaps in the two squads. 'Usual call-offs' he says, stirring memories both of that bit in the Parable of the Rich Man's feast about all with one consent beginning to make excuse and of the charity football episode in *Porridge* where they're promised a couple of Goodies and end up only with wrong 'uns.

At noon there's to be a talk by Professor Willie Stewart, the Glasgow-based scarlet pimpernel of neuropathology. Prof Stewart is also planning to keep goal for the H4C team and will wear those goalie gloves given by Dr Gates in the hope that both they and he might be fit for purpose.

Bill had already decided — 'while he still had the capacity' says his wife — that his brain should be donated to Dr Stewart's bank. Judith and the prof had further discussed it just a few days earlier. 'Professionally Willie is absolutely fantastic and we're so grateful for all the work he's doing,' she says. 'I want to say publicly how sensitive and how empathetic he has been to my family.'

His talk's introduced by Dr Sally Tucker, another H4C trustee, who talks with manifest affection — just as she had outside that Diet Coke café in London a couple of months earlier — of Bill Tucker, her footballer father. Again she recalls how her dad taught her to kick a ball over the house and to do the *Daily Telegraph* crossword. 'He was well known for being good in the air, a prolific header of the ball. He probably headed the ball 65,000 times in his career. That's what causes it,' she says.

The charity's principal aims, says Sally, are to support families who've members with football-related dementia, to have a voice in medical research and to educate younger people. 'I just want them to understand how fragile the brain is,' she adds.

She also cites Nancy Reagan, wife of the former US president, who famously said of her husband's dementia that it was the long, long goodbye. 'I have never heard a better description of the experience. My dad is my inspiration for H4C.'

Some in the well-filled room are themselves medical or scientific professionals. Professor Ian James, a psychologist based in Newcastle, compares the human brain to a blancmange - 'If you start throwing it around the oven, something bad is going to happen.'

Though Dr Stewart keeps it pretty simple — he self-effacingly calls it a slide show, though technology may have moved on a bit — many present won't have been subjected to so much science since second form physics at Spennymoor Grammar Technical School.

Though he doesn't mention it, possibly he's also read a report in that morning's *Sunday Times* about a £7.65 million award scheme, aimed not least at 'mavericks,' seeking to find the elusive answer to Alzheimer's.

Kate Lee, chief executive of Alzheimer's Research UK, tells the paper that she's 'absolutely convinced' that the problem will be solved by 'some bloke in an outhouse in Hull' or by a 'crazy woman genius in Cleethorpes.' Why neurological research tilts towards Humberside is unclear.

Dr Stewart talks of different approaches, of his FIELD study — 'one of my better acronyms' — and of differing views. 'The only thing that unites people is that if you're getting hit over the head, or hitting yourself over the head, over and over and over again, there's not going to be a good outcome. We all want to keep football going, but we have to find a way to make it safer. It's the 75,000 headers during a career that we need to worry about, not the two or three concussions. If a club tells you it isn't important, go and find another club.' Progress, he says, has been 'glacial'; there's no mention of crazy ladies in Cleethorpes.

The goalie gloves are handed over by Judith Gates with the perhaps optimistic hope that he will prove as safe a pair of hands between the posts as he is in that Scottish laboratory. He also agrees (again) to a proper chat in Glasgow about all that's going on. Whether or not he's from that line of what euphemistically might be supposed error-prone Scottish goalkeepers, we shall no doubt see after lunch.

While others enjoy their food, Spennymoor's junior teams stage an exhibition on the field of how football can be played, enjoyably played, without headers. Upstairs in the executive lounge, John Stiles is still passionately proselytising over the curry. 'What's going on is a nonsense,' he says. 'There's a killer disease. It's killed thousands and it will kill thousands more. We have to do more.'

Tony Mowbray, recently appointed Sunderland FC's head coach — introduced as 'manager' but that's old money — is due to kick off the game at 3pm but has been around since II, patiently answering questions, participating in everything. Outside the main entrance, an elderly Sunderland supporter presses his nose against the glass like an impecunious child, Just William perhaps, outside a sweet shop. William would have wanted sherbet lemons, the old chap wants an autograph.

Told of his presence, Tony goes outside at once. 'Hello, sir,' he says. Top bloke, the last time I'd met Mowbray was on Burns Night 2005 when he was manager of the Edinburgh-based club Hibernian. He was born and raised in Redcar, watched Bill Gates as a boy, bought boots and tracksuit at Bill Gates Sports and would himself be perpetually heading a football in the back garden. 'My dad was a scaffolder. He made this contraption for heading practice, the poles bent into shape at the steel works.'

Though a bit wary of what might be supposed scare mongering — 'you don't bite the hand that feeds you' — he soon warms to the theme, himself worried that he might yet become a dementia victim. 'I feel sharp and bright now, but who knows what's around the corner.'

For now he believes that heading in the professional game, or at least in training for the game, has been much reduced. 'I've never coached it, I don't think many do, and I've not seen one of those steelworks heading contraptions on a Football League ground — but there's still a big message for the younger generation.

'Football is never going to go away. It may change a bit but that would have to be global, approved by Fifa. It isn't just football, it's rugby, boxing, other sports. I'd like to see a good look at all of them.'

As the silhouette parade takes to the field, the names of 113 former players known to have been afflicted with dementia are tolled over the public address. Many are well remembered, from Joe Mercer to Stan Mortensen — Blackpool's hat-trick hero in the 1953 FA Cup final –from Don Revie to Alf Ramsey. Bob Paisley, Bill Shankly, Ron Yeats and Ronnie Moran may at various times have comprised two-thirds of the Liverpool boot room, so it is appropriate that the lugubrious litany is followed by a recording of *You'll Never Walk Alone,* the Merseyside anthem impeccably observed.

Former Middlesbrough and England centre forward Alan Peacock, now seriously affected by dementia, is among those saluted. Tony Mowbray visits him regularly. 'We used to have lovely chats,' he says. 'Now I'm not sure he even knows who I am.'

The afternoon's only problems are that the microphone's playing silly beggars and that there appears to be just one football between two squads anxious to warm up. Both are rectified. 'Microphone problems follow me around,' says BBC sports reporter Andy Sixsmith, the day's MC, cheerfully.

H4C play the immodestly named Team Solan All Stars, headers from set pieces outlawed in the first half and all heading in the second. Seemingly eager to justify their billing, the All Stars are going through their opponents' defence like a fork through the half-time cheesecake, and there is a suspicion that Dr Stewart believes there to be a prohibition on not just using heads, but hands. I'm behind the goal for the All Stars' second in a 6–1 win, just out of earshot of the prone professor's reaction. A Glaswegian imprecation? Maybe not. Suffice that he should not consider giving up the day job, something for which medical science would be immensely grateful.

Alix Popham has had to come off. 'Tight hamstring,' says the ironman, ruefully.

It's also good to see former Fifa referee George Courtney, Spennymoor lad and proud of it, running the line. Once famously as fit as a butcher's dog, George is now 81, nurses a gammy knee and other age-old ailments, but still shifts a bit. 'It was an emergency, more call-offs,' he explains. Though the pace of play may not be supposed torrential, it flows remarkably well, nonetheless.

Team Solan receive the Bill Gates Trophy, former pros Mickey Barron and Tony McMahon get man of the match awards, Judith Gates says that she's delighted at how it's all gone. 'The crowd's again a bit disappointing but the media have been terrific and the bigger picture is that football will again be made aware of the message we're trying to get across,' she says.

It's also been a thoroughly enjoyable day, even for those of us who can only dream of a new pair of goalie gloves.

Bill and Judith Wedding Day, November 26th, 1961

Bill and Judith living a wonderful life in the Cayman Islands.

Celebrating 50th wedding anniversary - a golden celebration of a golden life

Bill's final game for Middlebrough and last time he headed a football

A young man with incredible talent. Photo: Sunday Pictorial.

England's most sought after teenager and National team captain

Bill's final season at Middlesbrough under Jack Charlton. Photo: Jim Larkin Fotos

Another fantastic clearance v Leicester

Unbeatable in the air. Photo: Larry Ellis

Another successful headed clearance. Photo: Sport and General

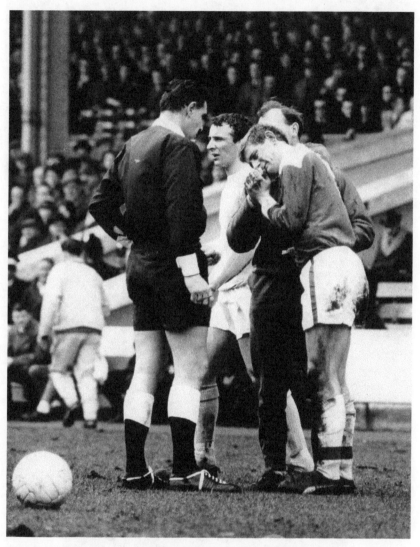

Treating a bang on the head with smelling salts! Photo: Sun Copyright Photograph

Dean Bank School team 1954–55

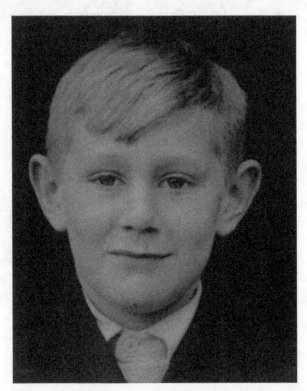

The son of a coal miner

From Ferryhill to Machu Picchu

The proud Boro philanthropist helping children around the world.

20.

'IT VERY MUCH REMINDS ME OF THE SMOKING DEBATE. EVERYONE KNOWS THAT IT'S WRONG, UNWISE, BUT NO ONE SEEMS TO DO MUCH'

The late Dr David Jenkins, the firebrand former Bishop of Durham, told me on the occasion of his 80th birthday in 2005 of two resolutions as he stood on the doorstep of his ninth decade.

The first was never again to drive more than ten miles from his retirement home in Teesdale, the second never again to make a train journey which involved changing at Birmingham New Street.

At the time it was wholly understandable. New Street station was a saturnine and subterranean sinkhole wholly unsuitable for elderly members of the episcopate as indeed for many others. These days, happily, New Street is born again, changed greatly for the better.

It's to Birmingham that I'm headed to talk with Dr Michael Grey, another leading researcher into sport-related brain injury and the man who came up with that pesky 'Scores' acronym. 'I regret it, I will never have an acronym like that again,' he'd told the League Managers' Association webinar, but these guys are acronymbies (and it's better than some of the others, anyway).

There's just one problem. The bus into Darlington is so late that the train's departing as I arrive. Dr Grey cheerfully puts things back an hour — like almost everyone else encountered across these cognitive question-and-answer sessions, a thoroughly accommodating guy.

Introductory emails have stressed human interest rather than the nooks and crannies of medical science. 'Quite right, too,' Dr Grey replies — but what journalistically suggests itself as the principal human interest story carries as excess baggage a terrible, indeed fearful, irony.

Though never much of a footballer during formative years in Canada — 'my career lasted about 15 minutes, broken clavicle'- he was an enthusiastic ice hockey goal tender, almost able to skate before he could walk. 'One of my earliest memories is sitting in the kitchen and my mother asking when I was going to start hockey,' he recalls.

There'd been three concussions, each time rendering him unconscious — 'you had to be unconscious for it to be taken seriously' — mostly resulting from what apparently is known as goal crashing, a testing time for the tenderfoot.

'I still vividly remember waking up one time and seeing the bright white lights coming slowly into focus. Someone asked how many fingers he was holding, I guessed correctly that it was two and that was it, they immediately had me back on.'

That he stopped playing at 16 had more to do with an absence of enjoyment. 'I'm not a big guy and I was getting hit lots of times. They wanted to win too much, the fun was going out of the game.'

Two of his sisters played soccer, as for differential reasons we shall briefly call it, at a fairly high level. One suffered 17 concussions, the other 11. One of them, he says, is already worried about the possible signs of dementia.

So Michael took enthusiastically to cycling, fit enough and good enough to contest events across Europe, until the time that he came at high speed over the handlebars. The injuries to his body mean that he may need a replacement shoulder, damage to his head potentially yet more devastating and already resulting in severe migraines.

The ardent campaigner for greater brain health in sport fears that he, too, may be developing early onset dementia. Michael Grey is 56. All right to include that in the book? 'Yes' he says, 'I think you should.'

We meet in a coffee shop near the cathedral. Dr Grey having headed into the city by car, not bike. He holds neuroscience research and teaching posts both at the University of East Anglia, alongside Michael Hornberger, and at the Queen Elizabeth Hospital in Birmingham. His partner is a barrister.

As well as a leading role in Scores, based at the University of East Anglia, he gave evidence to the Digital, Culture, Media and Sport inquiry into concussion in sport and helped found RECOS — meaning Repetitive Concussion in Sport and seeking to improve diagnosis. While RECOS may not be a perfect acronym, did he realise that it was an anagram of 'score'? No, he insists, he didn't. He's no longer directly involved.

The first person in his family to go to university — 'it took me a very long time to graduate, I didn't enjoy it' — he took further degrees in Denmark and Finland but self-effacingly insists that he speaks only English. 'I had four or five goes at Danish. It didn't work.'

Scores seeks to compare cognitive decline in former footballers over the age of 40, male or female and amateur or professional, with healthy non-players of similar age. So far around 300 have signed up, more than half ex-players, committing to a 30-minute home-based quarterly online test for a minimum of ten years.

The research could pick up signs of neurodegenerative disease potentially years before symptoms might become apparent and refer participants for further investigation where appropriate. Some, he hopes, will be able to take part for 30–40 years. 'I expect

I'll be departed by then. All of us decline, but most of us at a much slower rate.'

Familiarly, a big challenge is funding, that decade of research anticipated to cost £1.3 million. Though the League Managers' Association has been particularly supportive, he admits over a second coffee to having been 'stonewalled' quite a lot.

My feeling is that football should be working together to address these problems. Fund raising is quite frustrating but I'll work with anyone.

I'm not a football expert but I see a really beautiful game that can still be beautiful with heading removed. Football would still be one of the best sports around if you kept the ball on the ground. If you look at the beginnings of football it was quite brutal, a bit like Gaelic football. It changed, why can't it change again? I would very much like to see heading removed from the game or, if not, for people to be much more aware of the risks.

Heading the ball is a real concern, but there's a lot more to it than that. A lot of injuries are head to head, head to arm, head to pitch. People inside football have been very reluctant to address these things, at least until very recently, and to change.

It very much reminds me of the smoking debate. Everyone knows that it's wrong, unwise, but no one seems to do much. I feel very strongly that the business of football is being put before player welfare, and that has to change.

Like many others, Michael Grey seeks increased awareness, greater education, particularly among young people. 'It's a risk management issue. We need to better understand the risk and then get that message across. Young sports players need better to understand what it is they're getting into.

'From a scientific point of view there's a growing body of evidence to support these concerns but some of the governing bodies are in denial. A proportion of them are taking it seriously but there are still people I come into contact with who say all the right things but then act differently. We need to do what is best for the players and best for the game.'

He recalls the case of Jeff Astle, briefly and uniquely seems almost lost for words. 'Industrial disease...killed by football. That was 2002 — 20 years ago...what's happened since?'

Dr Grey also promotes regular NHS-funded neurological testing — 'We test our eyes every two years, why not our brains? It would help so much' — but insists that he'll stick to the science and leave the lobbying to others. Judith's so much better at it than him, he adds.

Two months after our meeting, Scores releases results of research comparing cognitive function among 145 former professional footballers with members of the general public. It was supported by the PFA, showing that footballers aged 40–50 out-performed the larger, general group — 'we know that regular exercise is really good for brain health,' says Dr Grey. 'It's when they get to 65 that things start to go wrong.

'The over-65s performed worse when tested for things like reaction time, executive function and spatial navigation. These are early warning signs for deteriorating brain health.'

They need, he admits, a bigger picture and deeper insights, perhaps following some of the former players for 30 or 40 years. 'There's a long way to go yet.'

21.

'THE CONCUSSION IN SPORT GROUP HAS CONTROLLED THE NARRATIVE FOR 20 YEARS, AND IT HAS COME TO THIS'

Delayed by Covid, the sixth conference of the Concussion in Sport Group — scheduled every four years, last held in 2016 — took place in Amsterdam at the end of October 2022. The three-day gathering attracted 600 delegates, paying 500 euros apiece, and a rather large pachyderm. The elephant in the room was called Dr Paul McCrory, who was not present.

Dr McCrory is the neuropathologist to whom Chapter Seven referred, the CISG's chair until his resignation in March 2022 and lead author of four of its five consensus statements, broadly and consistently sceptical of a cause-and-effect link between repetitive traumatic brain injury and CTE.

The Concussion in Sport Group is supported by many of the world's leading governing bodies, including the International Olympic Committee, FIFA, World Rugby, the International Ice Hockey Federation and the International Equestrian Federation. Its post-conference consensus statements are said widely to have shaped thinking on brain health among both elite and amateur athletes.

The report following the 2016 conference seemed almost to summarise the others, still supposing links to be inconclusive. 'The CISG has controlled the narrative for 20 years and it has come to this' says Judith. 'They have been discounting any research which doesn't fit that narrative. They will only talk about that agenda.'

So sometimes it had seemed in Amsterdam. In the *Daily Mail*, Chris Sutton, a former England international who followed his father Mike into Norwich City's canary colours, wrote of applause in the room at the 'ludicrous' suggestion that repetitive head impact wasn't directly linked to neurodegenerative disease. He wrote, too, of a shambles, of dismissive attitudes from so-called specialists.

Sutton had good cause for concern. Mike Sutton, his father, died with dementia on Boxing Day 2020, aged 76. Chris has no doubt that the principal cause of death was industrial disease — that is to say, football.

Judith shares the frustration. She was there at the conference with Dr Sally Tucker, her fellow H4C trustee and co-founder. A few days later, Dr Gates is back, abounding in conference talking points but with other things on her mind, too. Bill, inexorably and inevitably, has further declined both cognitively and physically. The man who until recently had an inexhaustible compulsion to walk is now ambulant only with a wheeled walking frame and, even then, only with careful supervision.

Tuesday November 15th will be the day that his wife has long dreaded but knew would come, when finally he must leave that lovely house and birdsong garden in Castle Eden for a specialist care home near Darlington.

She talks quietly about the agonies of it all, public detail unnecessary. 'It's not how we'd envisaged ending our days but the care home seems a very good place,' she says. 'At least Bill should be safe.'

The Repercussion Group, a global forum of scientists, medics and advocates with which Judith Gates and Sally Tucker are closely associated, published a 'positioning document,' greatly critical of both the CISG and its consensus statements, a few days before the Amsterdam conference. It spoke of 'years of failure to warn, to act and to be forthright' and of 'inconvenient truths'.

The most inconvenient of all, the paper suggested, was the direct link — though not yet scientifically watertight — between repeated head impact and neurodegenerative disease. Too many of the CISG, it supposed, had links to sport's governing bodies. The paper also wanted the approach to be patient-centred and not sport-centred.

'The increased neuropathological issue of multiple concussions and multiple sub-concussive impacts that can lead both to chronic symptoms in the short term and neurodegenerative diseases in the longer term has not received adequate attention during the consensus process.'

Back in 2001, Paul McCrory had just been appointed editor-in-chief of the *British Journal of Sports Medicine,* published by the BMJ group. 'There is no scientific evidence that sustaining several concussions over a sporting career will necessarily result in permanent damage' said an editorial at that time.

By the Spring of 2022, FIFA had expressed 'great concern' at the manner of his resignation from the CISG chair while the Australian Football League, with which he had worked closely, announced a comprehensive and independent review of McCrory's work. The BMJ had retracted nine of his articles and added 'expressions of concern' to a further 74.

After retracting a 2005 editorial piece, the BMJ group cited 'unlawful and indefensible breach of copyright' of another academic's work. 'The scientific record relies on trust and BMJ's trust in McCrory's work — specifically the articles he has published as a single author — has been broken,' they added.

McCrory insisted that any plagiarism had been 'neither intentional nor deliberate' and on at least one occasion blamed an editing error.

'The ramifications are immense,' Judith told the *Guardian* ahead of the 2022 conference.

Delegates had even been told that they shouldn't use Twitter from the conference. 'I found it bizarre and offensive to be told that,' she adds. Both, she and Sally Tucker, had managed to speak, both protecting the microphone in the manner of a hungry mastiff guarding its favourite bone. Judith, of course, had what she called 'lived experience' to share, right back to those fearful migraines when Bill was still playing football for Middlesbrough.

'I told them a bit about Bill, you should have seen their faces. The dilemma is that if you challenge some of these people, they put up barriers,' she says. 'Even at conference they were taking decisions in huddles, they don't like dissenting voices. We're not thoughtlessly calling for change, we're not in the blame game, but we're saying to the CISG that they should have more voices at their table.'

The latest consensus statement is due several months hence. How it defines 'consensus' may be particularly interesting.

Judith heads back to Castle Eden and to her desperately unwell husband. He probably won't know who she is or that she's been away. On the football front, there'll be another major development within days, she says, and there'll be more of that in the next chapter.

22.

'HOW PATHETIC THAT 30 FORMER FOOTBALLERS ARE TO SUE THE FOOTBALL ASSOCIATION OVER NEGLIGENCE. . . . '

Well, it should have been a brave new chapter, but response to the announcement that families of 30 former professional footballers are to sue the game's governing bodies over brain health issues seemed perversely to have little impact.

The Times afforded it three paragraphs at the foot of a page — somewhere the lacrosse results might normally have been — the BBC a perfunctory piece on the website. Even the *Daily Mail,* long a standard bearer for the cause, relegated the news to the bottom third of a sports page.

A run-of-the-mill report of a League Cup tie between Manchester United and Aston Villa received far greater prominence.

The problem of swaying — even alerting — public opinion may have been illustrated by a letter in the *Mail* four days later from a gentleman in Somerset. 'How pathetic that 30 former footballers are to sue the Football Association for negligence over possible brain injuries. These men all chose football as a career. No one forced them to play the game professionally, so they should not be compensated if their choice later turned out not to have been the best one for them.'

A few days after that, on November 23rd 2022, news that over 300 neurologically affected former rugby union and rugby league players — represented by Rylands Garth, the same specialist sports law firm as the footballers — were about to serve legal papers on the games' 'chiefs' attracted altogether greater coverage.

On November 28th the *Sunday Times* reported both the death of Scottish international rugby player Doddie Weir after a six-year battle with motor neurone disease — rugby union players 15 times more likely to contract MND, remember — and carried another column on the subject by the excellent David Walsh.

Tellingly, if a little breathlessly, it was headed 'For all the tragedies and mounting litigation, rugby still hasn't learnt its lesson. If there is any way to keep an important player on the pitch, teams will still find it.'

Head for Change had pondered bringing forward the release of a documentary to coincide with the news of football's legal action, but instead contented itself with a press release making ten proposals that sought to address the issue. They included the appointment of a concussion ombudsman, that head impacts in all training be 'minimised, monitored and regulated' and that a game-wide independent fund be established to provide financial support for players at every stage of their 'dementia journey,' particularly including funding for full-time care.

John Stiles, featured in an earlier chapter and interviewed by the *Mail*, repeated that football had killed his dad. 'I hoped dad's death would be the catalyst for fundamental change but it's wearying to seek to convince the FA, the PFA, the Premier League and the English Football League to act with decency.' The headline on Chris Sutton's short piece was blunter: 'This could wreck the FA but it's their own fault.'

What did Stiles make of the media coverage of the news? How many more might be joining the legal battle? 'We expect hundreds, we call this the first cohort,' he says, though aware of the advice that any success could still be years distant.

'It's no-win no-fee, the lawyer doing the work now. To be honest I'm not over-arsed about the money, it's the principle. It's just one part of my fight for justice, and I'm not giving up. Sometimes I feel like I'm banging my head off the door. I just want to do something.'

ITN had asked to send a reporter around, then cancelled. 'They said most of the reporters were in Qatar for the World Cup,' he says.

The action by footballers and in some cases their families is against the FA, the Welsh FA and the international rule-making body IFAB. They claim negligence on the grounds that the governing bodies failed to protect the players from brain injury caused by repetitively heading a football.

The Letter of Claim alleges that the authorities were negligent in 27 different areas, including failure to reduce the amount of heading in training and matches, failure to monitor and treat suspected concussions with the use of independent doctors and failure to enforce adequate return-to-play protocols.

The Rylands Garth website covers some of the ground, warning that litigation is 'notoriously slow' and that 'realistically speaking' any trial would not be for a number of years. 'That being said,' it adds, 'we will be pushing for an early settlement.'

They believe, it adds, that dementia in contact sports is an industrial disease — 'similar, say, to working in a factory and suffering hearing loss.' Are they, they ask themselves, looking for change in sport in any way? 'As a sports law firm we are, clearly, pro sports. But by potentially commencing litigation, we hope to help present and future players by raising awareness to help bring about change to make their sports safer.'

Head for Change, its rather cranial logo carrying the mantra 'Be part of the solution,' said in its media release that the charity 'recognised the concerns of families that have led to legal action.' It was, they added 'a wake-up call for the sporting governing bodies to work together constructively to fulfil their duty of care to all retired, current and future players.' The ten actions 'to protect players' were:

- That every sport publicly acknowledge that research evidence 'demonstrates the link between repetitive head impact and chronic traumatic encephalopathy.'
- A multi-media campaign with the message 'Heading harms your brain' should target all stakeholders.
- Every stakeholder should learn about the dangers of head impacts and CTE.
- Head impacts in all training should be minimised, monitored and regulated 'with particular reference to academies and foundations.'
- Head impacts in matches should be reduced and monitored 'to minimise harm to players.
- Concussion protocols should be fully implemented, temporary concussion substitutes introduced and an independent concussion ombudsman appointed.
- An industry-wide independent fund should be established to support players with dementia — 'particularly including funding for full-time care.'
- Affected ex-players and their families should be provided with ongoing emotional, psychological and practical support. 'Dementia,' it added, 'is a long and painful journey.'
- Brain and other physical changes from repetitive head impacts should be the subject of independent, player centred, precautionary research 'which does not expose players to further harm.'
- Diagnosis, possible treatment and cures for CTE should be the subject of urgent independent research 'in order to provide hope for ex-players... who have justifiable concerns about their future brain health.'

23.

'IF THIS WAS THE SHIPYARDS, I'M TALKING ABOUT ASBESTOS, THE TRADE UNIONS WOULD BE CALLING THEM OUT BECAUSE OF THE RISK TO THEIR HEALTH'

Many will be familiar with a verse from the sixth chapter of St Mark's gospel: 'A prophet is not without honour save in his own country, in his own house, and among his own kin.' A prophet, yes, but what of a professor?

Dr Willie Stewart, honorary professor both at his native Glasgow University and at Pennsylvania's Ivy League learning seat, too, is a globally eminent and internationally acknowledged neuropathologist who has long seemed central — crucial, indeed — to this narrative.

Earlier described in jest as the scarlet pimpernel of neuro-pathology, he has at last found 60 minutes among crowded hours for a chat in his laboratory office at the Queen Elizabeth University Hospital in Glasgow.

There's still a problem, however. The railwaymen are on strike, then suddenly aren't, though the emergency timetable is barely even chronological. The day previously, Dr Stewart's PA gently suggests a rearrangement. The offer is declined though I still feel a bit like the least prescient of the Three Little Pigs when stumbling out of the house at 6 15am.

Dementia still makes the news, *The Times* reporting a slightly paradoxical US study that more people have the disease than ever before but fewer at any given time. An interesting exercise in news values, a larger headline reports 'All England (Tennis) Club in talks over easing rule on white underwear.'

It's November 8th and Glasgow's already decked for Christmas, markets ablaze, mulled wine and pulled pork. It's 15 degrees and a chap in shorts and T-shirt is playing *Jingle Bells* on a ha'penny whistle. He still seems a little ahead of his time. The taxi driver from Queen Street station drops me as requested at the neurology department, a huge building on a vast campus.

The receptionist is friendly but puzzled. She's never heard of Dr Stewart, asks my name and date of birth instead. I explain that I'm not a patient. Finally she directs me to another reception desk, further into the building. The lady there appears equally bemused. It seems akin to the doorman at Walt Disney Studios asking 'Who's Donald Duck?' or the stewards at the Scottish parliament never having heard of the thistly Ms Sturgeon. (If they haven't now, events will dictate that they will have ere long....)

Finally the receptionist accesses the computer's innermost secrets, discovers that Dr Stewart is in a different but no-less enormous building several hundred yards away and summons one of those land train buggies now familiar on the sea front at Ayr (and elsewhere) or carrying US presidents (and about three dozen G-men) around the links at St Andrew's.

Advised of the urgency, the driver hits the accelerator. Soon we're doing 5mph. Thirty seconds into the appointed hour I'm finally delivered, Dr Stewart affable and welcoming but clearly a man to whom an hour means 60 minutes and not a moment more.

To that end there's been a technological breakthrough. After 57 years of mining Pitman — once there was a certificate recording

120 words a minute though not necessarily, as Eric Morecambe might have observed, in the right order — I've bought a little voice recorder, about the size of a small cigar and in line to make its debut. It sits almost eloquently between us, to the interviewee as old tech as an abacus but to the interviewer one small step. We've made it at last.

Dr Stewart further proves amiable, erudite and patient. Probably he didn't read my blog after his goalkeeping experience at Spennymoor, in which it was suggested that he shouldn't give up the day job and, truth to tell, was highly unlikely to be asked to.

Many now seek his counsel, among them Kevin Sinfield, the extraordinary former captain of Leeds Rhinos rugby league club whose diminutive friend and former colleague Rob Burrow — 'my little mate' Sinfield likes to call him — has motor neurone disease.

The English and Britain international's fund-raising challenges — 'increasingly insane' the *Sunday Times* supposed — had amassed around £8 million when this was being written and were also attracting increasing publicity and a clamour for his knighthood. After speaking with Dr Stewart, he also offered his much-battered brain for research after his death. 'Do what you need to do with it' said Sinfield. 'I don't think anyone will want my knees.'

In his autobiography, called *The Extra Mile* and published at the end of May 2023, Sinfield would echo all that had been headlined about rugby's existential crisis, both codes already reporting a significantly reduced number of players. 'What hasn't helped is the coverage of the concussion issue. It makes things tough for contact sports and at some point the balance might tip too far and we'll end up with other societal problems because people aren't exercising or playing team sports.

'My worry is that in 20 years time there's no rugby left and society has a much bigger problem with, for example, obesity. I'm not sure about rugby's longevity.'

Whatever might befall him in the future, added Sinfield– who'd suffered two major concussions in playing days — he wouldn't be following the litigation route. 'I wouldn't be where I am today, living a life that is able to give me fulfilment, but for rugby.'

A few days before our meeting, Willie Stewart had attended the CISG conference in Amsterdam — his first, rather reluctantly at that — and came away unimpressed. 'My sense is that there were far more people in the room not connected with professional sport who had far more understanding than those on the platform. I think the leaders of that group were the last bastions of resistance to change.'

At the start of the sessions, there'd been big images of the leaders. 'It's basically the same guys getting older and older. None of the committee was a heavyweight in the field of brain injury, far from it.'

The chat's preceded by the pretty evident explanation that I'm neither a medical nor a scientific man and that some questions might edge towards the ignorant. He smiles. 'I used to tell my students,' he says, 'that the only damn fool questions are the ones that you don't ask.' OK then, how old are you? 'Journalists' he sighs with perhaps a degree of mock exasperation. '53.'

The Field study, hitherto described as both ground breaking and game changing, was — of course — an acronym. It stood for Football's InfluencE on Lifelong health and Dementia risk, he says, and it came to him while on a bike ride. Lesser cyclists might just wonder where the next pub was.

They're all acronymble, these guys. Somewhere among these researches, somewhere on the banks of the Clyde, I came across BAD, the first two words 'brain' and 'action,' perhaps particularly appropriate in North-East England where — as in 'bad with the beer' — it simply means to be unwell.

There's also a familiar old joke in which Geordie asks his mate if he's still watching Sunderland play — the teams are interchange-able, of course. 'Nah' says his mate, 'they never came to see me when I was bad.'

Trouble is, I can't remember what the 'd' stood for.

Michael Hornberger and Michael Grey, Dr Stewart's fellow neurologists, are also keen cyclists, of course.

Published in 2019, the study by Dr Stewart and his team compared the brains of 7,626 former footballers with 23,028 from Scotland's general population. It concluded that the footballers were 3.53 times more likely to die from a neurodegenerative disease than the non-players. They were 5.07 times more likely to die from Alzheimer's, 4.33 times more likely to have motor neurone disease and slightly more than twice as likely to develop Parkinson's.

The incidence was greatest among defenders, lowest among goalkeepers — who, of course, have a more hands-on approach to such problems.

'As of October 21st 2019, a line was drawn in the sand for those who had been sticking their heads in it,' wrote Kieran Gill in *The Beautiful Game and the Ugly Truth*.

In October 2022, shortly before we meet, the Glasgow Brain Injury Research Group, which Dr Stewart leads, published a similar study focused on rugby players. It showed that they had more than twice the risk of a neurodegenerative disease and 15 times the risk of motor neurone disease.

'I am genuinely concerned about what is happening in the modern game and that if, in 20 years time we repeat the study, we could see something even more concerning,' he tells the media. 'Rugby has talked a lot and done a lot about head injury management and whether it can reduce head impact during training. These conversations have gone on a while and the pace of progress is pretty slow.

'Instead of talking about extending seasons and introducing new competitions and global seasons they should be talking about restricting it as much as possible, cutting back on the amount of rugby we're seeing and getting rid of as much training as possible. Things like that have to be addressed pretty rapidly.'

Head for Change is formally in partnership with the Glasgow Traumatic Brain Injury Archive, known more familiarly as a brain bank. Though they acknowledge that 'sometimes uncomfortable' decisions have to be made in order to help others, H4C's three trustees — Judith Gates, Melanie Popham and Sally Tucker — have all agreed that their loved one's brains can be donated, too.

Willie Stewart played rugby as a youngster, not least because — like Michael Hornberger and Michael Grey — he professes to have been useless at football. 'It was Glasgow so everyone at school played football but I was dreadful. I used to play in defence or in goal and that was because my only skill was in catching the ball or knocking people to the ground. I was no good at controlling it.

'At Spennymoor I didn't want to play in the outfield with the risk of too many injuries and humiliations. As it happens, I got plenty of the latter.'

In his Glasgow childhood, of course, all wanted to know if you were blue or green, Rangers or Celtic. Perhaps in the interests of self-preservation, he usually dodged the question. 'I found it easier to say Partick Thistle. That didn't offend anyone very much, so I got away with it.'

Rugby appealed intermittently. 'I wasn't terribly good at it but I played until I was 19, gradually training less and playing more rarely. I remember going to one game when they brought in one of the under-18s, the scrum collapsed and he broke his neck. I was standing there thinking why on earth am I involved in something so potentially damaging as this and actually not enjoying it very much.'

Had the thought occurred before? 'No, not really, funnily enough. It was more just general health and safety. At university there were plenty of other sports — bit of badminton, bit of basketball. You could find plenty of other ways to keep fit and healthy without risking rugby.'

He retains a Glasgow rugby season ticket. Does he wince — cringe, even — at some of the things he sees? 'There's no doubt that elite rugby has a very short path life. No sport in the 21st Century can afford to have injuries at the rate it does, it's unsustainable. Take away concussions and just look at the impacts, the sub-concussions. Young men and women are harming their futures by participating in these matches. There's no way that can continue.

> There are two routes for rugby now. One is that they continue and don't change and parents and families or whatever will just say that the game is no longer fit for purpose.

> Rugby will become a game like heavyweight professional boxing. It will become a niche sport, a bit like American football, a game for a few teams played at a high level. That's rugby's future if it doesn't change. Yes, they want to look after players as much as they can but they also recognise that it's an entertainment industry. Are people entertained by what they see?

> If they think that people are going to be entertained by heavyweight rugby then schools and kids and families are going to stop playing it. They don't want to see their sons and daughters exposed to that level of injury.

> It's a bit like, rewind 50 years, sons and daughters being sent into the boxing ring. We now realise the damage that it did...

He remained an enthusiastic cyclist — 'a great escape when I was growing up, you could just jump on the bike and disappear in the days before all the traffic there is now. Me and my mate would just go off on bikes when we were 12 or 13 and come back at tea time having had a bottle of Irn Bru and a Mars Bar maybe 20 miles away.'

In 2005, however, he was not only seriously injured in an accident when a car turned into his path but gained first-hand experience of the difficulty of diagnosing concussion.

'I was riding into work. It was the last couple of miles, I got hit by a car and found myself in the road. I tried to get up and realised there was something wrong with this hip. It turned out to be my pelvis and being not far from the hospital, there was a bus behind me with lots of people going there for work, and just behind that a guy on a motor bike who was working in the casualty department. 'I had a whole emergency response team around me looking after me. I was whisked off to hospital where they found out pelvic injuries but no mention of anything to do with the head.'

The following day, a medical student who'd been part of the roadside response looked in to see how Dr Stewart was. 'He immediately detected that firstly I had no idea of what had happened to me and secondly that my behaviour at the scene was bizarre. He described me as being like in a pub on a Friday night, I was so disconnected while lying on the floor with a broken pelvis — and that was before they got me with the morphine. Basically then the penny dropped that I had concussion which hadn't been picked up. They were managing down just one pathway, what was happening to the pelvis.

'Then they saw a picture of the car that had hit me, apparently the front end written off, at which point the casualty team decided I might have a brain injury and scanned me from top to bottom.'

It took months before he was happy getting back on the bike. 'It was tough,' he admits, 'not painful but psychological.'

Unlike Dr Michael Grey, his two-wheel mishap recorded earlier, Dr Stewart has no real worries about long term issues. 'If I were being honest, I would be less worried about that single injury in my late 40s than I would be about the multiple injuries when I was playing rugby. It's the repetitive impact and the cumulative exposure that's the problem.

'Back in 2005 cyclists were quite a rare breed. Since Covid there are a lot more out on the road than there were. People are a bit more understanding, a bit more tolerant, cars give you a bit more space. I'm enjoying my cycling again.'

He'd always liked science at school — 'arts, dreadful' — looked at what might be a natural progression. 'It was like asking your GP what he did, visit a few hospitals,' he recalls. The first person in his family to study medicine, he's been followed by his two daughters — one a junior doctor on the same campus, the other still at university.

'I was intrigued and fascinated all the way through university, particularly the neurological science — how the brain worked, how nerves worked. The lecturer was introducing us to the concept of how messages were transmitted along nerves. It's just physics in action.

'I spent all that summer picking up books on popular science, mainly neurology, half of them probably still in this room. I just thought it was amazing how the brain works. That probably hasn't changed for 30 years or more.'

What manifestly has changed is the profile. Though the Glasgow Brain Injury Research Group is very much a team effort, Dr Stewart is its acknowledged leader, its standard bearer, spokesman and champion. Most medical men prefer, however metaphorically, to hide behind a surgical mask. Is the high profile helpful?

> There's no point in people doing research if it doesn't translate into some change and influence what's happening with patients on the ground. What we are doing is informative, I think — enlightening, I think — but it has to be communicated properly.

> If we find that footballers are three-to-four times more at risk than non-players and publish it in a journal which no one picks up then what's the point? We need people to know it's there. Communicating in a way that's accessible to everyone engaged in sport to me is important. There's no point in doing this work unless we try to translate it into some kind of meaningful action. What we know about head injuries and impact in sport is utterly useless if we sit on our hands and do nothing about it. We need to see the change happen.

In his talk before the Spennymoor match, he'd described progress as 'glacial,' and probably hadn't factored global warming.

Any sign of a further thaw from sport's governing bodies? He turns, once again, to rugby.

'Four or five years of counting the same number of injuries year after year after year tells us that nothing is happening and that sport is not learning lessons and nothing is changing. They'll say their head injury protocols are second-to-none and that they've done all this research on tackles and introduced new laws about red cards and infringements. None of that has worked. It's all about saying they're doing all these things but actually they're not changing anything for the fellows on the ground.'

The simplest thing, he supposes, would be to minimise contact training. 'Players know how to play rugby, they don't have to be destroyed just to learn how to tackle on a Saturday. What they do need to do is look at the global programme and say that these 30-odd matches we're involved in is not sustainable. Get rid of as much as possible and if they can't do that then say that every player must have at least an eight-to-ten week block when they're not playing rugby.

'Professional rugby in England has been counting injuries for the last 20 years and the last four or five years the injury level has been the same. It tells you that for all the good work they've done in terms of recognising injury and taking players off, what hasn't changed is the rate of injury. There's nothing to protect the players. All they've done is spot the injury and that has to change.'

He'd once described football's injury protocols as a shambles. What did he mean? 'Football's current head injury protocols are dreadful. Another era. Football needs to get into the 21st Century. You can't assess a possible brain injury in 30 seconds or a minute on the pitch. You need to remove a player and say that if there's doubt you sit them out. If you look at football, before they introduced concussion subs, the problem wasn't the doubt it was the sit them out.'

Perhaps happily for the professor's blood pressure, the interview had taken place a week or so before the Iranian goalkeeper's fearful head blow — after which the medics tried to let him carry on regardless — against England in the World Cup.

'If your player is running away from you saying that he wants to play, the ref wants to restart and the crowd is baying for football to continue then you are going to go with the path and let him stay on. Medics and physios need to take the decision in the dressing rooms, away from the pressure.

'After another ten years and a couple of World Cups I think we're going to see heading training a thing of the past, or a very rare event, maybe once a week. Head injury management in football will be considerably changed and concussion management will be in line with other sports.

'Sally Tucker's dad headed the ball 70,000 times in his career, maybe 1,000-1,500 of those in matches. You can look at what's happening in terms of head impacts and say let's get rid of the 69,000.'

Is he ever accused of being a spoilsport? 'Dementia's a terrible disease. At the moment we have no treatment for dementia or effective therapies for dementia. The only way successfully to deal with dementia is to stop people getting it in the first place.'

Clearly quite a lot frustrates him, what (I ask) bloody well annoys him? He allows himself a laugh of the sort sometimes supposed sardonic. Conversations with the FA and the RFU are more balanced and more advanced than in other parts of the world, they're really trying to change things, he says.

What really bloody annoys me is that the great developments in UK sport aren't spreading to global sport. Why aren't FIFA saying let's look at what's happening in England and Scotland and stop heading the ball for under-12s? Why is there such a backward and retrograde position? Why is World Rugby conducting a symposium only last week which basically sought to deconstruct the idea that repeatedly hitting your head can cause real damage? Why is rugby not saying that they accept this as a problem?

The PFA and such organisations, they're the trade unions, they should be stepping up. If this were the shipyards, I'm talking about asbestos, the trade unions would be calling them out (on strike) because the risk would be too much for their health. The PFA doesn't really stand up and say that regular head injuries are damaging players.

They should be putting their foot down, demanding change on behalf of their members but they're not doing that. They sit back, there's the odd press release, but don't do much. They should be saying dammit, you represent the players, you do more.

It's coming up 2pm. Like a diligent referee, he's looking at his watch. It's as Kieran Gill observed, that there are lines in the sand and heads in the sand but, for now, the hourglass sand's run its course.

Not three weeks later there's a major — some might suppose momentous — announcement from the Scottish FA that professional footballers will be forbidden to head a ball for 24 hours either side of a match and that training with repetitive heading will be restricted to one day a week.

Scotland had already become the first country in the world with the same concussion protocols for all sports, centred on the 'If in doubt sit them out' dictum. The SFA announcement cites the Field study, says that their concern is for the safety and wellbeing of all players. It makes the second item on the BBC evening news, after Covid-centred insurrection in China.

There's a BBC Scotland website analysis, too: 'It shows that the message is getting through, the experts are taking no chances. The evolution of skills and tactics has meant fewer headers in the game anyway, but if the changes continue, due to mounting scientific evidence and pressure, it isn't difficult to imagine the game in the future without any heading at all.'

The SFA is based, of course, in Glasgow. Remember those earlier words about severely curtailing heading in training? The prophet is not without honour after all.

In June 2023 the University of Nottingham published a similar study called Focus, an acronym so neat and so obvious it's a wonder they didn't sell it to the highest bidder. Many of its findings are remarkably similar to those of the Glasgow team but, since this is cautious academics we're on about, they prefer the expression 'broadly in line.'

Funded by the FA and PFA, the Nottingham study among 460 former players again found that ex-footballers were 3.5 times more likely to develop a neurodegenerative disorder and that 2.8 per cent of footballers in the study already had a medically diagnosed neurological condition as opposed to 0.9 per cent in the control group. Former players, however, were less likely to have Parkinson's and none in the study had MND.

The BBC sought the FA's view: 'The FA has led the way in taking steps to help reduce potential risk factors within the game and establishing industry leading concussion guidelines,' they said. 'These include introducing the world's most comprehensive heading guidelines at every level of the amateur and professional game in England.'

They spoke to Adam White, PFA brain health chief, too: 'These studies ensure that targeted and evidence-led action can be taken to support and protect players at all stages of their careers,' he said. 'Continued involvement in this type of research will remain absolutely vital.'

At almost exactly the same time the media carried the news that Sir Alex Ferguson, proud Scot and one of the great football managers of all time, was a signatory to an open letter to the Scottish government to regard heading-related illness as an industrial disease (which, of course, is what had been happening since the Jeff Astle inquest 20 years before).

Other signatories included former Scottish national team manager Willie McLeish. 'You have to respect it,' he said. 'The science guys are not often wrong.'

There was also an email from a potential reader of the book, attaching a magazine report of a Swedish study among that country's top level footballers between 1924 and 2019. With the exception of the good old goalie, it concluded, the group was 50 per cent more likely to develop Alzheimer's or other forms of dementia.

It wasn't a football or even a medical magazine, it was *Woman's Weekly*. The message is getting across.

24.

'WE WOULD HAVE EXPECTED THE FOOTBALL ASSOCIATION TO HAVE BEEN PUBLICLY HOUNDED BY THE PROFESSIONAL FOOTBALLERS' ASSOCIATION. . . '

Portcullis House is a huge government building on the Victoria Embankment in London, connected by an underground tunnel to the Palace of Westminster, which it serves. Said to have cost £235 million, it was opened by the late Queen in 2001 and has offices for more than 200 MPs plus very many more staff.

Its name derives from the great gate which symbolises the UK parliament, latter day security necessarily more sophisticated. Airport-style safeguards include baggage scans and body pat-downs, though none may have been prepared for the occasion when Dr Stephen McGinness's wife and son joined him for lunch there.

Asked to remove his jacket, the lad revealed a T-shirt with the potentially disconcerting message 'Russian spy'. Quickly he was asked to resume his jacket, quickly his dad vouched for citizenship and sanity. He got his lunch.

Dr McGinness is a Scot whose principal academic qualifications are in microbiology and biochemistry but who has worked in parliament since 1998. He is (or was at the time of our meeting) clerk to the Digital, Culture, Media and Sport Committee, chaired by Julian Knight the Conservative MP for Solihull, which in July 2021 published a report — cogent and compelling, direct and sometimes almost dismayed — called Concussion in Sport. A crucial paragraph appeared on page 19 of the 40-page document:

> *Football engagement with the issue of concussion, both in England and internationally, has taken too long and its current prominence is due to the campaigning of organisations like the Jeff Astle Foundation and prominent spokespersons like Chris Sutton. We would have expected the Football Association, as the national governing body, to have taken a stronger, sustained interest in the issue after the coroner's verdict on Jeff Astle's death. We would also have expected the Football Association to have been publicly hounded by the Professional Footballers' Association, whose key concern should be player welfare. Over the past 20 years neither the Football Association nor the Professional Footballers' Association have fought hard enough, or publicly enough, to address this issue within the broader football community. They are, however, only part of a broader failure to address the issue of acquired brain injury in sport.*

A House of Commons working group had produced another report on safety in sport in 2002, almost 20 years earlier, since when precious little appears to have been done, a matter to which the latest publication fairly diplomatically refers. 'The government regularly flirts with the concept of greater statutory regulation of sport. The Culture Secretary will often threaten legislation, which rarely materialises.'

They were concerned, it added, 'that there is a history of the government looking into issues of sporting safety and failing to follow through with practical interventions that would make a difference to the health and safety of those participating.'

The second report questions, amid much else, the role and the rigour of the Concussion in Sport Group and of its contentious consensus statements, and an absence of cohesion, not least in government, and a sometimes inadequately educated medical profession. Sport, it says, has a responsibility to ensure that elite athletes aren't allowed to trade short-term success for their long-term health.

'We recognise that will never be and can never be, 100 per cent safe.... It should, however, be expected that participants are aware of the risks involved and there is a precautionary approach to risk management. The government cannot avoid taking a proactive role in ensuring that this occurs. The government has a duty to ensure that sporting activity at every level bears no unnecessary risk.'

That it also calls upon the government to 'grasp the nettle' of greater regulation of sport represented a rare stumble into Cliché Country and may thus be forgiven.

I'd emailed Mr Knight, himself a former journalist, to seek an interview. The chair referred me to Dr McGinness, a Celtic supporter — 'you'd expect me to be with an Irish name like McGinness' — with whom there's then a most helpful telephone conversation.

He asks how long I'd like. 'You sound talkative, how about two hours?' I ask and, somewhat to my surprise, he at once agrees. Before proceeding, however, it should perhaps be explained that the parliamentary job title 'clerk' no more indicates a Bob Cratchit figure hunched over a very large ledger and a very small fire than the Secretary of State is a shorthand typist.

Rather Stephen McGinness is a chief executive officer and, clearly, a polymath. At the time we meet, November 2022, the DCMS committee is running seven different inquiries ranging from 'Non-fungible tokens and the block chain' — whatever they, or it, may be — to 'Connective technology: smart or sinister.'

We meet over coffee in the huge Portcullis House atrium, said to have been designed to look and feel like a ship and once adorned with rather a lot of rented fig trees, reckoned by Wikipedia to have cost £400,000 by 2012 but now disappeared, too big for their roots. Dr McGinness misses them: they created a sound baffle, he says

He proves engaging, affable, patient, knowledgeable and greatly courteous, though some things are off limits. The lengthening litigants' line-up? *Sub judice.* Parliamentary privileges? Best not tread on those honourable toes, either.

Resonantly restored, Big Ben chimes one as, punctually, he sees me through the security screen and off the premises. There's just one problem, rather a big problem, but we'll return to that a little later.

However greatly their prospects may be in jeopardy, journalists still love a good sustaining soundbite — yet more greatly if it comes both foaming at the mouth and metaphorically wrapped in red ribbon.

So with the DCMS committee's Concussion in Sport report. Someone — Dr McGinness denies paternity, supposing the progenitor probably to have been committee member Steve Brine, Conservative MP for Winchester — had rather incredulously suggested in the 2021 document that so far as health and safety protocols were concerned, sport had been allowed to mark its own homework.

The phrase headlined the media release, too, the committee unequivocally expressing itself 'astounded' that sport's governing bodies had been allowed to drive hands-free.

Though by no means restricted to football and rugby, the report conceded from the start that the media focus on dementia among 'football heroes' had increased public awareness of the potential for participation in sport — amateur, professional and what someone called Weekend warriors — to carry a long-term risk, other health benefits notwithstanding.

'While the current science cannot prove a causal link between dementia and sporting activity, it is undeniable that a significant minority of people will face long-term neurological issues as a result of their participation in sport,' the report added.

Evidence had been heard from boxers to bobsleigh riders — fearful sport, that. Monica Petrosino, a Team GB ice hockey player, told of her own head injury and of her fears for the future; Dawn Astle, whose father's death had seemed to concentrate so many minds back in 2002, was another witness.

'For almost 20 years now football has failed to act and failed to protect its players,' she said. 'If the sport is left to its own devices, as it is, it will do just what it wants to do. If there was a body overseeing the sport 20 years ago, when my dad had died, you would have been saying to it "You need to take these steps, you need to take those steps, and those steps would have been taken."'

Chris Sutton also appeared. 'It is really important that the government take ownership of this because the (Football Association) and the (Professional Footballers' Association) have not done anywhere near enough,' he said. 'They have not been interested in it because it does not benefit them in any way, shape or form.'

Five days after my meeting with Dr McGinness, Sutton was again voicing outraged opinions after Allreza Beiranvand, the Iranian goalkeeper, suffered a severe blow to the head in a collision with a team mate during the World Cup match with England. Treated for 11 minutes, Beliavand was then allowed to continue before deciding, shortly afterwards, that he couldn't.

'Football's concussion procedures are an embarrassment,' Sutton tweeted. 'I'll say it again, the football authorities do not care about their players.' BBC commentator and former player Jermaine Jenas described it as 'a joke'.

Similar concerns were raised a few days later when Wales player Nicos Williams got his head in the way of a pile-driver from England's Marcus Rashford. After concussion checks which seemed cursory but were within FIFA guidelines, Williams continued. It angered Headway, another brain health charity, who claimed that 'once again' team medical staff had been left with no option.

'Medics are being forced to make snap judgements under pressure, resulting in players being allowed to stay on the field despite the assumed presence or at least some doubt over potential concussion,' Headway's interim chief executive Luke Griggs told the BBC.

The refusal by FIFA and IFAB — football's international law-making body — to introduce temporary concussion substitutes was causing needless risk to players, he said. 'The rule is supposed to be "If in doubt sit it out" not "Play on and see how it goes."'

Williams continued for another 12 minutes, fell to the ground and was finally taken off.

The DCMS committee had taken written evidence from bodies as diverse as the British Horseracing Authority — jockeys said statistically to be more at risk than participants in any other sport– the English Cricket Board, the Rugby Football Union and the International Mixed Martial Arts Federation.

Head for Change also submitted written evidence — its goal, it said, to 'revolutionise' the way the present and future crisis around sport-related head injury is approached. It talked of the 'silent killer' within sport, of the 'ethical tightrope' which medics and researchers affiliated with sporting bodies were obliged to walk and of the need for more rigorous protocols around suspected or obvious head injury.

'Currently the desire to win is paramount, each player under constant pressure to continue to play despite head injuries.' Instead, it said player welfare should be 'the predominantly guiding principle.'

The DCMS report, simultaneously considered by H4C to be a 'turning point' but only a first step, had particularly and perhaps inevitably been impressed by the Field report and by its potentially game-changing conclusions. It stated, however, that while the report clearly showed that something needed to be done, it didn't say what should be done.

It also noted players' reluctance to leave the fray, again stressing the guidance of if in doubt, sit it out. 'The reality is that, for most people playing sports, there is no one to stop them except themselves, friends, team mates and family. That is how far down awareness of concussion and how to respond to it must reach to ensure people seek the necessary help and treatment rather than return to the field to the detriment of their long-term health.'

Former rugby World Cup winner Kyran Bracken, born in Dublin in 1971 and capped 51 times by England, had made a similar point, suggesting that the elite game should set a better example for grass roots players. 'The mode that they are in is exactly the same that you see in a Six Nations match where a player will be knocked out and then stand up and say he's not coming off because he's absolutely fine. What you see on TV is what you see on every single rugby pitch up and down the country. If you are at university and you are in the third team, you are not going to go to A&E when someone says you should. you are going to go out with the boys and you are going to train on the following Wednesday, aren't you?'

If made into a film it could be called *Carry on Regardless.*

Those from the parliamentary estate had agreed, though with a little dig at the fourth estate. 'There is a tendency for the press to laud athletes who sustain injuries and drag themselves back onto the field of play, even swathed in bandages,' said the DCMS, perhaps remembering former England footballer Terry Butcher, his white shirt bloodied, insistent on resuming despite a fearful open head wound in a 1980s international against Switzerland.

As the Jockey Club may (or may well not) have said, it shouldn't just be about getting straight back onto the horse. Professor Nick Webborn, a leading member of the 2002 safety in sport working group, wrote in turn nearly two decades later: 'We set forward a pathway to "assess, monitor and advise on the improvement of

standards of safety and medical provision within organised sport."
Government failed to act to bring this about.'

The 2021 report made numerous recommendations — committees can do no more than recommend — some with a suggested deadline of no later than the summer of 2022. They included those below — the temptation to italicise the dates, but quote marks will well suffice.

- Establishing a UK-wide minimum standard definition for concussion that all sports must use and adapt for their sport.
- That NHS England, in collaboration with the Faculty of Exercise and Sports Medicine, prepares — 'within the next 12 months' — a learning module on best practice for treating and advising those who present with concussive trauma and that all GP and A&E practitioners take the module 'within the next two years.'
- That the government mandate UK Sport — 'which uniquely in our evidence base considers the consensus statement by the Concussion in Sport Group as a satisfactory basis for concussion protocols' — to take a governance role in ensuring that all sports it promotes effectively raise awareness of the dangers of concussion.
- That a more precautionary approach is taken and that more of the money spent on UK sport is focussed on the athletes 'who are at the core of UK success in sporting endeavours.'
- That the government 'immediately' mandate the Health and Safety Executive to work with sports governing bodies to establish 'by July 2022' a national framework for reporting sport injuries with an obligation for any event which might lead to acquired brain injury to be reported.
- That the government convene its own specialist group on concussion to assess 'every four years' emerging science on the issue.

- That a UK-wide protocol for concussion across all sports be established 'within the next 12 months.'
- That the government 'uses its power' to establish a single research group into concussion and the government deliver a 'comprehensive communications protocol' to ensure that everyone in sport is aware of best practice.

We'd mentioned a problem. It concerned the voice recorder, that cigar-sized piece of technological kit that had made its debut in the interview with Dr Willie Stewart and, as a parliamentarian might suppose, had again been tabled in the presence of Dr McGinness.

The problem becomes evident when I adjourn to a pleasant Westminster pub called *The Speaker* and, almost speechless, discover that I've pressed 'play' and not 'record'. The only sound is of my five-year-old grandson telling a story — a rather charming story, admittedly — about a rabbit and a blackberry bush.

At least the dog didn't eat it.

Only two things may with necessary accuracy be recalled from the interview, the first that in several appreciative references to Dr Stewart and his potentially game-changing research he calls his fellow Lanarkshire lad Wullie, as in the tousle-topped termagant championed for almost a century in the *Sunday Post*.

The other's that Dr McGinness has reason to retell Billy Connolly's familiar story about why the late Queen believed that the world smelled naturally of wet paint, but I'm blowed if I can remember why.

Apprehensively emailed that evening, Dr McGinness is almost impossibly understanding, almost scripturally forgiving. Like accidents. These things happen, he says, sources one of those smiley emoji jobs, suggests firing a few written questions instead.

The 2021 report made several recommendations with a July 2022 deadline: had anything been put in place? 'I have not as yet made any analysis of what has been done with regard to the report recommendations but we will feed back to members deadlines like this when we discuss the future programme.'

Did any specific event or person prompt the 2021 report? Are words like 'astounded' familiar in such reports? 'I think there was a growing perception of the issue and the committee in one of its future programme sessions decided that it would inquire into it. Public oral evidence sessions revealed enough evidence to warrant a report.'

How closely can the committee or its officers monitor future developments? How minded are they to do so? 'The secretariat of the committee will be keeping a watching eye on everything we have made recommendations on in the past. But I can make no comment on what members may have said in private session.'

Dr McGinness also sends a link to a Billy Connolly cabaret, performed in front of a VIP audience, in which the paint job's said to be about 23 minutes in. 'I hope you find it informative and en-tertaining,' he says. At that very juncture I'm trying, with no great success, to precis a CISG report. The Big Yin, shall we say, proves diverting.

He's much younger, marginally less hirsute, lighter on his feet, talks of childhood in Partick and (like Willie Stewart) of support-ing Partick Thistle FC. 'I call them that because most Englishmen think they're called Partick Thistle nil.'

He speaks, too, of Scots who always turn off the television when they see the priest coming — 'priests think we're a nation of busted tellies' — and of the long years before he lost his virginity. 'I had to do it eventually, otherwise I'd have gone blind.'

The audience includes football folk like Jack Charlton and Lawrie McMenemy, fellow Scots entertainer Robbie Coltrane, Esther Rantzen, former weather girl Wincey Willis and the re-doubtable Ms Sturgeon. One chap looks like sixties singer Joe Brown, but maybe it's one of his bruvvers.

The royal painting comes precisely on 23 minutes, beats the hell out of the Concussion in Sport Group but without reference to the context in which Dr McGinness had thought appropriate to retell it.

Prompted, he says that he was likening it to how — 'in my opinion' — a select committee's biggest influence 'is often choosing to look into an area, prompting the government and regulatory bodies to go over all their regulations and policies in more detail than otherwise would be the case. As such, the committee sees a much cleaner world with dusted down, polished up policies.'

Bidding adieu beneath Big Ben's boom, he'd revealed that shortly he'd be moving to become clerk to the International Trade Committee. The excellent Dr McGinness will likely be very grateful.

25.

'I TRULY BELIEVE THAT THIS IS THE BEGINNING OF THE END. IT'S EXCITING TO THINK THAT WE WILL SOON HAVE LIFE-SAVING TREATMENTS TO TACKLE THIS DISEASE'

A fortnight after the unfortunate events in London, we've a day trip to Edinburgh — special place — which also gets off to a disappointing start. Though the train doesn't leave until turned eight o'clock, WHSmith's on Darlington station still has no newspapers. Inexplicably, they blame 'the football'.

It's November 30th 2022 and the 8.03 northwards is accompanied by the advent of LNER's 'Christmas menu', options including stollen-flavoured muffin and hog roast sausage roll — which is not just hog roast sausage roll but 'hand crafted' hog roast sausage roll. As the caroller might have supposed, however, the Holy Tide of Christmas has effaced what folk still call the British Rail breakfast.

No newspapers to peruse, I turn on the not-so-smart phone to the BBC website where the top item heralds a 'momentous' breakthrough in the long battle against Alzheimer's disease. In these pages, it will be recalled, the words 'momentum' and 'momentous' must be handled with the literary and clinical equivalent of a ten-foot barge pole.

The website sums a story from the *New England Journal of Medicine,* in which Dr Willie Stewart had first ploughed Field's findings, about clinical trials of Lecanemab, a drug which, it's said, 'can slow the destruction of the human brain by Alzheimer's.'

Though these things are as set about with caveats as a suburban back garden with leylandii, the boffins appear genuinely optimistic, nonetheless. There's a quote from Prof Tara Spiros-Jones, appropriately of the University of Edinburgh — 'the results are a big deal because until now a 100 per cent failure rate has been the norm.'

Since I don't have contact details for Professor Tara, and since it's unlikely in any case that she'd be able to pop out for a drop of Irn Bru and a haggis toastie, I head for the incomparable Oxford Bar and raise a cautious glass there, instead.

Back on Waverley station for the 17.00 homeward, it's finally possible to buy a copy of *The Times* Scottish edition, though it's tempting to ask what time they were delivered. The main story, what the oft-invisible inky trade still likes to call the splash, is also about the Lecanemab breakthrough, the headline supposing it 'historic' and the sub-head adding: 'Treatment paves way for Alzheimer's cure, say experts.'

The report adds that the news had been revealed the previous evening to a conference of some of the world's leading neurologists. They'd not just thought it 'historic' but 'historic and momentous,' to boot.

The Times further talks of the biggest breakthrough in a generation, of a disease which affects 900,000 people in the UK and of a Yale-led study which involved 1,795 people aged between 50 and 90 with early dementia. It quotes Rob Howard, professor of old age psychiatry at University College London: 'My heart says that this is wonderful news. This will encourage real optimism that dementia can be beaten and one day even cured.'

Professor Howard has also been quoted in Chapter 18, the man who memorably supposed that in his 30 years of dementia research they'd always been five years off a breakthrough.

It also quotes Professor Sir John Hardy, a colleague at UCL: 'I truly believe it represents the beginning of the end. We now know exactly what we need to do to develop effective drugs. It's exciting to think that we will soon have life-saving treatments to tackle this disease.'

On page 19 of the Scottish edition, at least, there's yet more of interest to Judith Gates who, it may be recalled, curates a caramel wafer convention back home in Castle Eden. Tunnocks, Scotland's caramel wafer kings for 130 years, have not only seen record turnover — rising from £56.6m to £72.1m, but posted pre-tax profits up from £255,000 to £5.5m.

What really takes the biscuit, however — the pun as puerile as it is irresistible — comes on page 64, the sports section, a lengthy piece headed 'Silence over radical heading plan tells a story,' and written by Michael Grant, the paper's Scottish football correspondent, whose online cv mordantly notes that he'd covered Scotland in a World Cup finals and two European championships 'and must be considered an endangered species.'

What intrigues him is that not 'a cheep of resistance' has been heard from within the game following the Scottish FA's heading restrictions announced a few days earlier and outlined towards the end of the chapter on Willie Stewart. The silence, he supposes, speaks volumes. 'No one is rolling their eyes about the snowflakes taking over. Any old player or supporter who might once have piped up has probably lost a former team mate to dementia. Every old centre half or big No 9 is worried about dementia now.

'The old stalwarts and warhorses from the 1960s, 1970s and 1980s have been conspicuous by their absence. Maybe as little as ten years ago there would have been a few up in arms about it, but not any more. How could they be when they are the ones whose contemporaries, whose great pals, are being picked off by neuro-degenerative disease?'

I sought permission from Grant and *The Times* to reproduce and acknowledge rather more of the piece than is customary. Michael replied that he was quite close to the story — a few years ago he lost his mother to dementia.

He talks, too, of Dr Willie Stewart's commitment and energy. I email Dr Stewart to ask what he makes of it all, the reply characteristically courteous but (let's say) academically circumspect. It doesn't change much of our conversation, he says. The line about today Scotland and tomorrow the world — paraphrased — may not be appropriate.

'What we've seen is a smart approach to head impacts in Scottish football, which is at the very least a pilot of a possible approach. What happens next in the game and how this will be put into practice will be followed closely and, of course, additional adjustments made as needed to continue progress on reducing head impacts.

'This is just Scotland, however. There is complete silence from global football. Real progress will only be made when the global game gets onside with the changes that the SFA, the FA and other national associations have been working on. Until then, nothing has really changed — other than headlines for a day or so.'

It could be decades, inevitably, before the results of precautionary measures in the early 2020s become clear — dementia can be a fearfully slow burner — but Michael Grant is convinced it's the right move and that temporary concussion substitutes must follow. 'Of course there is more to do (but) the direction of travel from here is towards the big one, an eventual ban on heading in games. It cannot be acceptable to ban repeated heading in training and say it's fine for defenders aerially to attack cross after cross for 90 minutes.'

It's a most compelling piece of writing, the sort of thing that H4C should send to every sponsor and supporter when tempted to suppose that the battle naught availeth, and it might never have been discovered had not WH Smith's on Darlington station been so incorrigibly after their time.

Back home, another slab of hand crafted hog roast sausage roll despatched en route, I emailed Professor Michael Hornberger who, two months earlier in Chapter 18 had underlined the need for caution but ventured that he could see many positive changes on the horizon. The m-word is ventured.

'We talked of frustrated hopes and of false dawns. I wonder if I might ask you for an additional paragraph of comment on what you make of the news re Lecanemab? Is it 'historic and momentous' as someone in *The Times* supposed or indeed the beginning of the end for Alzheimer's? Is this the game-changer that some suppose or are we still just ten minutes into the first half?'

The admirable Professor Hornberger replies almost immediately. 'I definitely think it is momentous. Yes, the clinical benefits of the drug are small and there are side-effects but it is the first time that a drug has been shown to change the disease trajectory of Alzheimer's. That in itself is momentous.

'The other important aspect is that this will now spur much more investment in future treatments for Alzheimer's disease, so overall I think it's very positive news — but we're still in the first ten minutes of the first half.'

26.

'VARIOUS FAILINGS OVER A PROLONGED PERIOD OF TIME'

The Professional Footballers' Association, originally the Association Footballers' and Trainers' Union, was formed in 1907 by Manchester United players Billy Meredith and Charlie Roberts after a team mate's sudden death during a reserve team match. Its aims included opposition to the maximum wage, then £4 a week.

Roberts, the club captain, was a Darlington lad who'd played Northern League football for Bishop Auckland, signed for United from Grimsby Town for a pretty astronomical £600, had won three England caps in 1905 though was never again invited to fly St George's flag after becoming part of the union.

Among other things he is remembered for defying the FA ruling that shorts should not be worn above the knee — Charlie's barely covered his midriff — and for standing for the local council as a Conservative.

Wretched coincidence, he was just 56 when he died in 1939, days after seven-hour brain surgery following 'extended dizzy spells'.

Meredith was a 48-times capped Welsh international who'd been suspended for a season for (unsuccessfully) trying to bribe one opponent and for a month for kicking lumps out of another. Neither action seemed overtly fraternal. During a long career, he was also noted for chewing on a toothpick during matches, though for reasons which may only be imagined.

We've heard quite a lot about the PFA thus far into the book, and it's to be hoped will hear more as caution's fetters loosen, though the Association has seldom been far from the news. As recently as 1997 Rachel Anderson, an agent to several Sheffield United players, was refused admission to the PFA's annual dinner on the fairly evident grounds that she was a woman. Told the following year that she would again be unwelcome, she successfully took legal action.

At the time that this chapter was drafted, however, there were what euphemists like to call communication difficulties. Compared to the FA, mark you, the Professional Footballers' Association may be a model of openness and promptitude. More of those Wembley gentlemen shortly.

For the moment, and as manifestly playing for time as a 93rd minute team with a single goal lead, a few reminders of things that in the book have already been said about the PFA. It should on no account be considered a charge sheet, though some might suppose it an indictment.

'I thought the PFA was fobbing us off. It was only when (my dad) went on television that they got back in touch. They sent us a booklet, mainly about knee replacements and things and advice on how to fill in forms. As if we hadn't filled in enough forms. They swatted us away like mosquitoes,' — Dany Robson.

'The PFA used the usual delaying tactics. Another one less for them to worry about. Sorry, but this stinks', — Chris Sutton after Jimmy Robson's death.

'We're gaining momentum but what we need is a lot more from the FA and PFA. Footballers should know the risks and there's a long way to go', — John Stiles.

'*The PFA has shown complete disregard and cowardice. I hope they are brought to book. They have shown no compassion,*'— Eileen Haselden, widow of former Rotherham and Doncaster Rovers player John Haselden.

'*It was like "You know, many people get dementia,*"'— Jane Beresford, daughter of Gordon Barrett.

The PFA Charity is wholly unfit for purpose and has lost the credibility any charity should have. The FA should form a new charity, very much based on making the game safer', — Dr Judith Gates.

My dad was always very supportive of the PFA and I think they've failed families and football participants in general. It wasn't an easy meeting,' — Dr Sally Tucker.

We would also have expected the FA to have been publicly hounded by the PFA whose key concern should be players' welfare. Over the past 20 years neither the FA nor the PFA has fought hard enough, or publicly enough, to address the issue within the broader football community', — the DCMS committee report on concussion in sport.

The PFA seems latterly much to have changed, been converted even, possibly as a result of something game-changing that happened on an away trip to Damascus. This from their website in December 2022: 'The PFA is committed to giving football families living with dementia the support they need, and making sure that they are not left alone and without help.'

And this: 'Our PFA family advisers will work closely with you and various dementia support specialists to build a strong network that gives you and your family emotional, practical and financial support to face dementia with dignity....The wellbeing of current and former professional footballers is our utmost priority.'

And this: 'We believe in the unifying power of football in society. We protect players' rights, represent their views and provide support through a wide variety of educational, financial and wellbeing services.'

If an application was for financial support, the website added, families would be asked to fill in a form....

For more than a third of its 115-year existence, the PFA was led by Gordon Taylor, a diminutive former winger with Bolton Wanderers and Birmingham City among others who was chairman 1978–81 and chief executive for 40 years thereafter — supposed on his Wikipedia page to have been the world's best paid trade union official. He retired in 2021, aged 76, with a salary and bonus package put at £3.1 million.

Taylor, in turn, claimed that the PFA had evolved into the best sporting trade union in the world.

In *A Delicate Game*, Hana-Walker Brown spoke to Dr Mike Sadler, who'd written to Gordon Taylor in 1994 expressing concern over possible links between repeatedly heading a ball and dementia and suggesting a study comparing footballers with members of the general public. Taylor's reply was 'fairly dismissive'.

In 1997, following a *Lancet* study into those links, Dr Sadler wrote to Taylor again. This time, Dr Sadler said he didn't receive a reply.

Taylor had been appointed OBE in 2008 and given the Association's annual merit award — 'services to football.'

Dawn Astle, Jeff's daughter, had campaigned since 2002, when a coroner ruled that her father had died from industrial disease, for greater awareness of — and action on — the risks of neurodegenerative disease among footballers. She believed that the PFA had not shared her passion.

She'd also been angered after discovering that a 10-year study along the lines that Dr Sadler had suggested — started in 2001 and funded by the FA and PFA — had quietly been abandoned after five years.

'I've lost all faith in the PFA's ability to protect its members when it comes to dementia,' she told the *Wolverhampton Express and Star* in March 2019. 'The PFA is meant to support them, the union whose very existence is about player welfare, but for me has completely failed in its duty.

'They have let my dad down, they've let my family down, and they've let football down. They should have been the ones who fought tooth and nail for the players. If their own union isn't going to do it, who is?'

The internet offers a 55-second video clip of a meeting between Astle and Taylor at the PFA's offices in which she tells him that the PFA should be 'screaming from the roof tops' for its members and Taylor pleads that they haven't 'a fraction' of the resources of the FA, Fifa, Premier League and Football League, swiftly adding that he's not 'passing a buck'. At which point Astle walks out.

Subsequently she told the media that the PFA wasn't 'entirely hopeless', just over dementia, and that she'd be happy to work from a new era. So, quite remarkably, events were to prove.

In February 2022 she became what the PFA website terms 'project lead for neurodegenerative disease in football,' joined as 'family support coordinator' by Rachel Walden whose father, former Portsmouth wing half Rod Taylor, had also been confirmed by Dr Willie Stewart to have suffered CTE. They were key members of a new 'brain health' department dedicated to the care of former players with dementia.

The pair, says the PFA website inarguably, are 'well placed to help you process a difficult diagnosis and offer an understanding ear.'

Maheta Molango, made PFA CEO in 2021, said in a media release that his first formal meeting as PFA chief executive had been with Dawn and Rachel. 'These were tough conversations. I understand that families had felt let down.'

Among other things about which the PFA had had tough conversations, and had to answer even tougher questions, was its relationship with the PFA Charity, said to be the trade union's 'charitable arm' and perhaps most vividly remembered for paying almost £2m in 1999 for LS Lowry's painting *Going to the Match* depicting crowds at Bolton Wanderers. It was sold for £6.6 million in 2022.

In September 2022 the Charity Commission issued an 'official warning' to the charity — 'slapped them' with it said the *Daily Mail* — by then renamed the Players' Foundation, and said no longer to be arms-length but (to paraphrase) somewhere at yon end of a lengthy barge pole. It followed a two-year statutory inquiry — 'the Commission's most serious intervention' — into the charity's activities, possible 'conflicts of interest' and whether the Charity's activities had been 'exclusively charitable and for the public benefit.'

'The public rightly expects charities to operate to the highest standards,' said Stephen Grenfell, the Commission's head of investigations, monitoring and enforcement.

The report's publication had been unsuccessfully opposed in a High Court action by four of the PFA Charity's trustees, who were ordered to pay costs. 'A bizarre move that many saw as an act of desperation,' said the *Daily Mail*.

The report considered that 'mismanagement' had been committed — 'various failings over a prolonged period of time' — in connection with the Charity from its incorporation in 2013 to the beginning of 2019, including the occupation of the charity's property by (unnamed) non-charitable entities to whom it had neither charged rent nor entered into leasing agreements. The failure to charge meant that the PFA Charity was deprived of £627,000 'which could otherwise have been applied to activities which furthered its purpose.'

The Charity had also become the vehicle with which PFA staff costs were met. 'The Commission has considered whether further regulatory action is necessary in relation to individual trustees and will take appropriate steps in that regard,' the report added.

In a statement in response, the PFA Charity said that no other charity had faced such scrutiny. 'Every aspect of our work has been under the magnifying glass. It has been hard for all involved but we welcome the findings and are proud of the work we have done over the past nine years.

'We have mixed emotions. We are pleased that the charity can now move on but are frustrated that this has been hanging over us for so long.'

Molango, the PFA's new chief executive, a Swiss labour lawyer and former footballer said to be fluent in five different languages, has spoken of focusing on what matters to players 'rather than internal turmoil, bickering and fighting.'

He has also talked of 'a new level of transparency,' a concept with which I've been having a bit of trouble. I emailed the PFA press office in October 2022, seeking an interview. It was acknowledged by Dr Adam White, recently appointed the Association's 'Head of brain health' after being executive director of the Concussion Legacy Foundation UK, which he founded, and a man clearly on-message.

After a report earlier in 2022 found 'conclusive evidence' of the link between repeated head impact and CTE, Dr White told the BBC that the subject deserved recognition in the global public health discussion of preventable disorders caused by childhood exposure in contact sports like football, rugby, ice hockey and others. Repeated head impacts should be addressed in the same way as other childhood concerns like smoking, alcohol and sunburn, he added.

Dr White asked me what the book would be about. Candidly — 'the PFA, it should be said, historically comes in for criticism' — I told him. He then declined further involvement and referred inquiries to Ben Simpson, a former trainee with Port Vale FC and now the PFA's head of communications.

Might it be possible, I asked Simpson, to arrange a chat both with Mr Molango and with Dawn Astle who, having once walked out, had walked, head high, back in.

Subsequent interaction proved difficult. Three separate voice-mail messages went unacknowledged. Shortly before Christmas, however, we were at last able to arrange a briefing at PFA offices in Manchester for a couple of weeks into the New Year. Who said that January was always an anti-climax?

27.

'CERTAINLY THERE SEEMS TO BE RECENT HISTORY BETWEEN HEAD FOR CHANGE AND THE PFA'

Though the Professional Footballers' Association has a reputation for affluence, if not necessarily for opulence, first impressions of its offices in a quiet courtyard in central Manchester are distinctly proletarian.

Outside is a board identifying sundry other closely related companies and one of those little keypads which offer access to the initiated. Others, those without, must rattle a big brass knocker. I'm reminded of Scrooge's nephew, coming calling on Christmas morning.

The foyer's tiny, seating of the sort found in a railway waiting room (second class), deliveries dumped unopened across the few square feet of floorspace. The walls, here and elsewhere, offer football-themed artwork, often relating to the 1966 World Cup finals and often signed.

It's coincidental that, at the very hour I'm seeing Ben Simpson, a meeting of the International Football Association Board (IFAB) is taking place at Wembley to discuss the trial sanctioning of temporary concussion substitutes — a proposal supported both by the

FA and PFA — allowing a replacement while a player with a potentially serious head injury is medically assessed in the dressing room.

Without that protocol, it's claimed, the temptation is to play on and risk a second and more serious impact. If deemed fit, the player could return within ten minutes. As things stand, any substitution must be permanent. They expect a decision, a crucial issue, by 12.30pm.

The briefing, it's been made clear, is off the record (and so it will remain). In turn I several times express the ambition of an in-person and on-the-record interview with PFA people, particularly (again) Maheta Molango and Dawn Astle, though it would be interesting to include Dr White, too.

Ben's personable, amiable, knowledgeable and cautious. We meet in a conference room which may well have been the one from which Dawn Astle so memorably walked out on Gordon Taylor. I don't ask, nor notice — myopia again — if there's blood on the walls alongside the framed prints of glory days.

The morning's papers have been full of warnings — from a 'top health tsar', the warnings may also have been slapped — about the danger of bringing in cake to work. Ben apologises — sorry, should this be off the record? — but they've no cake. Nor coffee. Nor milk. Judith Gates would have had a caramel wafer mountain the height and breadth of the Cairngorms. Perhaps it can also be revealed that Ben's an Everton supporter and right now feeling pretty pessimistic.

On his laptop there's a 19-page briefing document which, for reasons of myopia not confidentiality, I'm unable to read. He promises to send it, partly a history detailing the Association's dementia-related research backing throughout the 21st Century.

It should in fairness be said that, in 2018, a group of senior medics based at the Nuffield Hospital in Leeds had written to the PFA in support of its then chief executive. 'We have known Mr

Taylor and his work for many years and he has at all times been helpful and considerate.

'The media coverage will, we feel, have caused distress to Mr Taylor and perhaps some anxiety among members of your Council. Hence our letter of sincere and deep support for him.'

The PFA had nonetheless conceded possible shortcomings in its evidence to the DCMS inquiry into concussion in sport — the one which expressed such surprise at its inaction. 'The PFA has always endeavoured to give the families the best support possible but we are not immune to criticism and are working hard to improve our service in this area,' they said.

'We had received public criticism from families who had accessed PFA support, where it was clear that the overall experience and the type of help they received had fallen short of expectations.'

Submitted in spring 2021, the Association's evidence showed a near-vertiginous rise in members who had died with a neurodegenerative diagnosis 2016–2020 — eight in 2015, five in 2017, 37 in 2020. They were aware, it said, of 275 members who had had a neurodegenerative diagnosis of whom 144 had died. They wanted to see reduced heading in training and rest periods between heading training sessions.

'The players' union believes in using the power of football to effect positive societal change and operates by the principle of caring for the interests of the game as a whole. The PFA and the PFA Charity have always been committed to a duty of care for all past, current and future members. The union has lobbied the football authorities to join with us on all aspects of health and safety in the game.'

There seemed, nonetheless, to be recent history — *frisson* at best, *froideur* at worst — between Head for Change and PFA. I try to assure Ben that I'm impartial, that the trade union's input into the book is an essential part of the narrative and not of the argument, that it's not an attempt to make them a sort of unisex Aunt Sally. Trust me, I'm a journalist.

We adjourn for a beer in the Britons Protection, a classic old pub barely 200 yards away which, ironically, is itself under threat. Ben insists upon paying, his phone on the table awaiting news — 'white smoke' he hopes, as might crowds outside the Sistine Chapel — from the meeting at Wembley.

Ben had himself been in London the day previously, facilitating recorded broadcast interviews — many of them with Dr White — offering alternative opinions dependent upon the outcome. It's how it works.

We part equally amicably — no smoke, no ire — but when the news comes, it's not good at all. Though the temporary concussion subs trial was supported not just by the FA and PFA but by players' bodies worldwide, it's been rejected by IFAB. 'No consensus could be reached,' says a statement; red rage billows with the black smoke.

Chris Sutton, never far from the back pages of the *Daily Mail,* labels IFAB the International Federation of Absolute Buffoons and calls for the players themselves to speak out. 'Their families will be the ones suffering further down the line and asking why they didn't put the players' safety first. The players have the power. Why aren't they using it?'

No less relentless, John Stiles in the *Telegraph* goes further, calling upon players to withdraw their labour in support of temporary concussion subs. 'If the players had a proper union they would be threatening to strike. If your health was being put at risk in any other industry, you would be talking about strike action. The model is broken.'

Judith Gates emails a simple message: 'We know that "second impact syndrome" is a significant danger if players experience further blows before recovering from a symptomatic concussion. Precautionary measures are needed — we wholly support the introduction of temporary concussion substitutes to allow a more detailed examination before return to play and we recognise that clubs may be reluctant to use the existing protocol, which provides for permanent concussion substitutes, because the player would not be allowed to return to the game.'

The Times gives it all a single paragraph, interred beneath a report of IFAB action (or otherwise) on extending the time that the ball's in play and on the video assistant referee, vaunted and oft-haunted.

On the record or off it, it remains to be seen if there'll be further word from the PFA and for how long the breath must be held.

28.

'WE'VE HAD THE AGITATIONS AND THE OBSESSIONS. NOW HE'S HAPPY AND SAFE. THAT'S SUCH A RELIEF TO US ALL'

Both physically and figuratively it seems important not to lose sight of Bill Gates, the now-unwitting instigator of the great cognitive crusade. The day gloomily foreshadowed, the weather appropriately lachrymose, he'd moved into the dementia care wing of the Middleton Hall Retirement Village near Teesside Airport on November 15th 2022.

At home, it had reluctantly been concluded, his safety could no longer be assured — not even with full-time carers. In the dementia wing, described as state-of-the-art, residents' movements are tagged. 'He seems settled here,' says Judith. 'We've had the agitations and the obsessions. Now he's happy and safe. That's such a relief to us all.'

Back in Castle Eden, she'd sat in Bill's accustomed place. 'I couldn't bear to sit opposite his empty chair,' she says.

Middleton Hall had asked her to write a potted biography of the Brasso-bright entrepreneur and tireless globe trotter, maybe a page, in order that they might sit down with Bill and know him better. 'Have you been abroad?' they asked. 'How long have you got?' said Judith.

Now it's early February 2023, the papers a couple of days earlier carrying the results of a 25-year study among 15,000 people by the Universities of Oxford and Exeter showing that even mild or occasional blows to the head in early life can lead to dementia many years later.

'These findings should send a clear message to policy makers and sporting bodies,' said Dr Susan Kohlhaus, research director of Alzheimer's Research UK. 'They need to put robust guidelines in place to reduce the risk of head injury as much as possible.'

I'm at Middleton Hall a few minutes before Judith is, prudently required by a pleasant young lady called Chloe to take a lateral flow test or some such Covid caution, these days (happily) not at the back of the throat but by shoving something akin to a raspberry Mivvi stick up a nostril. It's negative.

It's 11.45am and Bill's not long been up, late breakfast in danger of overflowing into 1pm lunch. Inevitably he appears further diminished, shrunk into himself. If he recognises me he is incapable either of acknowledging or articulating it. Not even the thought that at Middleton Hall it's fish and chip Friday — or the suggestion that, as all those years ago at Dean Bank, there might be scraps — seems able to animate him.

His room's spacious, thoughtfully and doubtless thoroughly equipped, a Middlesbrough FC shirt — 'Gates 5' — framed on the wall next to what's reckoned the biggest television in the place. From the patio window are extensive views of the grounds and, particularly, of the resident hen house and its incumbent pecking order. There'd been hens in Dean Bank, too. Judith had visited other care facilities but knew what she wanted. 'Bill had spent all his life among great views and open spaces. In some of the other places he'd have been looking at a wall.'

A couple of female fellow residents, chatting in a corridor, prove to be Middlesbrough supporters from former times. They remember Bill — 'Ah yes' says one, 'he played with John Hickton.' John Hickton was a centre forward. Centre forwards always were the fans' favourites.

Then Judith arrives, addresses him as 'William' and as 'honey', tidies his hair, pats his arm, kisses his cheek, produces from the sort of copious handbag of which Lady Bracknell would have been envious a great catalogue of mounted photographs of happy times past, each carrying a large-print caption. Visibly, he brightens.

One's a picture of Bill with a Seychelles tortoise. 'Put your thumbs up if you think the tortoise is the best looking,' says Judith. Slowly, the thumbs turn towards the sun. Another image is of the sumptuous dining room, half the size of a football pitch, of their friends' 120ft yacht off Cayman. Their own boat was called *Harry C*, after Harry Curry, her father. 'It was much smaller than that,' insists Judith.

A third photograph shows Bill and a former Middlesbrough team mate. Judith asks him who they are. 'Me and Spraggon,' says Bill, accurately. They're the first words he's spoken — memory's embers, maybe, but adroitly and affectionately stirred.

Ten months ago Bill would walk obsessively, if erratically. Now he shuffles behind a walking frame, when able to fathom — an understandable difficulty — which way round it goes. The day previously, their son Nick had taken his dad for a walk in his wheelchair around the Hall's 'stunning' 45-acre grounds.

The retirement village also has a fully equipped gym, a spectacular swimming pool, restaurant, library, community allotment, art studio, photography group. bird hide and goodness knows what else. 'Stunning,' it might in passing be added, has in recent times seemed an idly and inaccurately used adjective, and never more than on this occasion.

On this Friday afternoon there are three of us in the relationship, as the late Princess of Wales almost said, though Bill's vocabulary is greatly limited and his cognition uncertain. Was it football, sport, which so comprehensively extinguished that once-incandescent flame?

Just the day previously, someone had sent a team photograph of Spennymoor United, 1974–75, to which Bill had briefly returned after ending his Middlesbrough career. Back then the Gates family had lived in Marske-by-the-Sea. 'There was an end-of-season party, we got a bus party up,' recalled former Moors team mate Brian Mulligan. 'He'd never drink alcohol himself, but there were some great parties at Bill's.'

We talk without response of Dean and Chapter colliery and of his dad's prize vegetables, of his energetic years as chairman of Saltburn Round Table and of the time he did a sponsored bike ride with Jimmy Savile. Perhaps it's just as well he can't remember that bit.

Judith also recalls that, like their elder son, both Bill and his own father had been born five months into their parents' marriage. 'I think we must be genetically disposed to it,' she adds, memorably.

Visitors have perks, too. I leave with a big box of raspberry Mivvi sticks, or their pharmaceutical equivalent. 'Next time you're coming,' says the charming Chloe, 'just shove one up your nose first.'

Judith and I head off to a nearby pub for our own lunch, another Fish Friday. We discuss the possibility of the FA or PFA ever doing what they've said they'll do, admire Middleton Hall and its people, try mutually not to mention momentum. Thereafter she's headed back to Castle Eden remotely to lead a gathering of H4C's support group for those similarly afflicted. Earlier that day she'd been in another remote conversation, discussing H4C's social media strategy with students from Teesside University. It's good to keep busy, she says.

29.

'THE CONVERSATIONS THEY'RE HAVING IN RUGBY THEY WERE HAVING IN BOXING 100 YEARS AGO'

The four-star Lancaster House Hotel, not unreasonably styled 'de-luxe,' is on that northern city's southern outskirts, near the M6 and the university sports centre. Outside it, 4.45pm on a grey Wednesday in February, Alix Popham and friends are unloading their kit after the third day of a 450-mile sponsored cycle ride from Cardiff to Edinburgh. They've earned their rest tonight.

They're riding for Head for Change, the aim to raise funds and awareness — 'much needed funds' says the publicity — and to reach the Murrayfield stadium in time for Saturday's Six Nations rugby match between Scotland and Wales. Each is meeting their own expenses.

The Just Giving page puts the target at £50,000. By the time that they reach Lancaster, around half way in mileage, they've not realised a tenth of the anticipated income.

The brochure produced to accompany the indomitable cyclists lists the Murrayfield match as part of the day six schedule: 'Watch Wales smash Scotland' it says. 'Vans back to Dalmahoy. Out for a curry.' No scraps.

It's now nearly three years since Alix, himself capped 33 times by Wales, was diagnosed with early onset dementia, believed to be the outcome of more than 100,000 sub-concussive impacts while a professional rugby player. This is the guy, of course, who 20 miles out on a greatly familiar cycle route had completely forgotten the way home. 'That was just one moment,' he insists.

In the brochure, Mel, his wife, recalls diagnosis day. 'That weekend I lurched from disbelief to fear, from anger to feeling numb. The tears started and they didn't stop. How could this be happening to us? We had such big plans for our future together.'

Now it would be impossible to tell that he's unwell, a slight stiffness in the gait wholly generated by the day's 64-miler from Warrington. 'It's sitting down that's the only really hard bit,' says the saddlesore cyclist.

The 'alternative' treatment — mentioned in Chapter 14, undertaken abroad and subject of non-disclosure agreements — remains 'very positive, very exciting,' Alix adds. Six other former players, similarly diagnosed, are now undergoing the same therapy.

He's joined on the ride by Gordon Barclay, Clive Hamilton, Shaun Chard, Gavin Evans, Brian Edwards, Dai Mathias and Gareth Passey, Gavin said to have done his best to get out of it by selling his bike and refusing to answer phone calls. They're great lads, all of them.

Gordon, known universally as Porty because of his birthplace in Portobello, an upper crust suburb of Edinburgh, is the only non-Welshman. A former Metropolitan Police officer, he now lives in Swansea. 'There's no way in a month of Sundays I could afford to go back to Portobello,' he says. So what of Saturday's match? 'Let's just wait and see,' he says, as canny as Scots can be....

They're joined as back-up by Jon Prince. Joel Bramwell and by Aimee Mathias, Dai's daughter, who's i/c sustenance and thus the equivalent of a ministering angel. The lunchtime fajitas were indeed manna from heaven, they agree, the fourth day thought of cawl — a Welsh lamb broth — yet more potentially invigorating.

'They don't do cockaleekie,' says Porty, wistfully.

The guys head inside to shower, to hot tub, perhaps just to collapse in a heap. There seems little need for the Lancaster House's fitness suite nor for the advertised opportunity to 'Stretch with Natalie.' These boys, goodness knows, are being stretched enough as it is.

They're upstairs for getting on 60 minutes, happy hour turned damn-near ecstatic, chance below to have a closer look at the brochure. There's a page headed 'You know you're from Wales when....' — You support any team that plays against England, you know exactly who Aneurin Bevan was and what he's famous for, conversations with Indian call centre workers don't end well — and there are the words of both the Welsh national anthem and something called *Calon Lan* which, apparently, comes off the bench when needed.

Alix and Dai are first down, glowing like an advert for a Badedas bath, looking no wearier than if they'd had a tea time dander along the Lancaster Canal towpath. Dai had joined Alix and other Welsh rugby players on a charity bike ride in 2016, got in touch with him again after hearing of his dementia diagnosis. Dai and Porty had also joined a ride from Edinburgh to Cardiff in 2020 in aid of the Doddie Weir Motor Neurone Disease Foundation, just 30 miles from the Principality Stadium when they heard that Covid had claimed the match.

When the 2023 ride was mooted, Dai contacted Alix seeking his support. 'I never expected him to ride it as well though, knowing Alix, I should have done,' he says. 'I thought it was only going to be a small event, very informal,' says Alix.

We'd last encountered him, of course, at the 'no heading' football match at Spennymoor in September, chaffed him for coming off with what appeared little more than a kick in the calamities. It proved to be a torn Achilles. 'The surgeon said it wasn't bad enough to operate but I was in a moon boot for six weeks. Horrendous. I was walking round like a dinosaur,' he says.

Dai's an experienced and accomplished cyclist, has three times pedalled across America, organised this one. 'It's still early days for Head for Change,' he says, 'but the biggest thing is education, letting youngsters in schools and rugby clubs know what the risks are, trying for more safety.

'The conversations they're having in rugby they were having in boxing 100 years ago; boxing is light years ahead of rugby. If you get knocked out in boxing you're stood down for at least 30 days, in rugby you can be back in a week without missing a game.'

Momentum, the murmured, perhaps misrepresented m-word? 'I think there is momentum but we're now at the stage where governing bodies are reluctant to do anything because of all the legal stuff that's going on. Not much is going to change while they're awaiting the outcome.'

Alix agrees. 'At the moment it's a game of chess between the lawyers and the governing bodies and it could go on for years. It's the lawyers who are controlling things now. There's a lot more to come out yet.'

He gives a similar quote to the *Mail on Sunday* a couple of days later, though the Sabbath paper is also able to reveal that he loves haggis and is looking forward to a haggis and bacon sandwich at journey's end.

Others join the group in hotel reception, a wintry dusk enfolding but spring very much in their steps. Most seem to drink something called Guinness Zero. They're not out drastically to change the game of rugby, they collectively insist: 90 per cent of the head damage results from long months of incessant training.

Dai points out that the NFL in America, perhaps brought to its concussive senses by successful legal action, now only plays four months a year. Rugby players might play and train for 11 months a year. It can't go on like that, he says.

It's coincidental that, while they've been on the road, probably somewhere atop the Brecon Beacons, Dr Ann McKee — a neuropathologist who is director of the Chronic Traumatic

Encephalopathy Center at Boston University — revealed that of the brains of 376 former NFL players which had been analysed after death, 345, 91.8 per cent, had CTE. Her department, she said ruefully, had 'no relationship' with the NFL.

Gareth Passey's down with the kids, too, looks so fresh he might simply have been playing carpet bowls. He runs a timber business, reacts amiably to my wife's suggestion that there might be a profitable sideline in wooden clothes props, says that he'll see her on *Dragons' Den*. Red Dragons' Den, presumably.

Then he becomes more serious. 'It's not just the game, it's training three or four days a week. There are so many collisions. You need to look after people so much better. It's crazy. They went over to professional level rugby and they didn't know how to handle it. It's day in, day out. Where's the duty of care? It beggars belief what's going on inside players' heads. If a player has concussion he needs to be out, and looked after, for a much longer period of time.'

Dai agrees: 'I talk to a lot of people about rugby and they're living in the dark ages. Rugby has always been seen as a sport of gladiators but they're not gladiators any longer. Most are just ordinary men and women who want to enjoy a game. We're not trying to do away with rugby, we're trying to make it better, make it safer.'

And Porty: 'In the Met we'd commend officers for doing stupid things, like chasing around on a roof. It's like that in rugby — you make a really stupid, really dangerous tackle and everyone says it's great. We need to influence the decision makers.'

And Jon: 'In boxing you have to have a medical certificate. A licence before every fight. In rugby you can just move around between clubs — no MoT test, no records, just play on. I watched the Steve Thompson documentary and just thought 'Oh God, what happens next?'

And Shaun: 'You have to change the culture, to say it's all right not to want to play on if you've had a concussion, to say it's all right not to be all right.'

And Clive: 'We all think we're bullet proof, don't we? I suppose Alix is evidence that we're not.'

What of the extraordinary Alix Popham? Physically and metaphorically, what gets him back on the bike? 'I think there's just a certain part of his character, the family, which is indomitable,' says Joel, his brother-in-law. 'He just has this spirit, this desire to compete and to win. When the diagnosis came it was shocking, but the way that Alix has dealt with it has been brilliant. I think he sees Head for Change as part of his long-term legacy, his whole focus just now. If some good comes out of it all then it will have been worth all the effort. If there's a miracle even better.'

And if you think Alix is driven, everyone agrees, then you really should see his wife. Back home near Newport, Mel Bramwell-Popham had dropped their daughter Darcy at Langstone primary school, where staff and children had been covering the 450 miles on static bikes. She's then headed into London to spend a few hours in the office, then returned to collect Darcy. If you think Alix is driven....

She'd written in the brochure that, having recovered from the initial shock, they determined not to accept the prognosis and the five-to-ten year management plan. 'We had to find a way. Alix has never been average at anything in life and he wasn't going to be an average stat with this.... We decided to make it my life's mission to find a miracle and keep Alix here as long as possible.

'From that moment forward, Alix and I let go of any anger. We can't change the past but we can change the future....We needed to help protect current and future players, to prevent any others being in Alix's situation in years to come and we wanted to do it in a way that would protect the game we both still love.'

Alix next plans an Iron Man event. Then there's a Channel swimming relay — rugby union against rugby league — and a sponsored cycle ride from London to Lyon in time for the Rugby World Cup. He states what looks pretty obvious: 'I feel good.'

So the conversation drifts back to *Delilah,* an admittedly improbable choice for an anthem, though it could just as easily warn of the Lorelei, luring the unwary perhaps even the idiotic, towards the rocks. 'Why, why, why' shriek one hundred tabloid headlines, outraged at the perceived treachery. 'It'll just be ridiculed, won't it?' says Dai.

Shaun says that he and his wife spent half an evening discussing it. 'There are probably 344 more important things (his estimate) for the Welsh Rugby Union to be discussing and they end up pulling the plug on *Delilah.*' 'It's a diversionary tactic and it's going to fail,' says Shaun. 'You know what'll happen don't you? The boys will just sing it even louder.'

The band of brothers, great guys attended by a ministering angel, head off for dinner around 7.30pm. The Lancaster House doesn't do cawl (or, for that matter, haggis and bacon sandwiches.) The hardest bit, they concur, is getting back on the bike next day.

The following morning they're off on the 78-mile leg to Carlisle, 4,500ft of climbing through the Lake District, Alix said particularly to enjoy the ascents. On the fifth day they'll be crossing the border — rain, wind and fog arriving almost on cue as they head towards Edinburgh.

By the end of the road the Just Giving page has clocked £6,740, a few days later stood at £8,440. Perhaps accustomed generosity has been affected by a similar and simultaneous ride for Doddie Weir charities, perhaps by the UK's magnificent response to the earthquake that week, in Turkey and Syria. They're hugely grateful, nonetheless. 'Awareness' says Alix. 'Awareness'.

It doesn't end happily. Wales are thrashed (smashed?) 35–7. A couple of days later, Welsh rugby players join much of the rest of Britain in threatening to go on strike for a better pay deal. The best are on £400,000 a year, plus bonuses for actually winning. There's no talk of danger money. However temporarily, the situation's resolved.

30.

'IT'S A SPACE WHERE WE CAN SAY WHAT WE WANT WITHOUT JUDGEMENT. WE DON'T HAVE TO BE GOOD GIRLS BEING BRAVE'

Described as a 'virtual coffee meeting,' Head for Change runs online support sessions called Extra Time to Talk for wives, partners and family of those with sport-related neurodegenerative disease. The H4C website talks of 'coping strategies', though it seems a sharing strategy, too.

They're talking this afternoon, what might be supposed a stream of consciousness — raw, honest, sometimes emotional and with little attempt by the eavesdropping author to get a word in, not even edgeways.

I join the Zoom meeting with the consent of all, led by Dr Judith Gates and joined by four others — three in the UK and a fourth in the USA. 'My ladies' Judith calls them, as might the county president of the Women's Institute.

Judith is not feeling at all well. Taking a short break in Florida — much needed — she has copped at once for Covid, barks rather than coughs, feels (she says) about 95 but holds it together, nonetheless.

The group, she reminds us all, is an opportunity to discuss the reality of living with sport-related neurodegenerative disease. 'One of the greatest satisfactions I have from it is the message from members that they certainly aren't alone any more. It's a space where we can say what we want without judgement. We don't have to be good girls who are being brave.

'I've described the group as football's heroines — and forgive me for being a bit emotional, because I'm not very well — because they're the ones who are in the front line, dealing on a day-to-day basis with what it's like, with all the issues around responsibility and guilt and all of that.'

Though lightly edited for reasons of clarity, brevity or privacy, what follows is pretty much a word-for-word account of a teatime conversation in February 2023.

Caroline:

'I actually live here in the USA. Originally, obviously, I'm from England. My husband, Bob, has Alzheimer's but he was also a professional soccer player, football player, for a couple of years in his youth.

'We're going through a really, really tough phase at the moment. Bob has aphasia, or dysphasia, which is getting gradually worse so communication is now extremely difficult which is frustrating on all levels for everybody. The agitation is increasing, he thinks that somehow he's in England,

'He was actually managing to verbalise that he wanted to sign up and play football again, for Grimsby. That verbalisation has gone. He can't actually say that's what he wants to do but we think that's what he wants to do. He goes through his papers and his box. He wants to get out. I've had to drive him around a few times, just for a little peace. He went for a CT scan last week because the decline is just like a snowball, it's getting bigger and going faster and faster and, like I say, he can't verbalise that now. He's just getting more agitated.

'He goes to a day centre which has a pool table. Each time I've picked him up he's been playing pool on his own, and he was a really good pool player. He's playing pool his way, he just hits any of the balls against each other, it's not correct. As soon as we get home he's really agitated, it's almost as if he's on a bit of a high, stimulation. He wants to go straight out again. The agitation at the moment is just really, really hard to deal with. From the first thing in the morning he's just agitated, says things are ridiculous and I say what's ridiculous?

'While he's in the bathroom I've started putting toothpaste on his toothbrush because otherwise he's refusing to clean his teeth. He was shaving, he had an obsession with shaving two or three times a day but now we've gone back to refusing to shave, refusing to shower. Then we go downstairs, he tries to put the television on but he can't work the remotes. He'll watch the news for a little bit while he has his coffee but then he starts rummaging around.

'Judith, you know the memory box with the photograph albums and the scrapbook. We've gone from looking through that to him not letting anyone look through it. He just wants it there, in view. He's started going through the drawers, going through my papers, rummaging around. He can't tell you what he's looking for or doing.

'Then there's Alexa: I've discovered that I can put it on from my phone because what's happening is he comes upstairs and whereas before he would say Alexa play — I won't say it because she'll start singing — he just sits in the chair and looks at it and gets annoyed and then I say you have to tell her that you want her to play whatever. Now when he comes upstairs I have to go on my phone and play something, so that it's automatically playing when he gets up there. He might sing a little bit but he can't even sing the right words now. He'll sing the tune but the words aren't correct. That language centre is really struggling at the moment.

'I'm a nurse, I'm OK with washing and all of that stuff. It's just the frustration. I'm going to be 60 in September and my daughters want me to go back to England for a break.

(Someone else talking) 'I've had a month. You get back to being a person for a while.'

'He can still say eff-off which he's never done all his life and that's ridiculous. It's just frustration, you know, but it's so hard. All those books which say don't get into confrontation, don't argue with them...it's impossible to do when you don't know what they're saying. I'm saying 'I'm not sure,' 'I don't know,' but he's getting annoyed with me because he thinks he's having a conversation. It's obviously not the right answer to whatever is going through his brain. It's so frustrating. I can't fill in the gaps any more. All I do now is just hug him and kiss him and that's the only thing I know how to do because it's awful. He's like pushing me away, he does the swatting motions. It's, you know, it's tough.'

Tina White:

'My husband Goff played football across seven leagues, semi-pro, had a lot of concussions. He was a prolific header of the ball, started being weird probably five to seven years ago. It took a long time to get diagnosed but he's got probable CTE and dementia.

'Goff always had a temper but he never hit me. Last Friday I had a cry day. I just cried. My son was here and he obviously hugged me and I said 'I just want my Goffy back.' We've had some workers here and they've been brilliant with him. I think he really enjoyed male company. We haven't had much shouting this week.

'I've managed to get him in the shower but he doesn't know how to wash, so I've like squirted the shower gel all over him and then I sort of do this dance outside to show him all the bits he's got to wash. I told him if you think I'm doing that dance every day you're joking. We had some

children's picture cards, one saying I love you. He said it. That was nice, you don't get much niceness these days.'

Goff wanders in, almost out of camera shot. 'Do you want to come to say hello to my ladies?' asks Tina. Goff says Hi.

'I've had breast cancer through all of this but when I rang social services for help they said Goff wasn't bad enough and they wouldn't give me any help. I've finally got someone in for a couple of hours.'

Pauline Blant:

'My husband is Colin, he's been a professional footballer for many years. I don't know when he started really but you look back and think probably there were symptoms many, many years ago. He has been diagnosed with Alzheimer's and vascular whatever and goodness knows what. He was a central defender so I think the evidence is there that he's probably got it through heading the ball.

'Two weeks ago on a Sunday.... I run a bath for Colin and then I wake him up. So I said come on, your bath's ready, I said hurry up and get in the bath and he said he wasn't having a bath. I said yes you are, I thought we're not having that one, so I got behind the door (to stop him getting out). He was trying to move me, physically move me out of the way. It went on for a good hour and a half.

'The bath was cold by the time he got in. I thought what am I going to do if this is the situation, knowing that could be the next stage of his journey. So the next day I emailed Adam White and David Ryan (both of the PFA). I thought I had nothing to lose, what could I do? I had a little bit of backwards and forwards with emails and eventually David Ryan asked me if I wanted him to come up. So I said yes.

'He's one of the family liaison officers, apparently he's got 90 families. He came up on Wednesday, he was very nice. He had lunch with us and asked what support we needed. He did get back to me with what he'd

written down and what he was forwarding to Adam, Dawn and Rachel. It was nice to have that kind of visit and put a name to a face. Whether anything materialises I don't know.

'I have noticed a big deterioration in Colin. He's extremely verbally aggressive. He doesn't do anything really. He likes to go to the coast but that ties me up to a 45-minute drive, maybe an hour there and 45 minutes back, by which time he's tired and goes to bed. He can actually stay in bed until the next morning, unless I go up and ask him to come down for something to eat.

'It's very lonely. It's just like living with the shell of the person he was. I can only see it getting worse. He doesn't make sense when he speaks, he's not interested in anything. He forgets that he's eaten, an hour after breakfast he'll have a jam sandwich. He's never been like that, he's never been a grazer. I just want him back, I really don't know who this person is I'm living with. I just feel that I'm a carer and when we had the bathroom incident I thought I can't do it but he wouldn't want a young person looking after him, a carer. I just feel trapped. It's hard to see how these men are going through their final years but on a plus point I did get answers from the PFA.

'I think I rubbed Adam up a little bit the wrong way because I really said that they were just waiting for these men to die. He tried to reassure me that that certainly wasn't the case but what evidence is there otherwise?'

(Judith Gates) 'You've had years of no response, haven't you?'

Pauline: 'Absolutely, or absolutely ridiculous responses. When I did ask for help they said they'd send him to this day centre but it was absolutely not suitable for Colin. I was honest, I said look, I'm going to the newspapers about it. He was a nice enough guy, to be fair.'

Linda Tucker — Dr Sally's mum:

My husband Bill played professional football for more than 15 years. He started showing symptoms when he was about 59. I thought he was just being a grumpy old man but it turns out that he has dementia. He was a prolific header of a football, a central defender.

I've had a long journey. Obviously he was very aggressive, changed from a very easy going gentle person to someone who banged his head on the walls, made holes in the walls, slapped his head, and attacked me several times. Some of that has settled but he's still slapping his head quite a lot. He doesn't bang it off the walls any more. He'll still go for me at certain times. He can't express himself in any way really. Even when he says yes, he doesn't know what he's saying yes or no to.

You have to try to gauge whether he's in pain or not. In the last six weeks he's been doubly incontinent which is another downhill trend. He has gone downhill and he's also not sleeping very much. He wouldn't go to bed again last night. He just walks around the house, he goes in the kitchen, he sorts all the food out, I have to shop daily, really, because I can't leave anything lying around. I did leave an avocado to get ripe and next morning there were big teeth marks where he'd bitten into it. He obviously didn't like it and he'd put it back down again.

It's quite difficult. I'm very lucky in that I do get respite, 15 hours for Bill and 11 hours for me. It's going up to 21 hours for Bill and 15 for me but to try to get a week of respite has been an absolute nightmare. It got to the point where Swindon Borough Council asked if I would write to the PFA and ask if they would pay. I said they had to write not me, and gave them numbers and emails. The response which she had this week was that the Players' Foundation is a charity and while they strive to support the beneficiaries of the charity with provision of equipment they were afraid that they were unable to meet respite or care costs.

They are there really to make sure that they don't pay out, as far as I'm concerned. We managed to get some help from the PFA when Gordon Taylor was there, in fact it was probably best when Gordon Taylor was there in that respect because if you wanted some respite every week he would make sure you got some help with that. This new one that's come in now, they've taken it all away. They say help should be given by the local council but trying to get an answer from the local council is an absolute nightmare. I've been trying since April 2021 and we're now coming up to April 2023 and we're still not sorted.

They keep telling me I need to have a week off and they will give me, with my contribution, £640 a week. I just threw it back at them and said you find me a care home that will take him for £640 and they can't.

As regards Bill there's nothing left of him really. It's not just that he looks older, obviously, We don't get any conversation. I've taken him for a walk today, he's now started walking directly behind me rather than just to the side and the back. It's like caring for this stranger who you don't know and I don't particularly like him the way he is. It's very rare to get a smile out of him. In fact the carers get more smiles.

It's very, very sad, but it's very hard to get any support. The nearest care centre is Devizes, which is about 40 miles away, so I've got no chance. The local MP has said they've got a new integrated care board.... The care they offer when you come out of hospital is four half-hour sessions a day which is no use whatsoever for anyone with dementia. They could be flexible but they choose not to be. I think you're just up against it all the time and you shouldn't have to be. It's hard enough dealing with what they've got without having to hit your head against a brick wall every day.

He's got three pensions and two of them they've completely taken, his state pension and one of his smaller ones. I'm left with a portion of the other one which isn't sufficient to pay all the bills for the whole year. The money will run out. I have to pay all the bills, the total amount. You have to fight to get the care that you want and not the care that they want to give you. You have to fight for everything. The unfortunate thing is that the rules aren't the same all over the country.

None of the four has any doubt that their husbands' neurode-generative disease is a direct result of many years, day-in-day-out, repetitively heading a football. A power cut curtails some pretty horrific stories — and more graphic details, more lived experiences, arrive in the following days.

31.

'IT'S SO SAD THAT FOOTBALL WAS HIS PASSION AND IS NOW THE CAUSE OF HIS DEMISE'

I'd simply asked for a couple of biographical snippets. Pauline Blant, Tina White and Linda Tucker responded with very much more, graphic and oft-harrowing detail of what life's like when lived with someone with dementia and, very likely, CTE.

The accounts are abridged, chiefly when they overlap what was said in the Zoom meeting, but perhaps help explain why the momentum, and the manifest need for change, seems ever to increase.

Colin Blant, born in Lancashire in October 1946, was a well-travelled central defender whose clubs over a 16-year career ranged from Portsmouth to Workington and from Burnley to Darlington. Never a superstar, he was often described as 'workmanlike'. frequently as 'dependable'. That was then.

Pauline's email begins with thanks for taking the time to find out about the 'forgotten footballers' and about the 'terrible later years' when neurological illness ever more insidiously encroaches:

We were never ever informed that he was at any risk of developing this disease due to his career. I feel this is negligent, morally wrong and gross misconduct from many in football.

For many years we as a family tried to ignore the signs of brain damage, the main symptoms being forgetfulness, a lack of self-esteem and a lack of self-awareness. Eventually we could ignore it no more — getting the diagnosis was the worst day of our lives. What we would have given for the tests to be wrong.

Colin depends upon me and our daughter, Ashleigh, to try to keep him active and give him some quality of life. At times we still get glimpses of the husband and father we love very much. Sadly, these times are becoming fewer and fewer. Colin may have been aggressive on the pitch but off it he was calm, joyful and happy-go-lucky. He never ever displayed those horrible behaviours towards me and my daughter.

Pauline then describes a typical day, including the bathroom problems earlier outlined. He can't shower because of 'sensory' problems — 'for example he lacks the understanding of why you can't put a plug in when showering.' What she's trying to point out, says Pauline, is that ensuring her husband keeps his standards up is extremely difficult.

After trips to the coast he might head, fully clothed, for bed, first hiding his wallet in 'strange' places. Sometimes he won't get up again. 'This means that he will get up later at night or in the early hours of the morning. Sometimes he hallucinates or imagines that someone is in the house. He then proceeds to look for them — completely disturbing me and I find it so hard to calm him down.

'Sometimes he imagines that there is an animal, or a bird, trapped beneath the bed. He then upturns the bed. When I try to explain that there is no one or no creature he insists that there is and can be very verbally abusive. Eventually he will calm down and go back to bed. The next morning he is again difficult and starts searching for his wallet, completely upsetting drawers and cupboards. When I ask him to stop he resorts to abusive, aggressive language.'

If Pauline can't take him out, Colin gets restless and wants to go on his own — which he can't any longer. With a need for constant vigilance, outings become an additional burden. 'This is exhausting for me. I never get to relax or do anything for myself. Conversation is not what it was and lacks depth. Sometimes I feel like his entire memory — childhood, football, family, recent — has been completely wiped.

> *Where he was outgoing, interesting, full of life and funny — my favourite person to talk to — I now struggle to make small talk. He is a shell of the man he was, very isolated. There is nothing available suitably to stimulate him, like groups for men in similar circumstances. He has no male company and no group activities.*

> *We have asked for help from the footballing authorities and their support seems begrudged and minimal. They knew about this terrible industrial disease but once men suffer from it they are slow to step up and do what is right. We feel terribly let down.*

Godfrey Owen White, known as Goff, was what folk used to call a 'semi-professional' footballer, a term which should not be confused with 'amateur'. Semi-professionals *admitted* being paid, usually playing and managing just below Football League level. It still involved a great deal of heading practice.

'A prolific header of the ball,' says Tina, Goff's wife. 'He suffered multiple concussions in his twenties and was hospitalised on a couple of occasions but he still spent hours practising, heading that leather football. Though unable to diagnose until after his death, the consultant feels sure that it's CTE due to all that heading. It's so sad that football was his passion and is now the cause of his demise.'

Tina, who herself has suffered from breast cancer, then — like Pauline Blant — outlines a typical day, beginning five days a week with the arrival of a carer who washes and dresses Goff. 'I sometimes go for a walk or have a nice relaxing bath during this hour. If we're not going out he'll sit and watch television for most of the day. He cannot work the remote controls, so I have to change channels when necessary.

These last two weeks he has been following me all over the house, into the toilet, behind me when I'm cooking. He will move objects and ornaments to different rooms in the house. I regularly find odd things in his bed — banana skin, toilet roll, items of clothing. He spends some of his time sweeping up the same bit of dust. He can no longer make a cup of tea. I make all his drinks and meals.

He doesn't like being told what to do. I have to be very careful how I word things as he shouts a lot and can get aggressive. He can be affectionate and placid at times, but the mood can change in a second. I try to distract him with music, cuddles, food but things have got to a very unpleasant level where I've had to try to leave the house and call my neighbours or son. One time he attacked me with a broom and I had to lock myself in the bathroom.

Bedtimes are the worst. 'He has items arranged all over his bed. If I try to move any he gets agitated and shouts. He gets into bed fully clothed now. I try to put him into his pyjamas but it's not worth the battle any more. I tuck him in with teddy like a child and tell him I love him.

'This is the worst time of the day for me. I well up with emotion and the sadness of it all overwhelms me. I feel very sad and lonely. The man I've been married to for almost 50 years has changed and is lost to me.'

On other recent occasions Goff has waved a knife at Tina, thrown his coat at her and injured her arm. He has 'kicked off' in

Sainsbury's, throwing food around and shoving the supermarket trolley into other shoppers while swearing and shouting. He has left the house alone wearing just slippers and no coat — fortunately spotted by friends at the end of the road. At home he shouts, bangs doors and walls, stamps his feet.

If he goes into respite care, just to give Tina the chance of a decent sleep, every night is £123.42. 'I am concerned for the future and how I am going to meet these costs. Goff was a great guy and well respected, now there will come a point when I cannot look after him any more.'

And all, she says just once more, through football.

Linda Tucker apologises for a delayed response. She's had her hands full, she says. She and Bill married in 1974 — 'he was a kind, gentle, easy going, sociable man.' When his family began noticing changes, he refused to go to the doctor but was finally diagnosed in 2014.

> I now realise that he had been struggling for many years, most noticeably from the beginning of his fifties. Just before that he started refusing to believe things I told him. I was always wrong. This, apparently, is one of the early signs of dementia. He started saying he didn't like getting old, but I just put it down to becoming a grumpy old man.
>
> Then he became moody, irritable and very forgetful and was persuaded to see a doctor. A consultant diagnosed Alzheimer's and said it was down to heading a football.

In 2019, says Linda, they hit crisis point. Bill butted her. 'I've been yelled at, verbally abused, pushed, scratched and punched. That's not something Bill would ever have done. The kind and gentle man I married has changed into a stranger who I care for and don't particularly like. He looks like my husband but he's nothing like the man I married.'

He deteriorates almost daily. 'He sleeps a lot but not always at night. He often stays up all night. He eats anything that looks like food, so has to be watched 24/7. He now struggles when we try to get him out for a walk. He no longer recognises most people, no longer communicates. When he does try to say something it's usually garbled nonsense. It's all truly awful.'

32.

'THERE IS A FUNDAMENTAL ISSUE IF PLAYERS, UNIONS AND LEAGUES FEEL THAT LAWMAKERS ARE HOLDING THEM BACK FROM WHAT THEY COLLECTIVELY AGREE TO PROTECT THE SAFETY OF PLAYERS'

Ben Simpson cracks it. In the same Professional Footballers' Association meeting room in Manchester where on January 18th he and I had first bartered and bantered, Dr Adam White, urbane and articulate, waits upon his hour. If terms and conditions apply (and they do) it's simply that he can talk about the present and future but might hardly be expected to reflect upon the past, a country where things were done differently.

I'm even given a hardback PFA notebook, and a couple of PFA pens, though it's a couple of voice recorders which sit either side of the table, mutely and mutually suspicious. The wish similarly unspoken, I'm hoping we might have time for a beer afterwards.

'I'm sure different people at different times would call me difficult,' Dr White supposes towards the end of the interview. 'They would call me irate, they would call me challenging' — 'challenging' appears his favourite word, beating 'passionate' by a short head. He thinks, he continues, that he's a fairly decent, nice person on a personal level but not particularly forgiving. 'When I've got a job to do I'm going to get it done and I think that's probably why I was employed.

'I was employed to put people first. I was employed to be difficult with people when they don't do what they're supposed to do. I'm here to solve a problem. Sometimes I have to be nice and sometimes I don't.'

The problem, he adds with an optimism seemingly lacking among others in the field, can be solved within ten years. 'We have a real clear goal and that is to make dementia in football history, not because it would become hidden but because we'd have solved the problem. It's an ambitious goal. Whether we get there in ten years I don't know, but hopefully if we carry on shooting for the sky we'll hit the moon.'

As with Judith Gates, the 'doctor' prefix represents an academic 'doctorate of philosophy' and not a medical qualification.

As does Head for Change, and the no-less passionate Nick Gates, he emphasises the need for greater player education. Sleep, diet and lifestyle are each important, he says. 'We need to know that they understand the risks of heading a ball — I think we'll see a reduction in heading through their own volition. We need to put in place the best support we can for players when things go wrong so that if they get concussions they are able to access the best support possible to get through that journey in the safest way and fully return. I think last year we spent £1.8 million in education grants.'

How might they get the message across to young players who are complacent, or who believe that it'll never happen to them or that, if it does, it's 30–40 years and thus about three lifetimes away? 'I wouldn't want to call it complacency. I think it's, you know, that they don't know what they don't know. We have to remember that CTE wasn't being spoken of until the 2000s. Whilst there's a history of CTE over a century, no one was talking about it until 2005–06 and those first couple of cases from American football.

Jeff Astle died in 2002 and while there was concern we didn't really think about that until 2014.

> We've got a lot of work to do to educate people about this condition, on concussion, on the seriousness of the injury and making sure that we change hearts and minds and attitudes, considering this issue very differently.

> The way we do that is by education, by engaging with players about their brain health. I don't necessarily have all the answers but what I do have through an organisation like the PFA is access to our members because they're the ones who will have the answers and they're the ones who ultimately have the power to say that we're going to get you to take your brain health seriously.

> On the issue of heading it's their game so our responsibility, I believe, is to advise as best we can on everything we know about it and then they can make those decisions. When we do that with players now it makes them think and lots of them are reporting back on reducing the number of headers in training sessions because they don't want to put themselves at risk. The fastest strategy is going to be working with players.

Perhaps more surprisingly, he leans towards the view that football could be played without heading the ball at all. 'There are different ways of achieving that, aren't there? One of those ways would be to change the laws of the game. I actually think that the quickest way of achieving that is with the players. If players stop heading the ball, it will go out of the game. They might be allowed to, but if they don't do it, it doesn't matter. They aren't stupid people. These players care about their own health and their own wellbeing, so they will automatically remove it themselves.

'I don't think you would see any difference in the appeal of the game. Games change all the time, you know. I'm sure that somebody in the 60s, 70s, 80s, 90s said the introduction of the Video

Assistant Referee was going to be a travesty but it's happened and it's not a major issue.'

The interview's amiable, though perhaps he's still a bit wary. At one stage I offer the information that one of the Zoom meeting ladies had thought him a nice and a caring chap. 'It's not all bad, then,' says Dr White. 'I personally don't think I'm kind, compassionate, empathetic or any of those things. I care about this issue and it's easy to be compassionate when you care.

'When you sit and talk to these families [in America] whose children have taken their own lives in response to the challenges posed by CTE [subsequently shown in post-mortem examinations], and when you sit and look in people's eyes and listen to their truth it's going to be hard, but that's why I get up in the morning and go to work and why I'll carry on doing it. Yeah, it's important. Of course, it's important.'

The last time I was at the PFA, it may be recalled, they'd awaited as eagerly as the faithful beneath the Sistine Chapel chimney the word on the outcome of an IFAB meeting considering the experimental use of 'temporary' concussion substitutes and were pretty choked when the resultant smoke turned bitter black.

The argument, said to be supported by almost 80 per cent of players and 19 of 20 Premier League clubs, is that a 'temporary' sub would allow a ten-minute medical assessment in the dressing room with the possibility of the original player's return to action if deemed OK. A 'permanent' substitution could mean losing one of the team's best players without good cause.

It's wholly coincidental that IFAB's annual meeting should have been held two days before our second head-to-head and that the law-making body had again reiterated its commitment to an experiment with permanent concussion subs. The morning's papers are ablaze with indignation, and not just from England.

Luke Griggs, chief executive of the Headway charity, publicly questions FIFA's claim that players' health and safety always comes first. 'I think it's fair to say that FIFA, UEFA and IFAB have never taken the issue of brain injury in football seriously,' he says.

The PFA seemed to have been more guarded, restrained even and quoted Dr White: 'There's a fundamental issue if players, unions and leagues feel that lawmakers are holding them back from what they collectively agree to protect the safety of players. In terms of brain health and dementia this is a critical time for the whole of football.'

Guarded? The head of brain health demurs. 'I think I've shared my dismay at the decision over and over again. I'm really disappointed by it, angry at it, frustrated by it - but angry and frustrated because inevitably we're going to get more players on the field not being removed when they have a brain injury. Yes I'm angry and frustrated, that's my job. If the players want it then I feel we have to deliver it.'

Goodness knows why, I'd thought that he was American and am thus surprised to detect a west country accent. Born, raised and now back in Cheltenham, he also spent formative years in Devon.

His principal sport was rugby, he says at once — 'I was absolutely useless at football, probably still am' — and, truth to tell, the guy looks like a rugby player. A big lad, as they'd say in North-East England, and with little danger of being charged with exaggeration. It was as a rugby administrator that he made national headlines in 2016, allegedly barred from a big match at Saracens, while a member of the RFU board, after calling for an end to tackling in schools rugby.

Described as a 'safety campaigner,' he'd told the *Guardian* that the RFU was still very much an old boys' network for whom the notion of proscribing tackling in schools would be like turkeys voting for Christmas.

'They have this idea of doing things and they are embedded in the idea of 'that's what rugby is. It's a masculine sport and you can be injured walking down the street or feeding your goldfish.'

Before joining the PFA he'd also written a piece on a British Medical Journal blog addressing concussion in junior rugby but stressing that the chief attention should be on primary prevention. 'In other words we should focus on preventing the child's brain from getting damaged in the first place.'

Now a referee in the Rugby Union Championship, the game's second tier, he became the PFA's first head of brain health in October 2022, part of the perceived revolution under new chief executive Maheta Molango. The head hunters' website claims that it approached more than 500 people, interviewed more than 120, drew up a long list of 14 that dwindled to a shortlist of eight.

'A significant step forward for the PFA. He is passionate about player welfare,' said Molango at the time.

He arrived, says Dr White on the head hunters' site, in a 'particularly sensitive political context' What did he mean? More of that shortly.

Both appointed before he was, the new department includes Rachel Walden and Dawn Astle, both with intimate knowledge of the heartache of dementia, in family liaison roles. Former England international Jeff Astle, Dawn's father, died with dementia in 2002, his death tellingly ascribed by the coroner to industrial disease and prompting a determined and still unsuccessful campaign to have CTE in players formally recognised as such.

The Industrial Injuries Advisory Council is again examining the link between neurodegenerative disease and repeated head impacts. 'It's positive but they're looking at it with the wrong tools, it's like looking for stars with a microscope,' says Dr White. 'My responsibility as an academic, a scientist, is to go back to them and point out this incongruence of approach and hopefully they will take that advice on board. Our role over the next 12 months is to give them as much information as we can.'

Just the previous evening, Dawn's campaigning — she also founded the Jeff Astle Foundation with similar aims — had won her a 'special recognition' citation at the Spirit of Birmingham awards 'in acknowledgment of her efforts to raise awareness of neurodegenerative disease in sport.' Many other outstanding community and regional champions had been joined less explicably at the event by several castaways from Love Island, the reason for their washing up not immediately obvious.

Rachel's father, former Portsmouth and Bournemouth player Rod Taylor, was also found to have CTE after his death in 2018.

Adam White left college in 2009 and at once got a job in coach and referee development with the RFU. 'I was very keen on how we could improve sport for young people and specifically how we could get more young people into rugby,' he says.

He then trained to be a PE teacher but at the end of the degree course decided it wasn't for him. 'I really enjoyed the job but could see it would be tough doing it in 40–50 years time, teaching kids to throw and catch. I had been most interested in the risk associated with youth rugby and I was seeing an increasing number of injuries.

'At the same time, while still heavily involved with the governing body, I wasn't seeing the change that was necessary or that they were taking the issue as seriously as I thought they should.'

His subsequent doctorate at Winchester University embraced concussion, head injury, youth sport and why so little seemed to be changing. He spent a couple of years lecturing at Oxford Brookes University and in America in 2019 met Drs Rob Cantu and Chris Nowinski — the latter a one-time professional wrestler with good cause to worry about brain health — who ten years earlier had founded the Concussion Legacy Foundation with the mission statement of never resting until sport was safer and effective treatment for concussion and CTE was developed. 'Our vision, it added, 'is a world without CTE and concussion. Safety without compromise.'

Dr White co-founded the UK offshoot — the Americans call it a chapter — of the Concussion Legacy Foundation, particularly focusing on what he likes to term lived experience. Already there's been plenty of that with the PFA.

He talks of that ten-year dream, of resolving issues — neurological, financial, familial — within that timescale. A bit optimistic? 'I'm passionate about it and I hope to be in a place at the PFA in ten years time when I feel like my job's done. If we're at a point where I feel like I've done everything I can do then it's only right that I move on somewhere else. I'm certainly not looking to move on from here until we've solved the problem and I hope that's in three years, I hope it's in five years, certainly in ten years.

'I think I've described myself as a cause-driven person and I think we have a cause that needs driving. So that's what we're trying to do here. The union has helped a lot of people but in essence I'm in one of those really weird jobs where I want to make myself redundant. If I didn't have that outlook, I'd be the wrong person for the job.'

So what of the particularly sensitive political context (fear of damaging the game, together with the need to protect the coporrate money-making machine that is professional football) paraded atop the head hunters' trophy cabinet? 'All around us in the sporting world — concussion, CTE, brain injuries — we're at a point where we have to do something and it's a challenge. We've got to do more to prevent the issue, do more to support players who have concussion, do more to support families who are living with the experience or the ramifications of long-term injuries to the brain.

'It's a time when we can really effect change here but like any marriage it has to work from both sides. I certainly bring some expertise and some drive and some passion but I wouldn't have joined an organisation that wasn't equally wanting to buy into that partnership. At the PFA there was definitely the feeling that now is the time we can get our teeth into it and start to effect change in sport. It's a challenge.'

Individually and collectively, there seem to be a lot of players in the brain health field — some of them pretty formidable attackers — might it be getting a bit crowded? Dr White probably didn't get where he is today (or spend so much time in the United States) without seeing a curve-ball heading his way. 'I wouldn't say it's too crowded at all, to be honest. We need more people in this fight. We need more academics, more scientists, more research funding, more organisations educating, more public campaigns.

'I don't think it's always as cohesive as it should be. I think people working closer together in partnership would be better but I certainly don't think it's crowded. We need more people doing more.'

Whatever the size of the PFA 'pot' — estimated at up to £60 million — it's now controlled by the Players' Foundation, a separate charity. Dr White backs calls for a game-wide fund — and again appears to echo H4C — to help players' families meet health care and related costs. 'I think it's absolutely right that, as a union, we push for that and absolutely right that the players, the leagues, the clubs, the governing body look after and improve the quality of life of former players.

'We could be there in a week or two, maybe a month or two, maybe a bit longer,' he laughs.

'If it was my choice we'd be launching it tomorrow because, being blunt, I'm sick of hearing about families who are desperately in need not getting the support they need. It's heart breaking, you know, really tough, to hear about the desperate needs these families are going through. If that £60 million was in the PFA's account then I can assure you we'd have had a care fund a year ago. We wouldn't be pushing for this; we'd be doing it.

'If we had complete control of that money then a significant proportion would already have gone towards a care fund. The frustration from families is absolutely understandable. We want a proportion of that money going not just to caring for players with dementia but on a variety of issues. Absolutely I would like to see access to that money and I hope that the Players' Foundation now do support players.

'If we got the message now that we could launch (a fund) in an hour, we'd launch in an hour. So I'd like the other football stakeholders to hurry up, because families are desperate right now.'

The week after our meeting, Dr White is again quoted in some of the more thoughtful newspapers following Swedish research into neurodegenerative disease among former top-level footballers over there. Reported in the *Lancet Public Health Journal*, the study at Karolinska Institutet assessed 6,007 men who'd played in the period 1924–2019 against 56,168 non-coms.

Reflecting but by no means surpassing Dr Willie Stewart's findings, the study found that 'elite' players were 1.5 times more likely to develop neurodegenerative disease than those who hadn't played. The exception was goalkeepers, who rarely head the ball, and whose brain health was similar to that of non-players.

'It has been hypothesised that repetitive mild head trauma sustained through heading the ball is the reason that footballers are at increased risk, and it could be that the difference in neurodegenerative disease risk between these two types of players supports this theory,' said Dr Peter Ueda, an assistant professor at Karolinska. The footballers were nonetheless found to have a slightly longer than average life expectancy, probably linked to their level of physical fitness.

Quoted in the *Guardian,* Dr White repeated his call for the Industrial Injury Advisory Council to recognise dementia as an industrial disease. 'We are doing all we can to improve the management of head trauma,' he said.

Dr Richard Oakley, assistant director of research at the Alzheimer's Society, said that more answers were urgently needed. — including how they could accurately predict who was likely to develop dementia after traumatic brain injury. 'Sporting bodies need this clarity so they can put in place appropriate measures to protect players,' he added.

Back in Manchester, it's doubtless coincidental, serendipitous perhaps, that the PFA's headquarters is about 200 yards equidistant from two of the city's finest pubs — the Britons Protection where I'd headed with Ben Simpson in January, and Peveril of the Peak, named after a Walter Scott novel, to which all three of us now retire unhurt. We raise a cheery glass, courteous if cautious, and that's not challenging in the least.

33.

'HEAD FOR CHANGE IS DOING WHAT THE WEALTHY PLAYERS' FOUNDATION REFUSES TO DO'

Three weeks or so after the meeting with the PFA, the *Daily Mail* devotes space the size of a small swimming pool to the dementia in football debate.

Chiefly it concerns former Leeds United, Manchester United, Middlesbrough and Scotland centre half Gordon McQueen, a cheerily convivial chap briefly encountered back in the first chapter, whose neurodegenerative disease advances indelibly and whose daughter Hayley is a familiar Sky Sports presenter.

In brass-bold type across the top of the back page — coincidentally above news of Scotland's surprise win over Spain in a European Championship qualifier — shouts the emotive headline 'Players' charity has £60m but they still won't help my dad.'

Across two inside sports pages the headline's bigger and bolder yet and doesn't shout, it screams: 'To think of my dad as this big, strong strapping man.... He's been deserted in his hour of need.' Little need to wonder by whom Hayley McQueen thinks her father has been so badly let down.

The whole thing has been engineered by H4C, who've been given £9,000 raised at a football lunch in London, co-organised by former Arsenal and England man Paul Merson. H4C in turn made 'symbolic' £3,000 grants to the families of three former players — McQueen, Tony Parkes who spent much of his life with Blackburn Rovers and ex-Huddersfield and Bradford City man Allan Gilliver — in the expectation that it might fund short-term but desperately needed respite care.

'Head for Change,' said its chair, 'is doing what the wealthy Players' Foundation refuses to do. It shouldn't be left to Head for Change, a small and recently formed charity, to be the only ones helping families fund residential care costs.' A press release talked of families who were 'emotionally distraught and physically exhausted.'

The Players' Foundation, says the story, has declared assets of £58 million but had declined to provide such short-term relief. The Foundation and the PFA union before it, have long expressed the view, reinforced in a policy statement in February 2021, that care for former players with neurodegenerative disease and other long-term illnesses should be funded by governing bodies across the game.

The story's prominence provokes two immediate thoughts, the first that though several worthy organisations are active in trying to address issues around brain health in sport — and could possibly work more positively and more harmoniously together — H4C has become the militant wing, a real impetus for action, a real catalyst for change.

The second probably isn't a new thought at all. It's that the indomitable Dr Gates, a 77-year-old great grandmother in a far corner of Co Durham, is an awfully good person to have on your team.

It's the Players' Foundation, now surgically separated from the PFA, which Hayley McQueen specifically targets, though it was the PFA which told her that it had to consider her father's 'lifestyle choices', though the only one that should have mattered was 20 years as a hard-headed centre half. After that she declined to have further dealings with them.

The PFA had also reminded her that a football-related diagnosis couldn't be confirmed until at post-mortem. That may have seemed similarly unhelpful.

Allan Gilliver had spent much of his football career, on-field and behind the scenes, with Bradford City. Diagnosed in 2014, he told the *Bradford Telegraph and Argus* the following year that he'd been made repeatedly to head the ball every day in training. 'It hurt like hell,' he added.

Christine, his wife, had written to the PFA and to the Charity Commission — in the spring of 2023 still investigating the old PFA Charity — demanding answers. A petition urging action was signed by a dozen or more high-profile former players including Alan Shearer, Gary Lineker, Graeme Souness, Gary Pallister and former Manchester United and England goalkeeper Alex Stepney.

A week after the *Mail's* top-board splash the papers also reported that Preston North End player Ched Evans, 34, faced 'life changing' surgery and had taken leave of absence from football following many years of high-force head trauma. His condition, it was said, was 'usually found in American footballers and rugby players.' The other man's grass may be bloodier yet.

Gordon McQueen remained at the family home south of Middlesbrough, his wife and daughter asking not for money but for respite care. His bed has been moved downstairs, he has carers and is regularly visited by friends and former team mates. In November 2022 they thought they were going to lose him.

'It started with his balance, then his eating, then his swallowing,' Hayley tells the *Mail,* before returning her fire to the Players' Foundation. 'It has £60 million in the bank. What's it doing there? Collecting interest? What use is that?'

Judith Gates agrees. Among the most stressful things, she says, is families' concern over how residential care might be afforded.

'How will we fund it? What will happen to our savings? Will we lose our home? How will we manage? Families share an ongoing terror at the prospect of residential care costs for a disease that regularly attacks former players in their fifties and sixties.

'A charity doesn't exist to use its assets to make more assets. It exists to make those assets of benefit to its beneficiaries. These guys are suffering because of their profession. We only wish we could help more. We ourselves are living with this tragedy and we understand what families are going through. The guys are suffering because of their profession. The PFA Charity has a responsibility to look after players who have served the beautiful game so well. We are dealing with families stressed beyond limits; the dementia journey can be a long one, and it is hell.'

Dr Sally Tucker, Bill's daughter, shares the concern. 'Care costs are potentially monumental for families. It's the big elephant in the room.'

Gordon McQueen's nearing the end of an April week in a Northallerton care home, subscribed by Head for Change, when his old friend Eddie Kyle — 'an almost daily visitor' the *Mail* had said — comes for lunch at our village pub, the Shoulder of Mutton. We're joined by Tony McAndrew, an apprentice at Middlesbrough when Bill Gates was a senior and well-seasoned professional and another old friend of Gordon's.

Eddie's from Kilbirnie, the same Ayrshire town of 7,000 or so as was his stricken mate. 'He might have played for Scotland, done awfully well, but he was still just a big daft lad frae Kilbirnie, never changed a bit,' he says. 'It's so sad to see him now, sitting in his wheelchair, barely able to speak except in single words and nine out of ten of those you struggle to understand.'

He retains some comprehension. 'I take my laptop in and we watch football,' says Eddie. 'Yesterday there was a bad miss and I told Gordon even I could have scored that. He didn't say anything but just put his thumb down. OK, maybe I couldn't have scored it after all.'

Eddie's 73, three years older than his friend, was in the Kilbirnie Ladeside side when the young McQueen would pitch up at the end of first team training, anxious for a chance to make an impression. It's what the Scots call 'junior' football but on no account to be confused with child's play.

'Even then he had a beautiful left foot but for some reason the manager didn't like him,' Eddie recalls. Gordon joined Largs Thistle, moved to St Mirren and then on to Leeds United, a side in the 1970s as Scottish as haggis and neeps — five or six men like David Harvey, the goalkeeper, Eddie and Frank Gray, Peter Lorimer, Billy Bremner and big Gordon himself often collectively called to head back north for international duty.

'They'd get a couple of taxis from Elland Road to the station, stopping somewhere on the way maybe to get three dozen cans and 200 cigarettes,' recalls Tony McAndrew. 'Bill Gates was pretty unique in those days in that he neither smoked nor drank. Look what's happened to poor Bill.'

Like Hayley McQueen, Tony takes strong exception to the PFA's reference to lifestyle choices. 'What's liking a drink to do with anything? Gordon's dementia is almost certainly caused by heading a football hundreds of times a week, not by liking a drink and a cigarette. That was unforgiveable.'

Before becoming assistant manager at both Darlington and Hartlepool, a Teesside travel agent and local radio commentator, Eddie Kyle had played that junior football — once described by the *Daily Record* as 'absolutely mental' — for Auchinleck Talbot.

Junior football proved particularly to be a man's game when Auchinleck played Cumnock Juniors, a former pit village a mile-and-a-half away, and never more so then when the auld enemies met in a Scottish Junior Cup quarter-final back in the 1970s. Ed scored both the victorious Talbot's goals. Even now a lady from Auchinleck still uses the social media handle 'Eddie Kyle's lovechild', even now a gentleman from Cumnock talks of Eddie 'Bastard' Kyle.

Lovely man, he grieves already the loss of the Big Gordon he knew. 'I was at his 60th birthday party, all night, what an occasion. Gordon was like that — loved life, loved people — it's so terrible to see the way he is now, and all because of football.'

The talk turns to rugby, and particularly to rugby league. It's agreed that, compared to football but with the possible exception of Auchinleck Talbot v Cumnock Juniors, rugby league is indeed a game for gentlemen played by ruffians. Tony recalls his time at Chelsea, when Fulham hosted an RL side which on one occasion had to use Chelsea's Stamford Bridge ground instead.

'A few of us thought we'd watch, sat right behind the dugouts,' he remembers. 'It was just licensed brutality, like Glasgow on a Friday night.' Glasgow on a Friday night? 'OK, pretty much like Glasgow on a Friday night,' he concedes, 'but I suppose that's not really licensed.'

Tony's 67, made well over 300 appearances in two spells with Middlesbrough and had 20 first team games for Chelsea. 'A player who would always make his mark on the opposition,' says the *Middlesbrough Who's Who,* with little elbow room for euphemism.

He also recalls a pre-season friendly, for Boro at Whitby Town, when he was still a kid and when at least a part of Bill Gates, 12 years older and round the block a few times, remained a miner's son from Dean Bank. 'There was a plate of biscuits at the end of the match,' Tony recalls. 'I was first to grab one and received a hell of a kick on the shins from Bill. He told me to wait until everyone else had had their biscuits.

'He was right. I was out of order. I might have been a professional footballer but I was just a kid. Bill was always one for maintaining standards, he's a very good man.'

Neither of the Scots was warned about the danger of repetitively heading a football, though they don't need telling now. 'At the end of every training session at Middlesbrough they'd just lob high balls into the penalty area for the forwards and defenders to fight over,' says Tony. 'We never worried about it and even if something happened to me now, I'd be grateful for those great days.

'The match balls were all right, quite good, but the practice balls were old, heavy as hell, chuggers we called them. You might sometimes get a headache, but we just put that down to the battered old footballs. You were usually all right next morning.'

Eddie had similar experiences. 'I'd go out on the town on a Saturday night and people would point out lace marks on my forehead. I just thought it was a sign that I'd been heading the ball right — a badge of honour, if you like.'

Limiting heading during a match might be difficult, they agree. Limiting it in training seems much more practical. 'They count pretty much everything else in professional football these days,' says Eddie. 'Why can't they count the number of headers — say a maximum 30 — then compulsorily sub anyone over that number? Maybe there are difficulties, but you'd certainly want to try something after what's happened to Gordon and to Bill.'

At the same time as all this is going on, the *Shields Gazette* ('trusted news since 1849') carries a story about John Tudor, a Newcastle United forward in the 1970s who formed a successful striking partnership with Malcolm Macdonald, the 20th Century's second Supermac.

Though his story would be familiar in Britain — fighting dementia for 15 years, no proof until after death of a football link, family desperate about care costs and critical of both FA and PFA — Tudor has lived for three decades in Minnesota, where he'd emigrated to become a coach.

Residential care in the USA can be up to $10,000 a month, an ambulance might be $3,500. His wife Anne told the *Gazette* that while he still had 'brilliant' manners — 'he'll never take anything from you without saying thank you, always open the door for a lady' — his condition was worsening. 'It's hard to accept that there isn't any help or support. He probably got this through his job, but we can't prove it.'

The Newcastle-based *Chronicle* had carried a similar story six months previously when Tudor's son Jonathan, emphasising that his dad wasn't one of the well-paid modern footballers who could retire in comfort, launched a Go Fund Me page to help support him. 'If it carries on like this for two more years that's it, everything's gone and we're completely broke,' said Jonathan. 'I want to see my dad get the care he deserves, but over here it's all business.'

By April 2023 it had realised $5,649 of its $20,000 target from 197 donations.

Gordon McQueen died at his home in the early hours of June 16th 2023, He was a big, friendly, hospitable man, once described by the *Glasgow Herald* as a blonde Clydesdale, whom first I'd encountered in 1996 when he'd taken a Middlesbrough youth team for a friendly to mark the Wensleydale League's 75th anniversary.

In 2012, a week after a 12-hour party marked his 60th birthday, we sat down for a proper chat. It had been what the Scots like to call a good swallee and on the familiar grounds that one swallee doesn't make a summer, he planned another party in Dublin.

He was recovering from cancer of the larynx, conceded a full and colourful social life, subscribed to the Edith Piaf philosophy of negative regret. 'If you go in with an ingrowing toe nail they'll still blame it on the beer,' said Gordon.

The sports pages mourned him hugely. Across two pages the *Daily Mail* headlined a 'towering colossus' and a 'Lionhearted warrior who never gave up fighting.' *The Times* talked of a man who was 'formidable, fearless and great fun.' Mike Keegan in the *Mail* also wrote of the perceived absence of meaningful help from the PFA and its successor charity. 'While grief will be a constant companion in the months ahead, there may well be anger at the deplorable lack of assistance Gordon received in his hour of need from a union to which he had diligently paid his dues.'

The following morning, Judith Gates appeared on *BBC Breakfast* alongside Northern Ireland international Sammy McIlroy, a friend and team mate from Gordon's Manchester United days. Sammy talked credibly of a 'fierce competitor' on the pitch and, off it, a meek chap who just wanted to make everybody happy.

Judith talked once again of the long goodbye and of the ever-growing body of medical evidence linking sports players with neurodegenerative disease. 'The science and the research is irrefutable. We just have to accept it.'

34.

'THERE IS A REMARKABLE CONSISTENCY OF SYMPTOMS ACROSS ALL THESE CONTACT SPORTS, AND IT IS VERY GRIM'

The hairy mammoth gestation of the average book suggests that it's probably wise not to try to estimate how many former professional football and rugby players with brain health issues are suing their respective governing bodies for negligence. It's an awful lot, nonetheless, several hundred and rising. A successful outcome would be seismic, a game changer in every sense.

Most claimants are from the two rugby codes. Most, perhaps almost all, are represented by Rylands Garth, a London sports law practice self-described as 'the leading law firm in the country on the issue of brain injury in contact sport' and said to be 'working with leading chambers and medico-legal experts.'

They believe, it adds, that dementia among contact sport players is an industrial disease — 'similar, say, to working in a factory and suffering hearing loss.' More than 20 years earlier, it will be recalled, the coroner had reached the same conclusion at Jeff Astle's inquest.

News of another potentially critical development came in July 2023: Heather Anderson, a 28-year-old Australian Rules footballer, was believed the first woman in the world to be discovered, after death, to have CTE. So profound the effect on her brain, she was believed to have taken her own life. Sixty former AFL players were already suing the governing bodies for sums up to £500,000 apiece.

The problem isn't just major concussions but, says Rylands Garth, lesser impacts 'and the relatively minor sub-concussions that sports people experience every time they play.' Richard Boardman, a partner, is leading the claims. 'There is a remarkable consistency of symptoms across all these ontact sports and it is very grim,' he says on the company's website.

Learned eyes no doubt also watched proceedings in the United States, where the NFL was obliged to pay hundreds of millions of dollars in compensation. 'At least one study has found,' adds the website, perceptively, 'that rugby is far more dangerous than playing American football.'

How long? Litigation is 'notoriously slow' says the Rylands Garth website and though they seek an early settlement, resolution could 'realistically' be years away.

How much? 'If one has permanent brain damage then it is reasonable to say that one's claims could be considerable. Depending on the severity of one's injuries, it could range between thousands and millions of pounds.'

Where would that leave contact sport? How could it resist fundamental change if continuing in the same way risked ever-escalating legal action (and, of course, many more fearful outcomes for its participants).

The Rylands Garth website also reproduces several media articles on the topic, ranging from *Mail Online's* exhausting 'Being hit by a modern-day rugby player is like being hit by a truck. How bone-crunching collisions have exploded as body-building professionals replaced beer-swilling amateurs of old' to the *Financial Times's* more concise 'Rugby faces existential crisis.'

Doubtless an example of what folk these days like to call FAQs — frequently asked questions — the website further wonders of itself if they're trying to change sport in any way. 'By potentially commencing litigation we hope to help current and future players by raising awareness to help bring change to make their sport safer.'

So that's a 16-stone 'Yes,' then. Even without the encircling pressure groups, if litigation is successful, contact sport could never be the same again.

Claimants include John Stiles, Nobby's activist lad, who talks of justice for people like his late father and of the need for fundamental change in an industry 'that continues to cause death and illness among thousands of players, past and present, every year.'

The claims against the FA, the FA of Wales and the International Football Association Board (IFAB) allege that the governing bodies 'failed to take reasonable action' to reduce the number of blows to the head — 'including failing to reduce heading in training and matches' — failing to allow an independent doctor to assess players with possible concussion and allowing players to return to the game when it was unsafe to do so.

'Guidelines' restricting 'high force' headers to ten a week in training weren't introduced until season 2021–22. IFAB's refusal early in 2023 to sanction the experimental use of temporary concussion substitutes was also likely to be exercising legal minds.

Former Welsh international rugby player Alix Popham, already featured in the book, is another high-profile litigant. Steve Thompson had by April 2023 been joined by fellow former British and Irish Lions member Dafydd James.

The rugby union players allege that the game's governing bodies were negligent in failing to take steps to prevent players from permanent injury caused by repeated concussive and sub-concussive impacts. 'It's a problem that isn't going to go away' Alix tells BBC Wales. 'There are things which could be done tomorrow to make the game safer but that's not going to be done. It's not just changes in the game but things which happen in the week — 90 per cent of my damage was caused in training and that needs to be looked at.

'It's not World Rugby, the Welsh Rugby Union or the RFA making decisions, it's the lawyers at the moment and they're playing chess with players' lives. The (authorities) need to make the changes and they need to be made now. Every day that goes by, current players are being endangered.'

Rugby League claimants include Nick Fozzard, a 6ft 3in and 17-stone former Great Britain prop forward who enjoyed a lengthy Super League career and who admits that he was attracted to the sport by its brutality. 'I was never told of any risks. No one said 'Listen, this is a really tough, tough sport, these are the risks, this is what could happen to you if you play it. I didn't know the score. I didn't know I was going to forget everybody's names or that it could change my personality.'

The RFL told the BBC that it took player safety and welfare extremely seriously and that it provided support to former players through its charity partner RL Cares. 'Rugby league is a contact sport and while there is an element of risk to playing any sport, player welfare is always of paramount importance.

'As a result of scientific knowledge, the sport of rugby league continues to improve and develop its approach to concussion, head injury assessment, education, management and prevention across the whole game.'

For mysterious reasons shortly (if unsatisfactorily) to be explained, the Football Association has declined to comment or, indeed, to help in any way with the writing of this book. A spokesman tells the BBC, however, that dementia is a debilitating illness which poses 'very difficult challenges' for those living with it and for their families.

This is a complex area and we are committed to finding answers through funding multiple projects to help provide a clearer picture and supporting objective, robust and thorough research.

The FA has taken important steps to help reduce risk factors that may be linked to head impacts in football, with industry-leading concussion and heading guidelines across all levels of the game.

The rugby authorities said in a joint statement that they 'cared deeply' for every member of the rugby family and had been saddened by accounts of players struggling with health issues. 'We care, we listen, and we never stand still when it comes to cementing rugby as the most progressive sport on player welfare.

'Acting on the latest science, evidence and independent expert guidance, we constantly strive to safeguard and support all our players. Rugby is a leader in the prevention, management and identification of head impacts and World Rugby also proactively funds transformational research, embraces innovation and explores technology that can make the sport as accessible, inclusive and safe as possible for all participants.'

Richard Boardman, with whom Head for Change has been communicating, offers an off-the-record interview, which is kind but a little disappointing. As a briefing encounter, it suggests not taking things much further. He tells the BBC, however, that the players they represent love the game. 'We aim to challenge the current perceptions of the sports' governing bodies, to reach the point where they accept the connection between repetitive blows to the head and permanent neurological injury and to take steps to protect players and to support those who are injured.

These proposed claims in football aren't just about financial compensation. It is also about making the game safer and ensuring that current and former players get tested so that if they are suffering a brain injury, they can get the clinical help they need.

Everybody, the lawyers included in this matter, are fans of these sports and our main priority is looking after these guys and female players with brain damage. They need urgent clinical support and damages for themselves and their families.

We ultimately want these sports to survive well into the future, but clearly urgent, immediate changes are needed.

35.

'WE APPRECIATE THE INVITATION TO TAKE PART IN THE BOOK, HOWEVER WE WOULD POLITELY HAVE TO DECLINE ON THIS OCCASION'

The Football Association, as might to even the least imaginative be apparent, has overall responsibility for all organised football activity in England. Effectively they are also the ultimate guardians of the game and its players. If you're trying to write a book centred around brain health in sports players, particularly footballers, then one of the first steps would clearly be to ask the governing body for help and guidance.

I've a chequered history with the FA, spanning from 20 years until 2016 as a fairly combative chairman of the Northern League. On one occasion, a big bad wolf from the compliance department (or some such tin soldiery) threatened action after I wrote in a blog that people who watched football from behind glass in centrally heated rooms were cissies. Probably they sniffed homophobia; they were advised to buy a dictionary. This time, however, things seemed to start quite well.

On March 30th 2022, just days after the caramel wafer conflab at Castle Eden, I emailed the FA's media department explaining what tentatively was afoot. 'The FA is clearly aware of the issues and, indeed, is increasingly active in trying to address them. With this in mind, I'm hoping that it would be possible to arrange a face-to-face interview with an FA official or committee chairman — ideally both — chiefly charged with addressing this clearly crucial issue. I anticipate that such an interview would form a central part of the book.'

However tersely, acknowledgment came within two hours. 'Thank you for getting in touch. We will come back to you on this.'

The months passed, spring to summer to autumn. No one came back. Further emails and voicemails went unacknowledged. The FA appeared to have taken an improbable vow of silence and strictly, almost monastically, to be observing it.

On October 11th 2022 I emailed yet again. 'It's been a while,' I said. 'You won't need me to tell you that the debate around brain health in football (and other sports) seems increasingly to gain momentum. The FA's role, it seems to me, is central to the whole situation. Is it possible to set something up?'

Someone else from the media department emailed soon after-wards, 'Can you please give me a call when you have a second?' Finding a forgiving moment, I did. Clearly the FA, supposedly wealthy, was having problems with its phone bill. More months passed. In January 2023, at last having acknowledged a voicemail message, the media relations people promised to come back to me by the end of the week.

On February 21st, several more weeks having elapsed without contact, I wrote again. 'It's now very nearly a year since first I asked the FA for both help and guidance on the *No-Brainer* book. I think you know the rest.

'From my perspective, it seems impossible to essay a book chiefly about brain health in footballers without major input and indeed guidance from the governing body. I really would welcome the chance to talk with someone about an issue which almost weekly gains momentum. Must I assume that it's not now going to happen?'

If the message were familiar, then so was the resounding silence which followed. A little over a week later I emailed a member of the FA Council, whom I knew quite well, in turn seeking help and advice but stressing — my italics at the time — that *the very last thing* I wanted was to be seen to be running telling tales to teacher. 'Apart from anything else,' I added, 'I'm pretty sure that it would be counter-productive.

'The book is now nearing its final stages and it seems to be utterly inconceivable that there should be no input from the governing body on so important a matter, fast growing in national consciousness.'

Within a few hours, coincidentally or otherwise, the head of media relations rang. For a few absurdly optimistic moments I anticipated a breakthrough at last. They weren't going to help at all, he said. There was plenty of stuff out there in the public domain, he said. What about all the resultant and greatly relevant questions? They simply refused to answer any.

A few minutes later confirmation arrived in a 25-word email unilaterally headed that it was private and not for publication. 'As discussed earlier, we appreciate the invitation to take part in the book, however we would have politely to decline on this occasion. Kind regards....'

My response was almost as brief, and definitely for publication. 'If an 11-month delay and countless unacknowledged calls and emails is the FA's idea of 'politeness', I really wouldn't like to see the governing body being rude.'

Arrogant? Ignorant? Perhaps rather appropriately a double header. For the FA, for all, it was the most protracted 'No comment' in history, and probably the most wretched.

So what next, you might ask (or might, at least, if not dealing with the FA media relations department). An initial attempt at googling 'Football Association' and 'dementia' leads firstly to sponsored content for a sheltered housing association for sportspeople — 'it is well documented that an increasing number of sports players are suffering from dementia and much has been written about the lack of action across the sporting landscape' — and secondly to the Alzheimer's Society.

The Alzheimer's Society had been announced as the FA's 'official charity partner' for seasons 2021–22 and 2022–23 following a 'competitive application process'. The partnership, said the media release, 'seeks to help to bring dementia out of the shadows and tackle the stigma surrounding the condition.'

Like by writing a book, perhaps?

Googled content then takes a further dander along Acronym Avenue, down which half those involved in the specialist medical field seem irresistibly to divert — the capital letters are the give-away. Who, for example, might have guessed that Nottingham University's much-quoted FOCUS study represents Foot, Osteoarthritis and Concussion in UK Soccer or for that matter that 'former footballers are two-to-three times more likely to develop knee osteoarthritis than the rest of humanity.'

Were comfort's crumbs needed it might in passing be added that another study showed that former pro footballers lived three-and-a-quarter years longer than those in a non-playing comparison group and were less likely to die of heart and respiratory disease or cancer, They were, of course, a lot more likely to die with dementia.

Who could imagine that the HEADING study undertaken by the London School of Hygiene and Tropical Medicine unravels as Health and Ageing Data In the Game of football or that BrainHOPE — another of the admirable Prof Willie Stewart's research initiatives — is more formally Optimising Brain Health Outcomes in former Professional and Elite footballers?

As education expands, it may only be a matter of time before one of the newer and more progressive universities offers a course leading to a Bachelor's (or possibly Master's) degree in Acronyms, a BA for the 21st Century.

Subsequent searching proves more specifically rewarding. If there's a thread through the FA's media pronouncements, frequently cogent and always comprehensive, it's of a complex subject and the need for caution. Truth to tell, the FA appears so cautious it might be stuck for ever on yellow.

Frequently its view on heading is framed as 'guidance' or 'guidelines'. A mealy-mouthed paragraph offering advice to players at the higher levels of the 'non-league' game and those in the Women's Championship 'encourages' them to follow the 'guidance' where 'practicable'.

From wherever their global travels might take them, Nick and Judith Gates might be heard yelling: 'You're the governing body — don't *guide* them, bloody well *tell* them.' Judith Gates has been known to harness the odd expletive but only, of course, in frustration.

Similar caution had followed publication of the Field study in 2019, the FA not unreasonably stressing that they didn't want it to deter people from playing football. 'The FA's independently chaired Medical and Football Advisory Group reviewed the findings of the Field study and don't believe there is enough evidence at this stage to make changes in the way that modern-day football is played at any level of the game.

'The (group) agrees that further research is needed across the game and we are committed to getting the answers to the questions we need to improve clarity. The (group) currently don't advise any changes in the rules of the game but they have supported practical guidelines which are common sense and in line with modern coaching practice.'

The Advisory Group also helpfully reminded players that there were lots of other things from which ultimately, they might perish — it stopped short of advising against crossing the road — and advised learning new skills with which to keep the mind active.

Like writing a book on football's supposed top priority without help or input from the Football Association? Like making bricks without straw?

At one point the FA posed its own questions, prompting another biblical allusion, the bit about physician heal thyself. 'Q: Is heading the ball the cause (of dementia)? A. The Field study can't show this but unlike concussion there is no evidence to show that heading can cause long-term brain damage.'

'Q. Should heading be banned in youth football? We don't have any evidence to suggest that heading in youth football would be more of a risk than at any other stage of a professional footballer's career.'

Other research may have been a little less surprising. 'Early evidence suggests that lower forces are produced when a ball is thrown to a player rather than kicked and when a player heads the ball from a standing jump rather than running onto it' — to which the only response may be 'Oh' and 'gosh' and 'really'.

Subsequent events were to suggest second thoughts.

Much has been happening, for all that, which makes it all the more curious that the Football Association seems to want to play hunt the thimble rather than publicly to confront that trumpeting and ineluctable elephant.

In July 2021 the Association introduced heading 'guidelines' aimed at all levels of the game and said specifically to be focused on training sessions where most heading occurred. It had been developed, said the FA, 'using a precautionary approach to protect player welfare where scientific evidence is limited and will be kept under review.'

'Recommendations' followed. In professional football, 'high force' headers — those from a pass of more than 35 metres or from corners, crosses and free kicks, should be limited to ten a week in training. The recommendation, it added, was 'to protect player welfare and would regularly be reviewed.' A similar restriction was recommended for part-time or grass roots players — a maximum of ten headers in just one training session each week.

'The aim of this guidance is to reduce overall exposure to heading without compromising development of technique or the role heading plays in the English game,' it said.

It said nothing about how such recommendations would be observed, encouraged or assessed though FA chief executive Mark Bullingham was again prompted to suppose them the most comprehensive guidelines anywhere, adding that the measures represented a cautious approach while they learned more. 'We are committed to further medical research to gain an understanding of any risks within football.'

Moheta Molango welcomed it, too. Their members' health and safety were paramount, he said, adding that the PFA would lead an 'engagement survey' with former players, their families and charities 'to design an appropriate support mechanism for former professional footballers'.

In December 2021 a new 'brain health action plan on understanding, protecting and promoting brain health' was announced between the FA, the Premier League, the English Football League and the PFA. The plan, it was said, focused on research, education, awareness and support for players.

'It will bring together all workstreams and resources more effectively to manage head injuries and further to understand links between the game and neurodegenerative disease... a consultation with key stakeholders which will help shape future work in this important area.'

The FA also announced a £2.4 million partnership with the Rugby Football Union and with Premiership Rugby to expand the Advanced Brain Health Clinic, a clinical service and associated research programme for retired elite rugby players. It was expected that the programme would also embrace former footballers.

Mark Bullingham again talked of an incredibly complex area of medical science which required exploration in many different areas of research. 'Until we have a greater level of understanding we are also reducing the potential risk factors, We have already done this for heading earlier this year by introducing the most comprehensive guidelines anywhere in the world covering the youth and adult games at al levels. This new joint action plan will further help build our understanding.'

Maheta Molango, then recently arrived at the PFA, was quoted, too. 'The PFA is committed to advocating strongly on behalf of our members while working collaboratively with football's stakeholders. A joined-up approach is necessary to improve the health and safety of our current and future members.

'A co-ordinated response is also required to provide comprehensive and dedicated support to our former players currently living with dementia and other neurodegenerative conditions. This is a vital and complex area. It has to be *the* top priority [my italics, his quote] for all involved in football.'

Before the 2022–23 season the FA took yet more positive — if cautious — action, following the restrictions on heading in training for under-12s with a ban on 'deliberate' headers at that level and below — consent first having been obtained from IFAB, the international board. The training restrictions had 'worked well', they said.

Like it was a kids' disco, leagues and competitions were 'invited' to take part, though it may perhaps have been a Sicilian invitation, one that they couldn't refuse.

As before, the FA's publicity set its own questions and provided its own answers. It seemed rather like marking their own homework, earlier familiar in a parliamentary context. There was even perceptive talk of an Insight Team and of 'exploring methodologies for capturing the experiences of young players.' It's possible they meant talking to them.

So why now? Firstly to align with training, said the FA, secondly to 'support the development of more skilful players — stay on the ball when in possession' and thirdly to 'mitigate against any potential risks which may be linked to heading the ball while research is ongoing in this area.'

Should the trial be a success, they self-answered, 'the aim is then to remove all deliberate heading from all football matches at under-12 level and below from the 2023-24 season.'

The penalty for deliberately heading the ball would be an indirect free kick, the first time that that sanction had been used for any reason in under-12s football. If the offence were committed by a defender in the penalty area the indirect free kick would be taken from the penalty spot and if it prevented an obvious goal scoring opportunity, the player could be sent off.

What, say, of the under-13s? 'Our expectation is that heading should not be introduced into under-13 training. If coaches feel it necessary to introduce the techniques of heading... we strongly advise a maximum of one session a week with light balls with a maximum of five headers, always unopposed.

'We will continue to explore further ideas, in consultation with stakeholders in the game, to reduce heading in youth football without fundamentally changing the fabric of the game.'

None of that, of course, touches upon the critical questions facing the men's and women's game, or the plight of many former players and their families fighting a losing battle with neurodegenerative disease, or the need for a much more cohesive approach to the whole issue than sometimes seems to be the case. I suppose it's no use asking now.

36.

'AFTER YEARS OF POLITICAL WRANGLING, ENGLAND'S FOOTBALL AUTHORITIES ARE CLOSE TO AGREEING A DEAL TO ESTABLISH A DEMENTIA CARE FUND TO HELP FORMER PLAYERS'

In the same mid-April week in 2023, two seemingly positive developments were announced, or rather one was announced and the other the subject of what a plumber might term a controlled leak.

The second offered real hope, the reportedly imminent establishment of an independent charity subscribed by most of English football's major stakeholders with a particular remit to fund residential care for those ex-players with a serious neurodegenerative disorder, that pernicious pachyderm in football's front parlour.

The first was a government report, via the Department for Digital, Culture, Media and Sport, raising awareness of how suspected concussion cases in grass roots sport should be handled. It was aimed at parents, coaches, referees and players.

'A culture change is needed,' said Professor James Calder, its lead author, though stressing that sport promoted both physical and mental health and that they didn't want to deter involvement. 'We need to recognise that if you've got a head injury it must be managed and you need to be protected, so that it doesn't get worse,' he said. 'There has now been a realisation that washing someone with the magic sponge is not the right approach. If you feel there is a concussion, that player should be removed.'

It's fair to say that Judith Gates was rather more enthusiastic, however characteristically cautiously, about the second than the first.

That same week a study from Manchester Metropolitan University reported on comparative cognitive testing between a group of 30 who'd headed 20 footballs and an equal number who'd done so virtually. The first group did not improve with practice their performance on a cognitive test while the control group fared much better. The group which headed the footballs also 'self-reported an array of symptoms commonly associated with concussion.'

The following week it was announced that a 'concussion spotter' would be employed at the women's World Cup in Australia and New Zealand in the summer of 2023 — as had been the case at the men's event in Qatar the previous winter — to look out for signs of players suffering from a head injury. In the case of that poor Iranian goalkeeper, they may not have had to look very hard.

They'd be based in a television control room but have direct access to pitch-side medics and they to team doctors. Women footballers, research had suggested, were twice as likely as men to suffer concussions.

Andy Massey, Fifa's chief medical officer, had said that it was easy for team doctors in the heat of the moment to miss signs of concussion. 'It will just make things an awful lot safer,' he said. 'Often in football matches you miss these, even if you're sitting in the front row. You have people walking in front of you, so it's easy to miss.'

The DCMS report was promoted with the familiar slogan 'If in doubt, sit them out.' Perhaps inadvertently, the opening paragraph of the BBC's website report embraced its essential incongruity. 'Anyone with suspected concussion must be immediately removed from football, rugby and other sports and rest for at least 24 hours under new guidelines for grassroots clubs.'

Must? Guidelines? Squaring those two might sustain a cognitive exercise of its own and probably at A-level.

If the player suffered 'red flag' symptoms — loss of consciousness, amnesia or difficulty in speaking — the report added, they should be urgently assessed by a pitch-side medic or else taken to hospital. That hardly seemed rocket science, either.

If intervention appeared less urgent they should ring the NHS III helpline, it said, drawing scorn from *Sunday Times* columnist David Walsh, that seasoned safer sport champion, particularly in rugby. Contact in junior and youth rugby should be banned in training and restricted to matches, he agreed. 'It should be a no-brainer. Instead there's advice to dial III.'

Dr Gates supposed that the report went nowhere near far enough. 'A bandage for sports,' she said, concerned that the 'guidelines' didn't extend to 'elite' sport, that it failed to address the issue of brain damage caused by repetitive head impact or how to make sport safer.

'In short' she said 'it falls way short of doing enough to address the problem. It is not wide enough or deep enough and certainly doesn't go far enough.'

The report, she added, had been designed to 'satisfice' — among her favourite words — rather than to satisfy. Lexicographically blanked by *Chambers Dictionary*, 'satisfice' has its precisely defined day in the compendious *Oxford English*. 'To decide on and pursue a course of action which will satisfy the minimum requirements necessary to achieve a particular goal.'

QED? 'In focusing on treatment as distinct from prevention it suggests a course of action designed to satisfy minimum requirements and fails to focus on the central realities,' she said.

'The slogan "If in doubt sit it out" is only relevant to the treatment of symptomatic concussions. It ignores the central scientifically proven cause of long term injury. The greatest danger is long-term head impacts, much more dangerous to long-term brain health than symptomatic concussions.'

Stuart Andrew, a health minister, said they'd be looking at how well the guidance had 'been absorbed and understood.'

The second development, the probable establishment of a football-wide dementia care fund was revealed by Sky Sports senior reporter Rob Dorsett on a programme in which both Judith and Nick Gates took part. Sky thought that details could be revealed within two months — 'before the summer'–the *Daily Mail*, not naturally optimistic, subsequently supposed that it might be within a month, a clout before May was out.

Around 200 former professional players suffered from neurodegenerative disease, Sky said, though the number was likely substantially to rise. Specialist residential care could cost between £60,000 and £80,000 a year. Though the Players' Foundation had given 333 grants to 77 players since 2020, they were means tested — nothing available to those with more than £23,000 in assets or bank accounts, excluding the value of their home.

'After years of political wrangling, England's football authorities are close to agreeing a deal for a new Dementia Care Fund to help former players,' it said.

The FA, Premier League, English Football League and the PFA were together engaged in talks. The Players' Foundation, not formally involved at that point, could later play a role by legitimately transferring some of its estimated £60 million funds to the new, independently administered, charity. The relationship between the PFA and the Players' Foundation had been 'very difficult', the report added — though both charities agreed that, if alone obliged to meet residential care costs of former footballers, they'd soon be bankrupt.

For its part, the Players' Foundation says: 'The Players Foundation is committed to supporting beneficiaries who have been diagnosed with a neurodegenerative condition,' adding that it works closely with an organisation called Dementia Information and Support Courses (DISC) to ensure ex-players are receiving all the help they can get from their local authorities. If they need extra support, the Foundation will 'consider any application directly related to improving conditions for a beneficiary living with a neurodegenerative condition.'

Since legalities were likely to be time-consuming, an interim fund, advised by independent medical experts, could be set up. The PFA would still have a 'crucial' role to play in providing 'practical and emotional' support.

The Sky website's update on April 25th was headed with a warning: 'Readers may find some accounts in this report upsetting.' Probably they meant some of Judith and Nick Gates's experiences and, especially, those of some of the members of the Extra Time to Talk group whose once-pacific husbands had been sectioned because of violent and uncontrollable behaviour.

Wife and younger son had talked of those days when Bill, the man who once they'd supposed might run and run, had walked compulsively, uncomprehendingly, almost ceaselessly. 'One day his body was all twisted because he'd walked it to exhaustion and we couldn't stop him,' said Judith.

Bill had also gone through a stage when he was 'literally scratching at his eyeballs' because he was trying to remove his contact lenses. 'I had to hold his hands and tell him that he hadn't worn them for years.'

Every family to which she'd spoken, she added, had talked of the elephantine (if you like) cost of residential care. 'It's with them from the day they receive the diagnosis. How are we going to keep our house? How are we going to pay for all of this? That hangs over their heads every minute of every day.'

Sky also found an anonymous official from a similarly unnamed football body: 'The new fund will be a huge relief to so many because the suffering of families is so great and weighs very heavily on all of us in the game. Even when this is up and running it won't be our best achievement — our greatest achievement will be for fewer footballers in the future to develop dementia.'

Change for the better? 'We are delighted,' said Judith Gates, 'that our proposals appear to have been acted upon.'

37.

'HE WANTED NO ONE ELSE FROM FERRYHILL, FROM SPENNYMOOR, FROM THE WHOLE WORLD TO SUFFER AS HE WAS SUFFERING'

Usually, if fortune favours, it's the film that follows the book. *The Billion Pound Game,* Paul Frost's 43-minute documentary, beat the book by umpteen episodes`and if ever there were a moving picture, it's this one.

Judith's interviewed as Bill watches from an adjacent armchair, close but wholly distanced. 'I miss my boy,' she says. 'I miss my cup of tea in bed, I miss the fruit plate he would make and bring to me, I miss being able to complain to someone who won't just think I'm being a pain. I miss my companion, I miss my friend, I miss my Bill.'

Watching Bill in the DVD irresistibly recalls William Wordsworth's *Daffodils:* 'And oft when on my couch I lie, in vacant or in pensive mood....' Look at the former England youth skipper, the irrepressible entrepreneur, the global adventurer, the proud husband and father. There's nothing there. He's vacant.

Frost, formerly a greatly popular front man on Tyne Tees Television's regional news programme, talks also to Bill's former

Middlesbrough team mates John Hickton, David Mills and Alex Smith. If not quite calling their old colleague a dirty bugger — perhaps Judith's recollection had been slightly awry on that point, perhaps blue pencils had subsequently been sharpened — they're pretty graphic, if occasionally euphemistic, nonetheless.

Mills recalls 'a real competitor' in the way that a mongoose might talk of a tricky opponent after ten three-minute rounds with a rattlesnake. Then he warms to his theme. 'In those days players had a licence to assassinate and I would put Bill in that category, a real no-nonsense defender. It was like a split personality — a gentleman, very approachable, off the field but a real driving force on it. Bill was the original physical player, capable of taking an opponent out of the game physically. He gave it everything he had as a player, I had a lot of respect for him.'

Hickton says that they didn't like what they called fancy-pants players, though they probably called them something different in Dean Bank. 'It was tough but things were tough in those days. You'd just get stuck in and do your stuff.'

Alex Smith: 'He was very tough but it was a tough game and you had to be. It was a very physical game, not like now. Now it's a very technical game.'

Then there's Hilary Maddren, featured earlier, remembering Bill's football advice to her son when younger. 'Bill just told him to kick the legs from under them. They can't run with no legs, he said. She laughs at the memory, talks too of an amazing guy, a very funny man, a lovely man.

It's a carefully astute film, interviews overlaid with stirring still and cine footage, monochrome from home. As she did about 75,000 words ago, Judith talks of the train trip to the Olympics, of the blonde from Shildon — 'I was second choice' — of the coins in the fountain and of the call box at the end of the road in Middlesbrough from which she'd ring home to ask her mother how to cook mince.

Chapter Thirty-Seven

Pregnant when barely 16, people told her that effectively her life was over. 'In a way that motivated me. I think you can say we proved the critics wrong.' She also recalls Bill's early awareness that repeatedly heading a football — '100 times a day in training' — could result in neurodegenerative disease.

Yet more vividly she recalls his diagnosis and his entreaty that they promise him two things. The first was that they 'optimise' his remaining years — 'we have done and continue to do.' The second — 'an indication of his generosity of spirit' — was that she and their sons take positive action. 'We knew dementia was a possibility but it was only when it became reality that we realised how difficult, how hard, football had been to him.

'He wanted no one else to go through this dreadful progressive disease, dementia, or for their families to go through what his had. He wanted no one else from Ferryhill, from Spennymoor, from the whole world to suffer as he was suffering.'

She talks, too — several times — of wanting to find solutions.

Much of the film is shot around the second 'no-headers' game at Spennymoor, Dr Willie Stewart talking before donning goalie gloves of the need for preventative action. 'It's taken us a century to get this far and where we are isn't much further than where we were back then.

'Headaches have been making headlines for more than a century but football always has this little escape clause — it's that more research is required before they do anything.'

Tony Mowbray, himself a teak-tough former central defender, recalls how heading was his strong point, too. 'Cleverer people than me somewhere down the line have some difficult decisions to make,' he adds. Gary Pallister, similarly qualified, echoes him. 'It's not a nice disease. People like the FA, the PFA, are going to have to take some big decisions.'

Back in Spennymoor, back where she belongs, Dr Gates may have the last word. 'The evidence is irrefutable, there's much more to be done. What we need now is action.'

In south Wales, Alix Popham and others –former team mates like Shane Williams, Ian Jones, Ryan Gough and Kieran Low — continue vigorously to train for the cross-Channel relay race, Union against League, now planned for October 2023, almost three years after his early onset dementia was publicly disclosed. Sky Sports plans a four-part documentary.

Sometimes they're in the sea, sometimes in a pool. 'I could swim to survive, maybe get to the side of the pool, but have never done long distance,' says Alix.

Whatever they raise for H4C — the target's £250,000 — will go, he says, towards care and support for affected players and their families, education from grass roots to the elite game and independent research 'including experimental treatments that could help individuals.'

Though it might hardly be supposed a warm-up, he hopes also to complete a sponsored bike ride from London Welsh to Lyon ahead of the opening game in the 2023 World Cup, Australia v Wales, on September 24th and in the company of double Olympic gold medallist and former world champion Geraint Thomas OBE.

Mr Thomas, as might be imagined, is a Welsh dragon, too.

38.

'ANOTHER CLICHÉ –SORRY — WE CAN ONLY PLAY THE HAND WE'RE DEALT'

On the sort of day and at the self-same hour about which Noel Coward wrote of mad dogs and Englishmen, Bill and Judith and I assemble to negotiate the book's final chapter. It's been 15 months, the approximate gestation of that belaboured hairy mammoth and still the birthing to survive.

The gathering had originally been arranged for May 8th, Bill's 79th birthday, but Judith had been unwell and prudently unwilling to risk contagion in a care facility. Recovered, she took a restorative and clearly beneficial holiday to Japan. 'A fascinating mix of high technology and ancient superstition,' she summarises.

It's now June 2023, timely because — what the television channels like to call breaking news — she's just had wind that the report into the Concussion in Sport Group will be published at 11.45pm this very evening, a curiously restless deadline, and that its contents will be far less supportive (less damning, some might say) than they'd hoped.

There may not be mad dogs around the Middleton Hall retirement village, but Dr Gates is in that regard distinctly unhappy, nonetheless. Cinderella shift and closing words notwithstanding, we probably haven't heard the last of it.

The much better news is that she is in discussion with former Arsenal and Manchester United player Viv Anderson — the first black footballer to represent England — who wants to donate a percentage of his new company's profits to help footballers. It's all very 21st Century, all block chains and fungibles.

Elsewhere major change is afoot. It has been decided that, while Head for Change will continue vigorously and effectively, Dr Gates will chair Head Safe Football, a new charity charity whose goals and ambitions solely emphasise football. She will no longer be a trustee of Head for Change. Judith is s also excited about Head Safe's new logo, a 'minimalistic' elephant balanced atop a football. Partly the significance embraces the elephant in the room — how many times might that phrase been used in the preceding pages? — partly a reminder that the elephant never forgets, though in the circumstances that might seem a little perverse. Probably there's a high-powered study group still working on the accompanying acronyms.

Though never without energy or initiative, she seems reinvigorated. 'There are still two years before I'm 80,' she says, though by no means setting a deadline. 'There's so much to do. I'm determined to do more, I have the energy. We're stepping things up. It's time for action.'

Bill, conversely, declines, sips silently and almost imperceptibly from a beaker of orange juice, seems cheered nonetheless to have his wife again at his side. Whatever his cognition of time and place, he speaks just two improbable words — 'Brian Kidd' — during our 75-minute gathering.

Brian Kidd, it may be recalled, was the young Manchester United player suspected of breaking Bill's jaw in an off-the-ball incident unseen by the referee during a late-1960s FA Cup replay at Old Trafford. Suffice — counsel for the attacker, not for the defence — that there may have been provocation.

Judith had driven down for the Manchester match, planned to return the same night, instead stayed at the hospital with Bill and wore his shirt because she had nothing with her. Another potential problem was that she'd not brought her contraceptive pills. 'The hospital kindly prescribed me some,' she recalls. 'It was the first time they'd delivered the pill to men's surgical.'

So we head out into the noonday sun, Judith gingerly propelling the wheelchair and making jokes about learner drivers. We stop by the hen house, in plain sight pass the bird hide, gaze perhaps enviously at the bowling green, admire the flowers. If care's essential, and money no object, this may be as good as it gets.

A couple of days earlier Bill had very gently been exercised in the retirement village's gym when he was recognised by one of the transport staff, a Middlesbrough FC fan called Andy. 'I saw Darren kicking the ball to Bill,' he emailed later. 'The next thing I knew I was also kicking the ball to a Boro legend. That's not something I ever thought I'd do. It absolutely made my day and is something I'll cherish forever. but it was heart breaking and emotional, too.'

Andy had also asked if Bill remembered the late Ray Yeoman, another fiercely competitive former Middlesbrough player of that time. 'Of course I do,' said Bill, much to his son Nick's relief. It was the most he'd spoken for weeks.

Middleton Hall has a smart restaurant called The Orangery to which Judith and I adjourn for a final on-the-record interview, the voice recorder conspired against by great clashing canteens of cutlery. Cared for and yet more greatly cared about, Bill remains in his wheelchair in another part of the complex, inattentively in front of daytime television. Whatever it is that's filling the unforgiving minutes, it's not football.

Judith drinks Pimm's, talks for an hour with accustomed cogency before following us to a nearby pub for lunch. 'We tried to shake you off,' says Sharon, my wife, jocularly. 'It's quite hard to shake me off, ask the FA,' says Judith as we cross the car park. Many others may now, and may yet, know it to be true.

The recorded interview embraces everything from Sisyphus, the poor chap in Greek legend condemned forever to roll a boulder to within feet of the top of a hill — what comes of getting on the vengeful side of the gods — only for the damn thing to roll back down again, to Joe Biden, the US president, who pretty much rolls down of his own accord.

To a degree, at least, she's still talking to the press, albeit over penultimacy and Pimms. A long spoon to sup with the devil? Before all this, says Judith, I was the only devil with whom she'd supped. 'I looked at particular newspapers and recognised what stories were likely to get traction with their readers. I tried to step into the shoes of the people with whom I was dealing and work on a win-win situation for us both. I've tried to give them what was beneficial to them in order to get our powerful message across. I promised Bill that I would try to do it.

'I've been appreciative of the support of the media and hopefully it comes from a shared credibility. I try to be absolutely transparent in what I do. What you see is what you get — I'm a great grandmother who tries to make a difference. The thing that I want I can't have, which is to have Bill back, so given that I can't have that, I have to try to make his legacy honourable in his name. That's my constant message. I'm not out there saying I want money for the Gates family, I want this or I want that. We've been solution driven and mission focused. We're out to try to tell a story in order that it might not be other people's story in the future.'

She talks of 2am ideas, of possibly working on a new slogan (if not necessarily an acronym) of action not words. Inevitably, however, the chat starts with the simple question 'How's Bill?'

'Almost every week something more has slipped away,' says Judith. 'He now has a hospital bed because his physical ability to get into and out of bed has gone. He speaks less and less but when he does speak it's extremely appropriate. We feel that it does take longer, but he still takes things in. You would see this morning, you watched his eyes going from side to side and felt he was engaging. At some level he certainly is.

'The thing I'm so grateful for is that he's peaceful. He's tranquil, he's accepting. The staff are so kind, so totally kind. I couldn't bear it if he wasn't settled but we know what the outcome will be because it's literally his brain not telling his body how to do things any more.'

How much medical knowledge did she have before this extraordinary crusade began? 'I didn't have medical knowledge but I had a kind of anecdotal knowledge and I was kind of half-prepared. I became determined to use the analytical, problem solving, critical thinking skills that I had developed as an academic and apply them to this particular topic. I went out and did everything. I went online, I approached people who were speaking online, I approached neurologists - I went out there and I tried to learn. I tried to make it a quick study but also a rigorous study in order to assimilate the information.'

Does she ever feel resentful? 'I feel resentful for what Bill has lost and what we have lost together. I strive very hard to be grateful for all that we've had but I don't want to come across as Mother Teresa. I strive to keep the balance between what I see as the good wolf and the bad wolf fighting one another. The bad wolf says this is unfair, this can't be happening, and the good wolf says count your blessings, look at what you've had.

'I feel resentful that change isn't coming faster and I feel extremely resentful that the CISG still raises question marks about causation. How many more players will be like Bill? How many families will go through it? This is the bit that makes me resentful because I know that corporate interests are still controlling.'

If she'd been asked at the start of 2021 what she'd like to achieve in the first two-and-a-half years of H4C, would she now be satisfied? 'I'd feel that we'd done something but I always feel there's more to be done, she almost guardedly concedes and then offers an anecdote.

'The guy in Spennymoor who brought the silhouettes back to our house after we'd had them on the field as a circle of honour to those who'd been affected said that none of his six grandbairns would ever head a ball. Now that for me is success. I mean there are other successes, like getting IFAB to modernise rules in order to minimise heading in training, but the voice of the man and woman in the street, the people who want to protect their grandbairns, that's success as well.'

What of the past 15 months, the time since *No-brainer* was conceived at that caramel wafer conflab in Castle Eden? What's been achieved, and what disappointed? 'One of my personal challenges is that I'm always aware of how much more there is to do and therefore I have to deliberately stop myself and say, OK, you're on a journey, how much ground have you covered. I do think that we've raised awareness. I do think we've created a situation where the topic isn't going to go away, it's only going to get bigger and more is going to get known about it.

To a certain extent there's less resistance with families to speak out, so we've tried to make it known that it's an illness, it's not something to be ashamed of. It's a disease that's happening to your brain but it could be happening to your knee or your arm. We've done some work in raising the barrier of public acknowledgment and saying that there are voices here which will not be ignored and if you try to ignore us we'll shout louder, we'll shout differently, we'll present different examples. I have real aspirations for the next couple of years.

If I can get traction on the slogan, I'd love to see a poster on every training ground, in every school gym. Only by raising that level of awareness across the board, with the general public and not just in professional sport, will we get the message through that the brain is fragile and everybody should be thinking how to protect it.

Might they ever consider direct action, waving placards or gluing themselves to Wembley Way or something|? 'Never say never. But it's not my style. We're focused on the solutions, not on breaking windows or carrying banners. We're focused on thoughtfully highlighting the issues and then stepping forward in a strategic, thoughtful way to do what needs to be done — but I do recognise that limited action can often bring about changes. I'm very aware of that.'

So what should bodies like the FA and the PFA now be doing? 'First of all, they should be looking after families that are affected. We gave those token amounts for welfare care because no one else has and we wanted to say to the sporting governing bodies 'Does it have to be a small charity which acknowledges the issue? What are you guys doing about it?' We recognise that one of the elephants in the room, for families certainly, is the cost of residential care. They're frightened to death of it. Sporting governing bodies have to grasp that nettle. I know there's been talk. I say "Show me the money."'

You're 78.... 'I have to be realistic and say that for all that I feel fit, active, driven, I can't talk about reason and not reasonably accept that I'm two years from my 80th birthday. Equally I take comfort from the fact that the President of the United States is up there with me. I haven't fallen down yet. I don't want to be ageist but I hope I would have sufficient self-awareness to feel that if I was no longer of benefit to what we were trying to achieve I would step back. I equally hope that in the next few years, just as in the last couple of years, I'll work with people younger than me who'll carry the torch.

'I don't think there's any danger of the boulder rolling to the bottom of the hill again. I think the momentum is such that there'd be such a backlash against that, How far up the hill are we? The problem is that I keep adding to the top of the hill. We're moving, we're moving in the right direction, but when we get to the top of the hill, what would it look like?'

Final question, final page: how much can you say you've enjoyed the past two-and-a-half years?

Enjoy is a strange word to use' says Judith before we head to the pub. 'I could say — what could I say? — stimulated by it, satisfied, and had moments of personal epiphany. 'Oh my goodness that's happened, I never thought it would.' There've been all of those, but I wish I didn't have to do it.

There's a song I've probably mentioned before, a Kenny Rogers song called Goodbye. It begins with 'All I wanted was you and me and the wind,' part way through it says 'I want forever back again' and the final words are 'I'm glad you came my way.' These phrases are all so true for me. I'm glad Bill came my way.

So that's my pathway. Have I enjoyed being on that pathway? I would rather not be on the pathway but — another cliché, sorry — we can only play the hand we're dealt. So given that this is what Bill was dealt, and what we were dealt, there has been satisfaction in trying to create a legacy that honours him, though I would rather not be doing it at all.

There's so much I enjoy doing and want to do in life, but this is my project to honour my husband. He's a good man, Bill.

And there it was all going to end....

39.

'WE ARE A CHARITY FOR EVERYONE — ALL AGES, GENDERS, PLAYERS AT EVERY LEVEL'

It's September 18th 2023 and at the end of Neale Street, the former pit terrace in Co Durham where Billy Gates forever kicked about with the boys, an avuncular elephant stands tethered to a tree.

It's an inflatable, if not blown up out of all proportion then a thick-skinned three metres high with tusks that wobble in the wind. The media, the telly boys, gather around, learn that the pop-up pachyderm has travelled overnight from Bristol in the back of a van — perhaps there were no jumbo jets — and that he answers to Eric.

Judith Gates wants to call him CTE, which may not be terribly catchy but would still be less of a mouthful than chronic traumatic encephalopathy, which is what it represents.

The following Saturday he'll be at a Co-op Funeralcare event beneath Tower Bridge — that has an 'elephant in the room' theme, too - then packing his trunk for a kids' party in the boondocks.

Neale Street's where young Billy and his contemporaries broke windows and held pig muck derbies, where they talked of poss tubs and fed the store horse, where Middlesbrough managers would periodically come knocking and where the bairns — as the second chapter recalled — might dig for victory in the gardens while their dads righted the world over the gate.

Externally it seems little changed. The gardens still grow, too, though these days they're called smart allotments — something to do with security — and again raise the question about what's so particularly smart about a carrot.

The remarkable thing on this moisty Monday morning is that Dean Bank appears so effortlessly to take the elephant in its communal stride, as if Eric came around as regularly as the Rington's tea man and like there was something better on daytime television. At the school up the road, the bairns continue accustomed playground pursuits rather than crowd the railings to wonder whether it might be Indian or African, and to argue educationally over its ears.

Eric remains hidden in plain sight. The now-familiar phrase about the elephant in the room has rarely seemed more appropriate.

It's the launch event for Head Safe Football.

Judith's joined by younger son Nick and by Hayley McQueen, the late Gordon's daughter, Sky Sports presenter and herself an avid protagonist for safer sport. 'No one's fully talking CTE, no one is aware of all the ramifications, the risks are woefully misunderstood,' Judith tells the gathering sheltering beneath trees from a September shower. 'It's putting lives at risk, there are no two ways about it.

'Head Safe Football is a charity for everyone, all ages, genders, players at every level, not just in the professional game. We are stepping out into the wider world of football. We want to future-proof football.'

She also says that they want action, not words, which is a mite disconcerting towards the end of a 100,000-word book with an elephantine gestation of its own.

Hayley's there with her three-year-old daughter who's a bit tearful, a bit anxious, around Eric. Her dad, she says, played

Chapter Thirty-Nine

football in a similar back street in Ayrshire. 'I want to make sure that my daughter's generation is aware of all the risks,' she says. 'I want my dad's legacy to be that of the dangers of heading a ball, particularly among youngsters.' The elephant looks a bit ruminative, as elephants tend to do.

The following morning, Judith and Nick are back at the Middleton Hall care village where they show Bill, now 79, photographs of the improbable elephant at the end of the street where he was raised. Often asleep, he opens an eye to the images. 'Good heavens,' he says, and doesn't say another word all day.

The Gates family thought that they could better fulfil their promise to Bill by concentrating specifically on football's own particular needs. The Head Safe Football website talks of the new charity's formation 'at the request of the football community to provide emotional and practical support, evidence-based knowledge and up-to-date research for all footballers and their families.' Among its aims is to 'mobilise and unite the entire football community to fight for action.'

Judith speaks of widening the discussion but of still supporting affected former players and their families. 'The problem manifests itself in past players but begins in youth. There's a need for precautionary, preventative and protective approaches. Head Safe Football is the charity for anyone who's ever headed a ball.'

The new charity is setting up CTE Trailblazers, teams or individuals who will implement Head Safe practices 'based on awareness of the fragility of the brain' and Football United v CTE, its members educated to combat or play against the disease. The first youth Trailblazers will be at the 1,000-member Killingworth club in Northumberland — the under-14 Oranges — whose players include the son of Deborah Johnson, editor of the NR (Neuro Rehab) Times. 'A great idea,' says Deborah.

Like the elephant, it's hoped that they'll never forget.

Much else is moving — probably a lot faster than Eric — not least the announcement by the Professional Footballers' Association

321

and the Premier League in September 2023 of a £1 million fund to support former PFA members and their families affected by neurodegenerative disorders. 'This is an important step forward but we continue to believe that there needs to be a football-wide responsibility,' says Maheta Molango, the chief executive.

The following week there's a compelling debate in the House of Commons and the launch of *Concussed,* a quickly acclaimed book by campaigning journalist Sam Peters on the issue of brain trauma among sports players, particularly in rugby. Peters quotes stricken former England rugby international Steve Thompson that Dr Paul McCrory, neurologist and plagiarist, is 'little better than a murderer.' Owen Slot, reviewing the book in *The Times,* contents himself with the observation that McCrory is a fraud.

There are stories that legendary former Everton player Mick Lyons, almost inevitably a centre half, is another dementia victim — 'too much heading the ball. You forget so much,' says Lyons — and that the Scottish PFA is considering setting up a brain health clinic. 'I believe that if we can find £1.4 million for VAR, we can find money to support players when they leave the game,' says Fraser Wishart, the chief executive. 'It would be hugely beneficial for future generations.'

There's also a whispering of awards. Paul Frost's film *The Billion Pound Game* — around the 'no-heading' match at Spennymoor Town back in 2022 — is among the nominees for a Tees Valley International Film Festival award to be presented by Robson Green on October 28th.

Two days earlier Judith Gates expects to hear if she's won a global award in the *NR Times* 'people's choice' category — 'created to recognise and reward excellence.' Judith, says the nomination, is 'highly innovative in her approach and uncompromising in her commitment.'

The parliamentary debate on September 14th 2023 is remarkable for its harmony, its civility, almost its affability, none a quality for which the House of Commons is renowned. It's jointly sponsored by Ian Blackford, the Scottish National Party member for Lochaber, Skye and Lochalsh and combative former SNP leader in the Commons, by Moray MP Douglas Ross — an assistant football referee at international level — and by miner's son Grahame Morris, whose Easington constituency in Co Durham includes the Gates family home.

Blackford supposes that the three of them would make a formidable half-back line — 'but if the member for Easington will allow me, I will take up position on the left.'

The chamber, thinly populated, generates a cross-party chuckle. It's as if the ankle-nipping Highland terrier has suddenly become House trained. 'Beneath the story lies a silent but devastating injury,' says Blackford. 'Many affected families are financially destitute.'

There's praise for the PFA/Premier League funding initiative, a promise of action and investigation from Stuart Andrew, the Leeds United-supporting sports minister.

Grahame Morris recalls Bill Gates's determination after his dementia diagnosis. 'It was too late for him,' Bill had said, 'but he wanted to plant a tree so that others might benefit from the shade.'

Judith plans to seek further meetings with Grahame Morris. 'He will be very useful. He understands.'

There is much yet to be debated, much more to be understood, very much more to be challenged and to be changed. There's a growing feeling of momentum, nonetheless, and like the innovative and uncompromising great grandmother, that can only be a great force for good.

40.

'IT'S HARD TO ENVISAGE OUR AUTHORITIES ALLOWING OUR SPORTSMEN AND WOMEN TO PLAY WHAT SEEMS DESIGNED TO HASTEN THE ONSET OF DEMENTIA'

Bill Gates's remarkable life ended peacefully on the evening of October 21st 2023, close family by his side. Sir Bobby Charlton, perhaps the most celebrated of England's 1966 World Cup winners, had died a few hours earlier, also after long living with dementia.

The papers married tributes to Bill with admiration for his widow's continuing determination to establish and to vivify his legacy. Some called him fearless, others combative — useful word, combative — yet others supposed him hard tackling, which might almost have been euphemistic.

The *Daily Telegraph's* obituarist thought him 'an imposing physical presence' and talked of his work, chiefly in Africa, with his younger son Nick's charity Coaches Across Continents. The football magazine *When Saturday Comes* wrote of a solid central defender and an imposing aerial presence. It had spoken to Judith about his torment.

'On several occasions he asked me or his son to get him tablets or a gun, she said. 'Suicidal ideation is one of the symptoms of CTE.'

Ian Herbert in the *Daily Mail* reckoned Bill a giant but praised also his wife's 'quiet appreciation of the loneliness and struggle that comes for the families of those affected.' The campaign group which Dr Gates founded had 'moved mountains in a way that had shamed the game,' he added.

Hundreds of other messages arrive from around the world — 'even the guy who filled Bill's car with petrol,' says Judith.

Middlesbrough FC fan Rod Liddle in his *Sunday Times* column talked of 'Billy' Gates, as Dean Bank playmates and old Ayresome acolytes always did, wondered for how much longer sports like football, rugby and boxing could continue in their present form. It followed a report two days earlier predicting that dementia cases in England and Wales would almost double, to 1.7 million, by 2040 — lifestyle chiefly responsible.

'It's hard to envisage our authorities allowing sportsmen and women to continue playing in a way that seems designed to hasten the onset of dementia,' Liddle wrote. 'So far they have not done very much about it.'

Four days after Bill's death, Judith and Nick are at the ARC arts centre in Stockton for the premiere of Paul Frost's *The Billion Pound Game,* the first screening of the four–day Tees Valley International Film Festival. There's no red carpet, no effervescing champagne, no paparazzi (so far as may myopically be observed) concealed behind the corporation lamp posts.

Former team mates talk in the film about a player with a licence to assassinate, of how he would physically take an opponent out of the game, of Bill's dislike of 'fancy pants' (though it was in the fancy pants, quite likely, that he kicked them).

At the end of the screening, Judith has a few words — 'We have a game created by human beings which is destroying human beings' — talks also of the 'phenomenal' staff of the Middleton Hall care home, some in attendance, who'd cared for Bill throughout the last desperately dwindling year of his life.

She'd also recalled those final months in *When Saturday Comes*. 'We got an occasional flicker of life when we put a ball in his hands. Even with his eyes closed, which they were 21 hours a day, he'd throw it. If we put a ball at his feet he'd always kick it. Having lost almost everything because of the game he loved, he still loved it to the end.'

Other issues yet intrude, several newspapers reporting in the days after Bill's death that PFA chief executive Maheta Molango has been given a £150,000 annual pay rise, to £650,000. Chief among the critics is John Stiles, Nobby's lad, offering the view in the *Mail* — beneath the headline 'Kick in the teeth' — that the £1 million 'dementia fund' launched by the PFA and Premier League is by comparison 'pathetic'.

'How can they possibly justify this?' asks Stiles. 'It's a slap in the face for all those families who are struggling to pay for care for their loved ones who are suffering because they played football.'

On the morning of Bill's funeral, *The Times* also carries a substantial interview with Stiles. 'People are dying unnecessary deaths. Heroes are dying before our eyes. The PFA should be talking about striking in my opinion.'

He'd known Sir Bobby since childhood — Uncle Bobby, he called him — and very understandably wouldn't be at Bill's funeral because Sir Bobby's coincided with it. There'd be an awful lot at the Boro boy's, nonetheless.

Bill's laid to rest at a family ceremony at the Durham Woodland Cemetery at 11am on November 13th, the day almost appropriately teeming, suitably lachrymose. A racing man might suppose the sylvan going heavy, a Dean Bank lad that it was awfully clarty. 'Bill would also have called it perfect playing conditions' says a chap in a Middlesbrough scarf. 'I can still see his sliding tackle now.'

Earlier in the day, the elephant no longer in the room but trumpeting ever more ineluctably beyond football's close–guarded portals, Head Safe Football has issued a press release insisting that they are 'more resolute than ever' in continuing the campaign to protect future generations.

'No other family should go through what we have been through,' says Judith in the media statement. 'By tackling the elephant in the room we can help eliminate this cruel brain disease from football. Bill cared passionately about preventing others from suffering such an avoidable fate.'

They'd brought him to the environmentally friendly burial place a couple of years earlier, sought his approval, and commit him now in a biodegradable coco leaf coffin, made from small stems of coconut palm leaf. Mourners place single roses, red and white inevitably, on the grave.

In time it's intended that his wife will reunite with him there, though the site, returned to nature, may by that time only be identified with the help of a Durham County Council microchip.

Laura Parks, the humanist officiant, tells the family gathering that the spot is perfect for Bill — 'he adored and appreciated the natural world; this is so utterly beautiful and natural a place.' She talks, too, of Bill's spirit, his sense of adventure, his humility and his endlessly warm and loving character, of his staggering legacy and uniquely incredible life.

From 12.30pm, the rain unrelenting, friends are invited to lay a rose of their own. The gentleman from the council, snug (if not quite smug) in wellies suggests that others may wish to change footwear, too. However, there are no boots, not even football boots, in the boot.

At 1.45pm, just 15 minutes before Sir Bobby's funeral service in Manchester Cathedral, a humanist service for Bill — 'to celebrate his life and mourn his death,' says the order of service — is held in the ballroom of the Ramside Hall Hotel on the other side of Durham. The invitation urges not to wear black, goodness knows it's black enough outside.

There are memory tables, too, photographs and football shirts, a Round Table tie not out of its wrapper, little monuments. It's a big room, and it's thronged.

Laura talks of a 'truly remarkable life,' of a man who was almost superhuman, of one of the world's leading lights. 'I can safely say that he was a success,' she adds. None demurs.

Judith, yet more eloquent in tribute, talks of 61 years, 10 months and 25 days of marriage — 'an imperfect, perfect marriage' — recalls again the unlikely romance that began amid the Olympic fountains of Rome. 'We could hardly have been more different if we'd tried,' she says, noting that she was a 'student nerd' trying to fathom the meaning of life and he was (it's not how she puts it) Spennymoor Grammar School's answer to Dennis Compton, the great all–rounder.

'Put a ball at my feet and I'd trip over it,' says Judith. 'I'm so physically uncoordinated, I can't even walk and chew gum.'

Partly, she recalls, she'd been attracted by the young sports star's sparkling blue eyes. 'Gradually, inexorably, unremittingly the light began to dim as the CTE spread like poison ivy. Torment and despair were evident in his eyes, increasingly duller.'

She talks, too, of the long, hard journey since diagnosis, of wishing 'forever' were back again. 'I had 12 years to prepare myself and I was really not prepared for the surge of emotion after his death.'

Hilary Maddren tells again of feckless advice to reckless youth, Nick Gates — watched by elder brother David — offers things that we mightn't have known about their dad, that he played tennis for the Cayman Islands as well as football for England, that he was far less able on the ski slopes — 'I've many a time picked him up off the snow' — that he may have over–celebrated his only hole–in–one on the golf course. 'It was only 127 yards,' says Nick.

He talks of his dad the adventurer, the ambassador, the be-friender, the man who hated exploitation and injustice, who went eyeball–to–eyeball with a silverback gorilla, who'd get up in the middle of the night to help baby turtles to the sea, who'd visited more than 100 countries with Judith but who, through all the millions and all the miles, never forgot that he was a working class lad from a pit terrace in Co Durham, still happy to dig the garden. 'My dad was my best friend' says Nick. 'He changed the lives of millions of people. I idolised him.'

There's music from Louis Armstrong — *Wonderful World* — from Kenny Rogers, *Goodbye,* from Elton John singing *The Circle of Life.*

It's recorded also that Bill's favourite foods were corned beef pie and scones with clotted cream, the former unaffected by perceptions of fine dining and the latter by his self–diagnosed dairy intolerance. Spread out in the next room, both help furnish a feast for the five thousand.

There's also a condolence book, though I don't sign it. *No-brainer* may itself be the longest condolence message in history, or just its most garrulous epitaph. More briefly, it was a vivid privilege to have known the real Bill Gates. May his legacy endure for ever.

MYTHS AND FACTS

MYTH	FACT
Football does not cause neurodegenerative disease	Footballers are 3.5 times more likely to die from a neurodegenerative disease than the average person.
The old footballs caused CTE because they weighed more.	Footballs have always been the same weight. Today they travel faster and are therefore more dangerous.
The risks are the same for men and women	Women are 1.9 times more likely to suffer from concussion than men and take an average 2 days longer to recover. Can we wait for 30 years for the research to 'catch up' before we put in place policies to safeguard women against CTE?
Correct heading technique will protect me from CTE	The brain shakes within the skull irrespective of the technique you use to head the ball. Therefore technique has no relevance to long term brain health.
Heading the ball doesn't hurt therefore it isn't doing me any harm.	There is a causal link between Repetitive Head Impacts and Chronic Traumatic Encephalopathy. The more headers you perform over your lifetime the more likely you are to develop a neurodegenerative disease.

MYTH	FACT
There is nothing that can be done to make football a safer sport.	Reducing exposure to head impacts will mitigate the risk of CTE.
Rugby does not cause neurodegenerative disease	Rugby players are 2.5 times more likely to suffer from dementia but they are 15 times more likely to develop Motor Neurone Disease than the average person.
Symptomatic concussions are the only and most dangerous type of head injury.	A concussion is an injury and with correct treatment and rehabilitation can be recovered from. CTE is an incurable disease caused by the cumulative forces of head impacts over a lifetime therefore Repetitive Head Impacts pose an even greater danger.
The new tackle rules in Rugby will prevent CTE	In 2023 Rugby's governing bodies introduced a new law reducing the tackle height from shoulders to below the sternum. Although this will not prevent CTE it is a good start in the campaign to reduce head impacts.
I never had concussion so I won't get CTE	CTE is caused by the cumulative forces incurred by receiving repetitive head impacts; these do not need to be symptomatic concussions.

AUTHOR'S NOTE

In appreciation....

As ever on these occasions I am chiefly indebted to my wife Sharon, to whom this book is dedicated, for her professional counsel and editing and for her enduring love and patience. She supposes that *No-brainer* has been a bit out of my comfort zone and she may have a point.

I'm grateful to Dr Judith Gates for asking me to tackle so vital and so essentially human a story, for the caramel wafer mountain which helped sustain it and for her forbearance and insightfulness while the boulder was once more being rolled up the hill.

I'm grateful to all those people across Britain who freely gave of their time to help the project and not least to Dr Stephen McGinness, then the clerk of parliament's Digital, Culture, Media and Sport committee, who so remarkably tolerated my technological ineptitude.

And I gratefully acknowledge all those sources — chiefly *The Times,* the *Daily Mail* and the BBC — who've helped build up what I hope is a compelling story.

Finally, a word about Bill Gates, a miner's son who became a millionaire. His decline has been terrible to witness and perhaps difficult for both of us to comprehend. He was a most remarkable man. I hope the book does him justice.

Mike Amos MBE
November 2023

MIKE AMOS

Mike Amos was for 55 years a journalist in north-east England, almost entirely on The Northern Echo, until made redundant at the age of 73. He has won more than 40 journalism awards, was named North-East Journalist of the Year seven times in 18 years, was an inaugural inductee in the Provincial Journalism Hall of Fame and in 2006 was appointed MBE for services to journalism.

Born in Shildon, Co Durham, where he served as local councillor, churchwarden and parish magazine editor, he retains a lifelong passion for Shildon FC but worries over where allegiance might lie should they ever draw his other favoured club, Arsenal.

For 20 years until 2016 he was chairman of the Northern Football League, the world's second oldest, and has written or edited several books about the league. Other books include Unconsidered Trifles, a 400-page memoir of life as a "jobbing journalist."

JUDITH GATES

Wife, mother, grandmother and great-grandmother: educator, university lecturer and international management consultant: activist and charity worker, Judith has led a full and varied life, culminating most recently in her work with Head Safe Football, her husband's legacy, a charity she founded to focus exclusively on the dangers of football related dementia. She blends extensive professional qualifications, namely a PhD in professional development and masters degrees in both education and business, with extensive management experience, and fires them with a personal passion to fulfil her promise to Bill Gates, her husband. Sadly, noting upon diagnosis that it was too late for him, he asked his family to ensure that no player in the future suffers from CTE. Judith has a promise to keep.

HEAD SAFE FOOTBALL

Head Safe Football is a unique charity focusing on football related brain disease, in particular Chronic Traumatic Encephalopathy. CTE is a progressive and incurable brain disease caused by repetitive head impacts, including headers. The severity, intensity and frequency of the head impacts are contributory factors. Symptoms may include aggression, violence, confusion, depression and memory loss, Unremitting, symptoms slowly worsen over decades and result in dementia. There is no reprieve, no escape. Head Safe Football provides emotional and practical support, evidence based knowledge and up to date research for all footballers and their families.

Publish with Us

We give writers the opportunity to see their work in print

We specialise in memoir, biography, autobiography and history,

but will consider other factual genres.

haythorp.co.uk

contact@haythorp.co.uk